C000302446

CHLOROMYCETIN

(Chloramphenicol)

THEODORE E. WOODWARD, M.D., and
CHARLES L. WISSEMAN, JR., M.D.

University of Maryland School of Medicine
Baltimore, Maryland

With the collaboration of

Harry M. Robinson, Jr., M.D., George Entwisle, M.D.,
Fred R. McCrumb, Jr., M.D., and Merrill J. Snyder, Ph.D.

Foreword by Joseph E. Smadel, M.D.

A Publication of

MEDICAL ENCYCLOPEDIA, INC., NEW YORK, N. Y.

Distributors outside U.S.A.:
Interscience Publishers, New York
Interscience Publishers, Ltd., London

This Monograph on Chloramphenicol

is Dedicated to

The School of Medicine, University of Maryland,

in recognition of its

Sesquicentennial Celebration of Medical Progress

in Teaching, Practice, and Research

1807-1957

TABLE OF CONTENTS

FOREWORD

This foreword provides an opportunity to welcome a monograph, long overdue, dealing with the discovery, development, properties, and therapeutic uses of chloramphenicol, the first of the broad-spectrum antibiotics to be employed in the treatment of human infections. It is of interest that the stimulus to the rapid accumulation of information in the large-scale production of the pure antibiotic from cultures of *Streptomyces venezuelae* came, for the most part, from the demonstrated efficacy of chloramphenicol in the treatment of rickettsial infections, first in experimental animals and then in man. The observation, made during the initial studies on Malayan patients with scrub typhus, that chloramphenicol also cured patients with typhoid fever provided the additional incentive for commercial development and approval of this antibiotic. During the decade since 1948, chloramphenicol has found its place in the treatment of a wide variety of other microbial infections. Such matters are discussed in detail in appropriate chapters in the monograph.

The fact that chloramphenicol possesses a relatively simple molecular structure accounted for its early synthesis and production on a commercial scale. More important to science, it permitted synthesis of stereoisomers of the biologically active substance and the preparation of compounds with various alterations and substitutions in the parent molecule. Using such materials, it was possible to obtain data on the mode of action of chloramphenicol and on those structural requirements of the molecule concerned with antimicrobial activity. It is worth noting that chloramphenicol itself continues to be the most active biologically of any of the compounds of the series.

Reading this monograph has given me considerable pleasure for, among other things, it has recalled the exciting days in the laboratory in 1947 and on the wards in 1948 when chloramphenicol revealed itself as the first really effective agent in the treatment of the rickettsioses. It is appropriate that this treatise has been prepared by Doctors Woodward and Wisseman, both of whom have added materially to knowledge about this antibiotic. Among Woodward's many contributions were those made when he served as physician-investigator of the original American group that made medical history in Malaya in 1948. Wisseman in a series of brilliant studies demonstrated that chloramphenicol produces its antimicrobial effect by interfering with protein synthesis. The authors are to be congratulated on producing a readable, authoritative dissertation which brings together information accumulated during a decade of experience with chloramphenicol and which places the antibiotic in proper perspective with other therapeutic tools in the treatment of the numerous infectious ills of man.

Joseph E. Smadel, M.D.

Associate Director
National Institutes of Health
Bethesda, Maryland

PREFACE

Chloramphenicol has the distinction of being the first antibiotic of wide antimicrobial range to find clinical use in human infections. After its original isolation from a soil *Streptomyces* by Burkholder, brilliant studies by scientists in the laboratories of Parke, Davis & Co. led to its characterization, purification, and ultimate synthesis. After these initial developments, an Army group headed by Dr. Joseph E. Smadel conducted pertinent pharmacological and biological tests, culminating in clinical observations in Mexico and Malaya. The part played by Dr. Raymond Lewthwaite, Director of the Institute for Medical Research in Kuala Lumpur, Malaya, and his group of devoted associates cannot be overly lauded. The productive teamwork developed at the Army Medical Service Graduate School and various medical institutions throughout the United States, Puerto Rico, Bolivia, Malaya, and other centers attests to the value of collaboration between the laboratory scientist and the clinical therapist, particularly during the early stages of drug evaluation.

Chloramphenicol was the first antibiotic to arrest, in a matter of hours, the clinical manifestations of the typhus fevers, Rocky Mountain spotted fever, and other rickettsioses. It is the only antibiotic useful for the practical treatment of patients with *Salmonella typhosa* infections. For these reasons, rather complete details, with appropriate documentation, have been presented in the chapters pertaining to the use of chloramphenicol in the rickettsioses and in the enteric diseases, notably typhoid fever.

The value of chloramphenicol soon became apparent for the gram-negative infectious diseases, including brucellosis, tularemia, and pneumonic plague. The pyogenic meningitides, particularly those caused by *Hemophilus influenzae,* yielded to chloramphenicol's action. This antibiotic is regarded by many investigators as a major weapon in the therapy of meningeal infections. More recently, chloramphenicol was shown to be of significant value in clinical disorders caused by gram-positive bacteria, i.e., pneumococci, streptococci, staphylococci, clostridia. Of particular significance is its current status with respect to specific treatment of staphylococcal disease and urinary tract infections.

Experimental studies with chloramphenicol have provided better understanding of: (1) the mechanism of action of antibiotics, (2) the antagonism between antibiotics that can develop for a specific microbe, (3) the patterns of resistance, and (4) the biological nature of bacteriostasis and rickettsiostasis. The basic concepts of immunity provided by the scrub typhus studies paved the way for interrupted or intermittent antibiotic regimens and supplemental vaccine administration as ancillary measures in augmenting the immune response. The future will decide the significance of these leads.

An attempt has been made to include a wide enough representation of the published material on chloramphenicol to present a well-rounded point of view. Obviously, the gamut of writings is not included since this herculean task was beyond the capabilities of the reviewers and would serve no useful purpose. Bibliographical selection among foreign publications is based primarily on the pertinence of the contribution. An objective viewpoint has been sought with respect to the role of chloramphenicol and other chemotherapeutic drugs as remedies for specific microbial diseases. The reader will undoubtedly not always adhere to the authors' opinion. Illustrative case reports, chosen because of their representative features, have been selected to aid the reader.

Obviously this monograph on chloramphenicol is merely a compilation of the contributions of many. In preparing these chapters we have leaned heavily on the writings and personal observations of the Army group and of our Baltimore associates. We wish to acknowledge, with appreciation, the original contributions of our colleagues, Drs. Joseph E. Smadel, Maurice C. Pincoffs, Robert T. Parker, Herbert L. Ley, Jr., and Miss Ann Merideth. Most of the publications cited as originating from the Department of Medicine, School of Medicine, University of Maryland, have been supported by grants-in-aid from Parke, Davis & Co. Dr. Elwood A. Sharp and Mr. Louis W. Lang provided invaluable assistance during the course of these observations. Mrs. Anna Wroten, Miss Bertha Reed, and Miss Phyllis Auffarth deserve thanks for their assistance in preparing the manuscripts.

| Chapter I | # History of the Development of Chloramphenicol |

By 1947 the successful application of the antibiotics penicillin and streptomycin to the treatment of certain infectious diseases had established securely a new era in antimicrobial therapy. This potent and dramatic effect on the course of many infections notwithstanding, it was clearly recognized that the range of antimicrobial action of each of these antibiotics was relatively restricted and that important diseases, such as typhoid fever, rickettsial infections, and most viral diseases, failed to respond to these impressive drugs. Therefore, the observation in 1947 by Burkholder that the growth of adjacent inocula of both gram-positive and gram-negative bacteria was inhibited on agar streak cultures by a new actinomycete, isolated from the soil of a mulched field near Caracas, Venezuela, was especially significant and was destined to lead to important advances in the realm of antibiotic therapy.

From culture filtrates of this new soil organism, later named *Streptomyces venezuelae,*[2] a crystalline antibiotic was isolated that was inhibitory for a wide range of gram-positive and gram-negative bacteria, rickettsiae, and the psittacosis virus.[1, 3] Its unusually broad range of antimicrobial action, low toxicity for animals, great stability, and effective absorption from the gastrointestinal tract[4] suggested that chloramphenicol,* as the new antibiotic was called, might become the first major antibiotic suitable for clinical use since the discovery of streptomycin. Indeed, this prediction was borne out by the early clinical trials, which established chloramphenicol as the first drug of real value for the treatment of rickettsial infections and typhoid fever. Its usefulness for the treatment of numerous bacterial infections was rapidly recognized. In this manner, chloramphenicol ushered in as its first member the present series of so-called "broad-spectrum" antibiotics.

At about the same time, workers at the University of Illinois independently isolated a *Streptomyces* from compost from the South Farm of the

---

* The trade name of Parke, Davis & Co. for chloramphenicol is Chloromycetin.

1

(II)

O_2N —⟨ ⟩— $\overset{H}{\underset{OH}{\overset{①}{C}}}$ — $\overset{NHCOCHCl_2}{\underset{H}{\overset{②}{C}}}$ — $\overset{③}{CH_2OH}$

(III)

(I)

FIG. 1. Chloramphenicol (taken with permission from Hahn et al.[14]).

University at Urbana, Illinois. It had properties similar to the organism just described. When these investigators compared the antibiotic that their *Streptomyces* produced with the newly isolated crystalline chloramphenicol from Parke, Davis & Co., they found that the two were identical.[5, 6]

The unique composition of chloramphenicol, i.e., the presence of organically bound chlorine and a nitro group, which are not usually found in naturally occurring compounds, was recognized early by the Parke, Davis chemists. This group later elucidated the structure of the antibiotic and developed a method for its synthesis that was suitable for commercial production.[7-9] Chemical synthesis, in contrast with microbiological synthesis, yielded a racemic mixture of two stereoisomers, only one of which possessed antibiotic activity. However, the synthetic antibiotic, when separated from the inactive component, proved to be fully as effective for the treatment of infections as the product obtained through the fermentation reactions of *S. venezuelae*.[10]

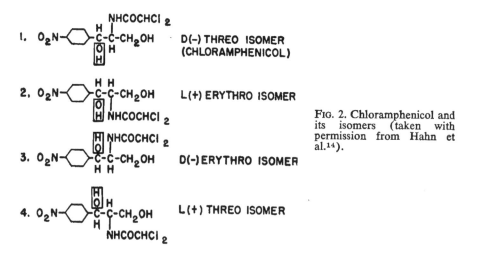

1. O_2N—⟨ ⟩—$\overset{H}{\underset{\boxed{\substack{O\\H}}}{\overset{NHCOCHCl_2}{\underset{H}{C}}}}$—$C$—$CH_2OH$ D(–) THREO ISOMER (CHLORAMPHENICOL)

2. O_2N—⟨ ⟩—$\overset{H}{\underset{\boxed{\substack{O\\H}}}{C}}$—$\overset{H}{\underset{NHCOCHCl_2}{C}}$—$CH_2OH$ L(+) ERYTHRO ISOMER

3. O_2N—⟨ ⟩—$\overset{\boxed{\substack{H\\O}}}{\underset{H}{C}}$—$\overset{NHCOCHCl_2}{\underset{H}{C}}$—$CH_2OH$ D(–) ERYTHRO ISOMER

4. O_2N—⟨ ⟩—$\overset{\boxed{\substack{H\\O}}}{\underset{H}{C}}$—$\overset{H}{\underset{NHCOCHCl_2}{C}}$—$CH_2OH$ L(+) THREO ISOMER

FIG. 2. Chloramphenicol and its isomers (taken with permission from Hahn et al.[14]).

Since then, the synthetic compound, identical in all respects with the natural product, has been produced on a commercial scale. Hence, chloramphenicol also became the first antibiotic whose chemical synthesis was economically and technically practical for large-scale production.

CHEMISTRY OF CHLORAMPHENICOL

Soon after chloramphenicol was isolated in pure form, it was recognized that the drug molecule contained a nitro group and chlorine in organically bound form, both features unusual for naturally occurring substances. Chloramphenicol is a crystalline compound, melting at 149.7 to 150.7 C. (corrected); it is optically active, $(d)^{25}$ D$=25.5°$ (ethyl acetate); and its absorption spectrum in water or 0.1 N hydrochloric acid shows an absorption peak at a wave length of 278 mμ. Its solubility in water is about 2.5 mg./ml. and in propylene glycol, about 150.8 mg./ml. It is very soluble in methanol, ethanol, butanol-1, and ethyl ether; insoluble in benzene and petroleum ether. Solutions in distilled water are highly stable, even upon boiling.[7]

In 1949 its structure was established, and confirmed by synthesis, by the works of Rebstock et al [8] and Controulis et al [9] as D(-)threo-*p*-nitrophenyl-2-dichloracetamido-1, 3-propanediol (fig. 1). Moreover, the roentgen-ray crystallographic studies of Dunitz[11] were consistent with this configuration. For discussion, the molecule is conveniently considered in three parts, as shown in figure 1: (I) the propanediol moiety, (II) the dichloracetamide side chain, and (III) the *p*-nitrophenyl group.

The two asymmetric carbons in the propanediol moiety give rise to two pairs of possible stereoisomers (fig. 2), all of which have been synthesized.[9] A strong relationship is found to exist between steric configuration and biological activity. Thus, only the isomer that conforms to the configuration of the one produced by *S. venezuelae,* i.e., the D(-)threo compound, or chloramphenicol itself, has any very significant inhibitory action on the growth of microorganisms.[9, 12] Further emphasis of the dependence of biological activity on configuration comes from the observation that the L(+)erythro compound, which has little or no effect on the growth of *Bacillus subtilis,* nevertheless inhibits the synthesis of the D(-)glutamyl polypeptide by this organism.[13] Conversely, chloramphenicol, the D(-)threo compound, which inhibits growth, has no effect on the synthesis of D(-)glutamyl polypeptide.[13] These observations would seem to have an important bearing on hypotheses concerning the way in which chloramphenicol produces its effects at a molecular level.[14]

The antibiotic molecule is vulnerable to attack by enzymes found in both animals and microbial agents. Thus, reduction of the nitro group to an amino group, hydrolysis of the amide bond to split away the dichloracetic acid side chain, degradation of the propanediol chain, and conjugation all lead to loss or reduction of antibiotic activity.[15-19] Moreover, a wide variety of alterations in the molecule have been made in different laboratories around the world, and in many instances some information is available concerning the relative biological activity of the new or substituted compounds. Information of this kind has been reviewed by Hahn et al [14] in an attempt to elucidate the structural requirements for antimicrobial activity in the chloramphenicol series of compounds. As a result of this analysis they arrived at the following generalizations.

1. The antibiotic activities of compounds in the chloramphenicol series are approximately proportional to the relative electronegativity of the *para* substituent of the aromatic ring but are not suppressed by changes in the molar volume of this ring system. The aromatic character of the ring structure appears essential for biological activity (see figure 1, III).

2. The antibiotic activity is specifically dependent on the steric configuration of the substituents attached to the two asymmetric carbon atoms of the propanediol moiety.

3. Variations beyond narrow limits in the molar volume of the electronegative head of the acylamide chain (see figure 1, II) abolish the antibiotic activity. Changes in the electronegativity result in roughly parallel changes in the growth-inhibitory activity.

Chapter II	Antimicrobial Activity

The discovery of chloramphenicol, the first of the broad-spectrum antibiotics,[1] gave promise of incorporating, in a single drug, therapeutic efficacy for infections caused by a wide variety of both gram-positive and gram-negative bacteria, as well as certain large viruses, and extending the therapeutic range to include, for the first time, infections of rickettsial etiology. Laboratory studies, using growth-inhibition techniques in the test tube and in experimentally infected animals, were undertaken to explore this amplified spectrum. Concurrently, clinicians began to use chloramphenicol in therapeutic trials in patients with infections caused by organisms against which chloramphenicol had not yet been fully evaluated in the laboratory. The purpose of this chapter is to summarize, correlate, and interpret, in so far as possible, these laboratory studies in such a way as to provide a useful concept of the range and nature of the antimicrobial action of chloramphenicol. Since these findings, at times, are at variance with clinical results, reasons for these anomalies are discussed.

Correlation between the laboratory findings and the results of clinical trials with chloramphenicol has been good in many instances, but inconsistencies have been encountered with this drug, just as they have been encountered throughout the history of the development of chemotherapeutic and antibiotic agents. Thus, the results obtained with chloramphenicol in the test tube, the experimentally infected animal, and the human being have not always been in close agreement. The typhoid bacillus, for example, was readily inhibited by chloramphenicol in the tube dilution sensitivity test,[20] and then, by chance, enteric fever in patients was found to respond to treatment with the drug.[21] Yet, the results obtained subsequently in typhoid-infected mice were not consistent with these earlier findings.[22] Similar inconsistencies have been observed with other infections.[23-25]

The reasons for the type of inconsistencies just mentioned are manifold and are not fully understood in all instances. However, it should be obvious

5

that in vitro studies can yield only certain basic information that is limited to the action of the drug in contact with microorganisms under specified artificial conditions of growth. Such tests cannot be expected to reproduce in detail all of various conditions of growth encountered in the body during infection or to compensate for the differences in drug concentration that may exist between the blood and other tissues, or between the fluids bathing the outside of cells and the interior of cells. Infection by a microorganism in an experimental animal may not be accompanied by the same mechanisms of pathogenesis or identical host-parasite interrelations as obtain in natural infection by the same organism in man. It is well known, for example, that the infection resulting from the intraperitoneal injection of artificially grown *Salmonella typhosa* into mice results in an overwhelming and rapidly fatal septicemia, which does not reproduce the unique relationship between the microorganism and tissue cells that is characteristic of typhoid fever in man. It is not surprising, then, that the results of chloramphenicol therapy of typhoid bacillus infection may differ between mice and men.

Prediction of the efficacy of any antibiotic in man from the results obtained in experimental animals must take into account differences that may exist between man and animals in the patterns of absorption, tissue distribution, and excretion of the drug. Thus, the administration of chloramphenicol to man results in maintainable high blood levels as well as excellent penetration into other body fluids, whereas in many common laboratory animals the rates of conjugation and elimination are much higher (see chapter III). For these reasons, many discrepancies exist between laboratory and clinical results, which, moreover, make comparison of chloramphenicol with other antibiotics on a weight for weight basis, in either the test tube or the experimental animal, meaningless from an applied clinical viewpoint.

IN VITRO RESULTS

The in vitro sensitivities of most of the commonly encountered pathogenic microorganisms are presented in table I. No attempt has been made to analyze the literature exhaustively. Rather, the results from several sources were compiled and series reporting large numbers of strains were included so that minor differences between reports and between techniques would be minimized. The percentages given in table I, although approximations, probably represent as reasonable an estimate of the occurrence of sensitive strains in so far as any attempt at tabulation of data of this kind can. The concentrations of 5 and 25 μg./ml. were selected because both these levels can be obtained in the body fluids of man, the lower with ordinary dosage schedules and the upper with increased dosage. When different nomenclature was used, species have been consolidated under the generic name, for example, *Proteus* species, *Salmonella*

TABLE I
Sensitivity of Pathogenic Microorganisms to Chloramphenicol

Organism	No. of strains	Per cent sensitive to:		References
		<5 µg./ml.	<25 µg./ml.	
Achromobacter species	119	8	38	26
Actinomyces bovis	3	0	100	27
Actinomyces israeli	18	100	100	28, 29
Aerobacter-Klebsiella	968	69	88	20, 26, 30-39
Alcaligenes faecalis	24	45	71	20, 33, 36, 38
Bacillus anitratum	163	4	4	40, 41
Bacillus anthracis	40	50	100	20, 30, 42, 102
Bacteroides species	115	62	97	43-45, 103
Bartonella bacilliformis	1	100	100	46
Brucella species	49	92	100	20, 30, 36, 47
Candida albicans	?	0	0	48
Clostridia species	51	42	78	49-52
Coccidioides immitis	?	0	0	53
Corynebacterium diphtheriae	185	100	100	20, 38, 54-56
Corynebacterium species	400	100	100	56
Diplococcus pneumoniae	178	99	100	20, 33, 37, 38, 57-59
Enterococci	596	61	83	33, 36-38, 59, 60
Escherichia coli	1114	68	87	20, 26, 30-33, 36-39, 59, 61
Hemophilus influenzae	203	100	100	33, 62-65
Hemophilus parapertussis	12	100	100	66
Hemophilus pertussis	110	97	100	20, 67-69
Leptospira species	6	83	100	70
Listeria monocytogenes	9	78	100	30, 71, 72
Malleomyces pseudomallei	6	83	83	83
Micrococcus pyogenes	5010	49	95	20, 30, 33, 36-38, 59, 61, 73-80
Mycobacterium tuberculosis	20	35	100	81, 82
Neisseria intracellularis	56	89	100	20, 84, 85
Neisseria gonorrhoeae	172	100	100	86, 87
Nocardia species	18	0	67	27, 29
Paracolons	77	33	77	88
Pasteurella species	18	94	100	30, 104, 105
Pleuropneumonia-like organisms	32	60	75	89, 90
Proteus species	867	22	74	20, 30, 32, 33, 36-39, 59, 91-93
Providencia species	25	—	92	93
Pseudomonas aeruginosa	774	1	10	20, 30, 32, 33, 36-39, 59, 91, 94-96
Pseudomonas species	42	5	60	95
Salmonella typhosa	120	81	100	20, 30, 61, 97, 98
Salmonella species	259	74	100	20, 36, 59, 97-99
Sarcina species	2	50	100	20
Shigella species	155	83	100	20, 30, 36, 97, 98
Streptococci (alpha)	149	96	99	30, 33, 36, 37, 60
Streptococci (beta)	189	93	98	20, 30, 33, 36-38, 60, 61
Streptococci (anaecrobic)	5	60	80	50
Vibrio cholerae	64	84	89	30, 100, 101

species, or, at times, under a name in common use, for example, paracolons, alpha streptococci, enterococci.

From table I the broad spectrum of chloramphenicol's action is apparent, notable resistant species being only *Pseudomonas aeruginosa* and members of the fungi imperfecti group. *Achromobacter* species, closely related to *Ps. aeruginosa* except in pigment production, usually are also resistant. Many groups are noteworthy because all strains tested fell within susceptible levels. It should be remembered that in all species where adequate numbers of strains have been tested, there has been much variation in sensitivity. The table can serve only as a guide, since for many species the single isolate from an individual patient may differ greatly in its susceptibility to the antibiotic from the susceptibility of other strains of the same species from other sources.

Although it is difficult to relate characteristics of organisms to their sensitivity, a number of interesting observations have been made. Toxigenic clostridia seem to be more sensitive than less virulent strains.[50] *Proteus mirabilis* is more sensitive on the whole than other *Proteus* species.[92] The occurrence of resistant strains of paracolon organisms is more common than the occurrence of resistant strains of the closely related *Escherichia coli*. Attempts have been made to relate antibiotic sensitivity and biochemical reactions within the coliform group (i.e., IMViC and sugar fermentations). Although it was found that organisms having biochemical characteristics of *E. coli* types, as opposed to *Klebsiella-Aerobacter* types, tended to be more sensitive, the results were not consistent.[106]

Resistance. In the presence of chloramphenicol, organisms on repeated subculture may acquire increased resistance to the drug in a stepwise manner, similar to the development of penicillin resistance.[107-114] The rapidity with which this resistance develops varies from strain to strain, as does the stability of the resistance in the bacterial population (mutant) when subsequently cultivated serially in drug-free medium. On the whole, highly resistant gram-negative mutants are obtained in this stepwise manner with relative ease, whereas the selection of highly resistant mutants in gram-positive organisms, such as *Micrococcus pyogenes, Streptococcus viridans,* and enterococci, is much more difficult. In general, laboratory experience suggests that resistance to chloramphenicol evolves with somewhat greater difficulty than to other antibiotics. One of the products of this type of approach was the isolation of a chloramphenicol-dependent variant of *Klebsiella pneumoniae* by Gocke and Finland.[110]

The development of cross resistance to chloramphenicol simultaneously on increasing resistance to the tetracyclines, and vice versa, has been reported but is by no means a uniform finding.[108, 112, 115-118] This, too, seems to occur more readily with gram-negative than gram-positive organisms. Cross resistance between chloramphenicol and other antibiotics has not been demonstrated.

Synergism and Antagonism of Combinations. Both antagonism and synergism have been demonstrated when chloramphenicol was combined with other antibiotics.[119-133] Such effects frequently occur in vitro when chloramphenicol is used in combination with streptomycin, penicillin, bacitracin, sulfonamides, or neomycin, but the results obtained with such combinations are unpredictable. They may be antagonistic, synergistic, or indifferent and may vary from species to species and from strain to strain. Combined effects, other than additive, have not been observed between chloramphenicol and the tetracyclines. Although Jawetz and Gunnison[131] have proposed a scheme to predict combined antibiotic sensitivity, results do not always conform to the predetermined pattern.

IN VIVO RESULTS

A summary of the treatment of experimental infections with chloramphenicol is given in table II. The efficacy of chloramphenicol in the treatment of rickettsial infections (which first led to interest in this antibiotic), as well as of infections of the psittacosis-lymphogranuloma venereum group, is clearly demonstrated. It should be emphasized that, in many of the experimental trials, certain pharmacological properties peculiar to chloramphenicol were not taken into consideration, so that results using chloramphenicol were not comparable to those obtained with other antibiotics. Thus it will be seen that results listed in table II indicating ineffectiveness in experimental infections often are not borne out when chloramphenicol is tested in these same infections in man.

Resistance. Although occasionally changes in the sensitivity patterns to chloramphenicol of commonly encountered pathogens have been noted,[169, 170] the failure of organisms to increase markedly in their resistance to chloramphenicol is impressive.[74, 171-178] This is in contrast to the changing sensitivity patterns observed with other antibiotics, and has been attributed to the more restricted use of chloramphenicol. Kirby and Ahern observed a decrease in staphylococci resistant to chloramphenicol from 20 per cent in 1952 to 6 per cent in 1953, and they attributed this to a lessened use of the antibiotic during that period.[179] However, this does not explain the consistently high sensitivity pattern maintained by staphylococcal strains isolated in hospitals where use of the antibiotic has not been curtailed.

Although little or no change has been observed in the sensitivity pattern of microorganisms to chloramphenicol, development of resistance does occur occasionally during treatment of an infection. Development of resistance while on therapy is most probably the result either of the selection of a resistant

TABLE II

Chloramphenicol in the Treatment of Experimental Infections

Disease	Host	Result	References
Amebic dysentery	Rat	Good	134
	Dog	Fair	134
Bartonellosis	Rat	Negative	138
Brucellosis	Mouse	Fair	135
	Mouse	Negative	136, 137
Cholera	Mouse	Good	100, 139
Diphtheria	Guinea pig	Negative	54
Epidemic typhus	Chick embryo	Good	3, 140-142
Feline pneumonitis	Mouse	Negative	143
Fièvre boutonneuse	Chick embryo	Good	140
Gas gangrene	Mouse	Fair	144
	Guinea pig	Good	49, 145
Herpes simplex	Mouse	Good	146
	Rabbit cornea	Negative	146
Klebsiella pneumonia	Mouse	Fair	23
Leptospirosis	Hamster	Good	147
Listerellosis	Mouse	Good	71
Murine typhus	Chick embryo	Good	140, 141
	Mouse	Good	141
Myxomatosis	Chick embryo	Negative	148
Nocardiosis	Chick embryo	Negative	27
	Mouse	Good	27
North Queensland tick typhus	Chick embryo	Good	140
Parapertussis	Mouse	Good	66
Pertussis	Chick embryo	Good	67
	Mouse	Good	66
Plague	Mouse	Good	150
	Monkey	Good	151
Plague toxin	Mouse	Good	152
Pneumococcal infection	Mouse	Negative	23
Primary atypical pneumonia (Eaton's virus)	Cotton rat	Good	153
Psittacosis-lymphogranuloma venereum	Chick embryo	Good	3, 154-157
	Mouse	Good	154
Q fever	Chick embryo	Good	140-142, 149
Rabies	Rabbit	Negative	158
Relapsing fever	Mouse	Good	159, 160
Rickettsialpox	Chick embryo	Good	140-142
	Mouse	Good	141
Rocky Mountain spotted fever	Chick embryo	Good	140-142
	Guinea pigs	Fair	141
Salmonellosis	Mouse	Good	99
	Chick	Fair	161
Scrub typhus	Chick embryo	Good	140, 141
	Mouse	Good	141
Staphylococcal infection	Mouse	Negative	23
Syphilis	Rabbit	Good	162-164
Toxoplasmosis	Mouse	Fair	165
Tuberculosis	Mouse	Fair	81, 166
Tularemia	Mouse	Good	24, 167
Typhoid infection	Mouse	Negative	22
	Rabbit	Fair	168
Vaccinia	Chick embryo	Negative	148

mutant from the original infecting strain or of the introduction of a resistant strain from an exogenous source. Acquisition of resistance as it occurs in vitro in a stepwise progressive manner seldom is encountered in vivo. Meads et al, however, have observed this in chronic urinary tract infections.[180] Other properties of coliforms, such as antigenic composition, colony morphology, and virulence, also may change under the influence of chloramphenicol.[181] The production of these variants has been accomplished in vitro when *E. coli* was grown in the presence of chloramphenicol and specific antiserum.[182, 183]

Synergism and Antagonism. Synergism and antagonisms have been demonstrated when chloramphenicol has been combined with penicillin or streptomycin in the treatment of mice infected with hemolytic streptococci, enterococci, Friedländer's bacilli, or *Ps. aeruginosa*.[126-129] Much of the literature deals with in vivo antagonisms, but in most instances these depend on critical selection of dosages and dosage schedules. Ahern and his co-workers have shown that the interference between chloramphenicol and penicillin could be demonstrated in the treatment of streptococcal infection of mice previously reported by others only when a single injection was employed. No interference was evoked when treatment was continued for two or three days.[130] The clinical significance of these experimental observations has not been evaluated adequately.

MODE OF ACTION

The over-all action of chloramphenicol on susceptible microorganisms is customarily referred to as bacteriostatic or rickettsiostatic rather than bactericidal or rickettsicidal (for example, see Smadel [184]). Indeed, with the conventional methods of in vitro testing, chloramphenicol usually is found to differ markedly from penicillin by its low capacity to kill bacteria. On the other hand, a slow but definite bactericidal effect has been observed with some frequency, and, on occasion, a rapid killing action has been described.[23, 185-188] In instances in which quantitative data are available, the bactericidal effect generally appears at drug concentrations well above the minimal bacteriostatic level.[189, 190] Moreover, the sensitivity of bacteria to the lethal action of chloramphenicol seems to vary greatly even from strain to strain of the same species. Thus, three strains of *E. coli* have been observed in which the action of chloramphenicol was predominantly bacteriostatic, slowly bactericidal, and rapidly bactericidal, respectively (Wisseman, unpublished data). Therefore, for practical purposes, the action of chloramphenicol would best be considered principally suppressive unless specific laboratory data are available that indicate a lethal action on the particular strain under consideration.

The precise mechanism(s) whereby chloramphenicol produces its inhibitory effect on bacterial growth is not yet clear. Presumably, this occurs through interference with some essential microbial metabolic process.

Numerous studies made along this line of approach have revealed an interesting variety of effects of the drug on different aspects of bacterial metabolism. Eagle and Saz[191] have presented an excellent résumé of the observations made by different investigators. However, much of the work points to a prompt, reproducible, and selective inhibition of bacterial protein synthesis as one of the major metabolic effects of chloramphenicol.[12, 191-195] This effect on protein synthesis occurs at minimal bacteriostatic concentrations of the drug and is not accompanied by comparable effects on nucleic acid and polysaccharide synthesis or energy metabolism.[12, 191-195] How chloramphenicol interferes with protein synthesis remains to be elucidated.

ASSAY METHODS

Colorimetric, polarographic, and microbiological methods have been used for the assay of chloramphenicol. Colorimetric methods utilize the reduction of the aromatic nitro group of chloramphenicol to an amino group and the determination of the resulting amine by a modification of the Bratton-Marshall diazo procedure.[196, 197] Results of these methods, as well as of the polarographic method,[198] include nitro-containing degradation products, so that erroneous results are obtained when these procedures are used for the analysis of materials, such as urine, containing high concentrations of these inactive products. Assay by the measurement of antimicrobial activity may be accomplished by turbidimetry, i.e., the 50 per cent inhibition of *Shigella sonnei*,[199, 200] and by diffusion plate assay, i.e., cup-plate method employing *Sarcina lutea*.[201]

Chapter III | Pharmacological Properties

Chloramphenicol is a stable substance that is readily and rapidly absorbed from the upper gastrointestinal tract. The relatively small size of its molecule makes possible easy diffusion of this antibiotic into tissues and body fluids and across different internal barriers. The distribution within the body and the metabolism of the drug are discussed in this section. The dosage forms, routes of administration, and side effects are discussed separately in succeeding sections.

ABSORPTION AND DISTRIBUTION IN BODY FLUIDS AND TISSUES

Chloramphenicol is absorbed rapidly from the gastrointestinal tract after oral administration of the crystalline compound.[202-208] For example, it is first detectable in the blood within about 30 minutes after ingestion of a single 1.0 Gm. dose. Concentrations are maximal in about two hours and then decline slowly over a period of several hours. With large single doses, i.e., 2 to 3 Gm., low levels may persist in the serum for as long as 24 hours. The maximal concentrations attained and the time required for the serum concentration to fall to negligible values depend on the size of the dose. As might be expected, repeated doses at four to eight hour intervals usually maintain serum concentrations within the accepted therapeutic range, and large doses repeated frequently tend to have some cumulative effect. In dogs subjected to traumatic shock, absorption from the gastrointestinal tract continues; however, effective antibacterial concentrations in the serum develop more slowly and peak concentrations are lower than in animals not in shock.[209]

The active form of chloramphenicol predominates in the blood; nevertheless, conjugated forms (*vide infra*), detectable by chemical but not by microbiological assay methods, are also present.[204] In solution, the antibiotic combines reversibly with albumin. Indeed, about 60 per cent of the drug probably occurs in protein-bound form in the serum.[4]

After chloramphenicol gains access to the blood, it diffuses rapidly into

13

many tissues and across a wide variety of barriers within the body. Animal studies,[204] however, indicate that the distribution is not uniform throughout all the tissues and body fluids. Thus, the highest concentrations are found in the kidney and liver and the lowest in the brain and spinal fluid. Systematic studies of the drug distribution in man are very limited in number. Gray[219] found the antibiotic to be present in lung, heart, liver, spleen, kidney, brain, and gut of 5 human bodies. Moreover, a review of the more detailed studies of individual tissues and fluids discussed in the following paragraphs bears out this general impression.

Chloramphenicol enters the spinal fluid with relative ease, even in the absence of meningeal inflammation.[64, 203, 206, 208, 211, 212] After a single 1 or 2 Gm. dose in adults, the antibiotic appears in the spinal fluid within two to three hours, reaching a peak concentration in four or five hours. The levels attained in the spinal fluid have been reported by some to range between 6 and 60 per cent, with an average of 27 per cent, of the concentration attained in the blood serum of normal children, while other investigators working with both adults and children frequently report a figure of about 50 per cent. This last figure approximates roughly the proportion of chloramphenicol that is not bound to serum proteins and is presumably more readily diffusible. Some investigators have reported a cumulative effect with repeated doses; others have not detected this phenomenon. In normal children it has been estimated that serum levels between 25 and 35 μg./ml. are required to achieve regularly a spinal fluid level of about 5 μg./ml.[206] It is important to note that with blood serum levels of 10 μg./ml. or less, chloramphenicol has been found only irregularly or not at all in the spinal fluid.[206, 208]

Limited published observations suggest that chloramphenicol penetrates readily into pleural and ascitic fluids. In one study, concentrations of 2 to 14 μg./ml. were detected within four hours after a single oral dose of 1 to 2 Gm.[212] The placental barrier is crossed with ease. Concentrations have been found in the fetal circulation that are between about 30 and 80 per cent of that in the maternal circulation. No toxic effects have been detected in the infants.[213, 214]

The drug penetrates into all parts of the eye.[215, 216] Chloramphenicol administered parenterally to the rabbit penetrates well into the ocular structures and is found in the aqueous and vitreous humors, cornea, iris, chorioretinal tissues, sclerae, optic nerve, conjunctiva, muscle, and lacrimal gland. Observations of this type in human eyes are more limited; nevertheless, they indicate that orally administered chloramphenicol passes very readily into the aqueous and vitreous humors. Moreover, chloramphenicol applied locally penetrates into the aqueous humor.

Chloramphenicol passes into the saliva where fluctuations in its concentration parallel closely, though at lower levels, those of the blood.[217] This probably accounts for the bitter taste experienced by some patients receiving full doses of the drug. There are divergent reports with respect to chloramphenicol concentrations in human milk. One group[211] found the level in milk to be about one-half that in the serum obtained simultaneously, while another group[218] failed to detect the drug in the milk of 12 women in different phases of lactation. The antibiotic concentrations in the urine and bile are considered in detail under "Metabolism and Excretion," since these are also routes for the disposal of the antibiotic and its metabolized forms.

A curious exception to the otherwise generally widespread distribution of chloramphenicol in the body is found in the study of Borski et al.[219] These authors reported that one hour after administration of a single 0.5 Gm. intravenous dose, when the blood level was within accepted therapeutic range, measurable concentrations of chloramphenicol were not found in the prostatic fluid, prostatic tissue, or semen. In contrast, penicillin, the tetracyclines, and bacitracin were readily detectable under similar conditions. Unfortunately, comparable information is not available for intervals longer than one hour after administration or after repeated doses of the drug.

PENETRATION INTO CELLS

The effectiveness of chloramphenicol in the therapy of some infectious diseases in which intracellular localization of the causative organisms is a prominent feature suggests that this antibiotic may penetrate into cells of the body in an active form. Although this point has not been proved unequivocally, a number of observations do point in this direction. For example, Glazko et al [220] reported that chloramphenicol and one of its hydrolytic products were associated in part with cellular elements of the blood, while the glucuronide derivative remained almost entirely in the plasma. The study of Magoffin and Spink[221] left unanswered the question of a bacteriostatic action on *Brucella* organisms located within leukocytes. Furthermore, Pramer,[222] who made direct analysis of cellular contents, demonstrated a slow but definite penetration of the antibiotic into cells of the alga, *Nitella clavata*. Perhaps the best evidence, though still indirect, that chloramphenicol enters cells in an active form is found in the recent observations of Bozeman et al[223] who demonstrated that addition of the drug to tissue cultures of MB-III cells infected with *Rickettsia tsutsugamushi* is followed by a rapid disappearance of visible organisms from the cells and by a prompt reduction in infective titer.

METABOLISM AND EXCRETION

Chemical assays indicate that 75 to 90 per cent of an oral dose of chloramphenicol is excreted in the urine within 24 hours after administration

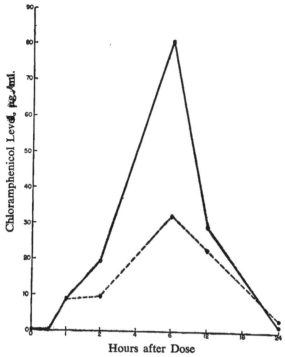

FIG. 3. Simultaneous chloramphenicol levels in blood and bile after a 4.0 Gm. oral dose (after Woodward et al[226]). The patient was a 65 year old woman weighing 85 Kg. ——— = blood; – – – – = bile.

in forms that retain intact the aryl nitro group; yet microbiological assays reveal the presence here of antibiotic activity equivalent to only 10 per cent or less of the administered dose.[202, 204] These data suggest that chloramphenicol is inactivated in the body. Indeed, chemical examination also reveals the presence of a hydrolytic product and a glucuronic acid conjugate of chloramphenicol in the urine, which actually form the major portion of the excreted products.[18] Of these, only the unaltered chloramphenicol has any significant antibiotic activity. Despite the relatively large fraction of the administered dose that is converted to forms not active against bacteria, urine concentrations of the active compound are relatively high, and peak levels of the antibiotic exceeding 200 μg./ml. have been recorded after a single 1.5 Gm. oral dose.[204] The principal mechanism in man for renal excretion of the unaltered chloramphenicol is probably glomerular filtration, whereas the inactive nitro compounds are apparently excreted largely by tubular mechanisms.[204] Probenecid does not affect the excretion of the unchanged antibiotic.[224]

A much smaller fraction of the administered dose of chloramphenicol is excreted in the bile.[204, 225-229] Glazko et al [204] reported total recovery from the bile by chemical assay of only 2.7 per cent of a 1.0 Gm. dose given a patient with a biliary fistula. The amount excreted in a form active against bacteria was even lower (0.14 per cent). Gray[225] found that the bile levels in a patient with acute cholecystitis who received 100 mg./Kg. chloramphenicol per day varied between 6 and 51 μg./ml. and that the total amount excreted in 24 hours ranged between 486 and 6222 μg. These observations are similar to those of Woodward et al [226] who reported that chloramphenicol was excreted in the bile at levels significantly lower than those present in the serum. Figure 3, which is taken from their report, shows simultaneous blood and bile levels. Other investigators[227-229] have found somewhat higher concentrations in the bile. Thus, while the bile appears to serve as a minor route for the excretion of chloramphenicol and its metabolized forms in man, forms of the drug that possess antimicrobial action are excreted in the bile in concentrations within the ordinary therapeutic range.

Only very small amounts of chloramphenicol are excreted in the feces.[206, 210] Gray[225] found that the amount of chloramphenicol detectable by microbiological assay ranged between 0 and 3 μg./Gm. of feces when the oral dosage of the crystalline compound was 30 mg./Kg./day; between 4 and 9 μg./Gm. when the dosage was 75 mg./Kg./day; and between 3 and 11 μg./Gm. when the dosage was 100 mg./Kg./day. In contrast, stool concentrations are much higher when chloramphenicol palmitate is administered orally instead of the crystalline form.[230]

There are significant differences in the pharmacological considerations of chloramphenicol between man and some experimental animals. For example, the rat excretes chloramphenicol freely in the bile in the form of inactive nitro compounds, chiefly the glucuronide. In this animal, the glucuronide is not reabsorbed readily from the intestine, and although a very small amount may be reabsorbed and subsequently be excreted into the urine, a larger portion passes to the cecum, where it is first hydrolyzed to chloramphenicol and then is reduced to inactive amines by bacteria. Some of the amines just mentioned are excreted in the feces and some are absorbed from the intestine and are subsequently excreted into the urine.[18, 19, 204] These observations in the rat illustrate the type of pitfalls that might be encountered if pharmacological, or even therapeutic, results obtained from animals were extended too freely directly to man without prior confirmation.

The major site of conjugation of chloramphenicol is presumed to be the liver. The livers of rats possess enzymes capable of transforming the antibiotic into inactive nitro forms. Moreover, the livers and kidneys of rats and guinea pigs also have the capacity to reduce chloramphenicol enzymatically to inactive aryl amines.[204]

SUMMARY

Chloramphenicol is rapidly absorbed from the gastrointestinal tract, attains therapeutic concentrations in the blood quickly, and diffuses readily into the cerebrospinal fluid and other body fluids. Indirect evidence suggests that chloramphenicol also penetrates into cells of the body in a form that has antimicrobial activity. The antibiotic is conjugated and degraded, presumably in the liver, and is largely excreted in both active and inactive forms in the urine, although it also appears in bile and saliva in lesser, although still therapeutic, amounts.

| | Dosage Forms and |
|Chapter IV | Methods of Administration |

Chloramphenicol is currently available in a variety of forms for oral, parenteral, and topical therapy of infections. Rapid absorption of the antibiotic after parenteral or oral administration and its prompt diffusion into extravascular body fluids make it particularly useful in the treatment of generalized infectious processes.

Chloramphenicol for oral administration is supplied in hermetically sealed capsules each containing 250 mg.* and in capsules of 50 and 100 mg. each. A tasteless palmitic acid ester of chloramphenicol containing 125 mg./4 ml. is available for use in the pediatric age group. As the antibiotic is quite stable, it is not necessary to refrigerate any of these preparations. Chloramphenicol should be administered orally to adults at the rate of 50 mg./Kg. body weight per day; children should receive larger amounts (75 to 150 mg./Kg. body weight per day) during the acute phases of generalized infections. Five to seven days of therapy will suffice for most acute infections. Dosage intervals of four to eight hours will assure body fluid concentration above minimum effective levels. Patients in whom gastric intubation is indicated may be given chloramphenicol suspended in a suitable fluid medium.

---

* The trade name of Parke, Davis & Co. for oral chloramphenicol in hermetically sealed capsules containing 250 mg. is Chloromycetin Kapseals; for capsules of 50 or 100 mg., Chloromycetin capsules; for a palmitic acid ester of chloramphenicol containing 125 mg./4 ml. suspension, Chloromycetin Palmitate: for hermetically sealed capsules containing 125 mg. of chloramphenicol and 125 mg. of dihydrostreptomycin sulfate, Chlorostrep Kapseals; for a microcrystalline form of chloramphenicol, Chloromycetin intramuscular; for intravenous chloramphenicol, Chloromycetin solution; for a solution of 0.5 per cent chloramphenicol in propylene glycol with 1 per cent benzocaine, Chloromycetin otic; for chloramphenicol as a dry powder with buffer, Chloromycetin ophthalmic; for 1 per cent chloramphenicol in a petrolatum ointment, Chloromycetin ophthalmic ointment; for chloramphenicol with hydrocortisone acetate, Chloromycetin-hydrocortisone ophthalmic.

Adequate serum concentrations of chloramphenicol have also been achieved after the rectal insertion of punctured capsules.

Hermetically sealed capsules containing 125 mg. of chloramphenicol and 125 mg. of dihydrostreptomycin sulfate may be employed in the treatment of intestinal infections and in the pre- and post-operative management of patients in whom bowel surgery is contemplated. Dosage should be calculated on the basis of the chloramphenicol content of the preparation.

For intramuscular use, a microcrystalline form of chloramphenicol is available in rubber-capped vials containing the dry powder, with which a suspension is prepared by adding 2.5 ml. of physiological sodium chloride or sterile water for injection. It is for intramuscular use only. This form of chloramphenicol has a repository quality and may not produce blood concentrations in keeping with the dosage given. Adults should receive 1.0 Gm. every 6 to 12 hours; children, 100 to 150 mg./Kg./day.

Chloramphenicol solution for intravenous use is packaged in 2 ml. ampoules each containing 500 mg. of chloramphenicol in a 50 per cent aqueous solution of N, N-dimethylacetamide. It should be used only in those instances where rapid serum concentrations of antibiotic are mandatory and oral therapy is prohibitive. It is not soluble in small volumes of aqueous diluents and dry syringes must be employed in its removal from the ampoule. Chloramphenicol solution should be diluted in 100 to 200 ml. of physiological sodium chloride or 5 per cent dextrose in normal saline by discharging the contents of an ampoule through a needle submerged in the diluent. Adults should receive 0.5 to 1.0 Gm. at six hour intervals at a rate not to exceed 20 ml./minute. The dosage for children is 75 to 150 mg./Kg./day to be given in divided dosage at six hour intervals.

Chloramphenicol is available in several forms for local application. For otic use, there is a clear, colorless solution consisting of 0.5 per cent chloramphenicol in propylene glycol with 1 per cent benzocaine. It is administered locally at the rate of 2 to 3 drops several times daily. Ophthalmic chloramphenicol is supplied as a dry powder with buffer, with which stable 0.16 to 0.5 per cent solution may be prepared by adding sterile distilled water. An ophthalmic ointment containing 1 per cent chloramphenicol in a petrolatum base is also available. Both types of preparations have also been incorporated with hydrocortisone acetate. In addition to the amounts of chloramphenicol just mentioned, the powder contains 25 mg. and the ointment 0.5 per cent hydrocortisone acetate. Chloramphenicol cream contains 1 per cent chloramphenicol in a nonirritating cream for topical use in the treatment of superficial pyodermas. It is applied locally to the affected areas four times daily.

The successful therapy of any infectious disease depends in part on establishing effective concentrations of antibiotic in tissue fluids. For this reason, adjustments in dosage should take into account the degree of sensi-

TABLE III
Simultaneous Chloramphenicol Concentrations in Serum and Cerebrospinal Fluid

Patient	Serum concentration, μg./ml.	Cerebrospinal fluid concentration, μg./ml.
1	79	37
2	55	17
4	20	11
6	11	7
3	56	26
5	20	7

tivity of the offending organism as well as the weight of the patient. Thus, while the usual daily adult oral dosage of chloramphenicol is 3.0 Gm., consideration should be given to the use of 4 to 6 Gm. daily when moderately resistant (15 to 50 μg./ml.) organisms are encountered. Administration of single oral doses of 1.0 and 2.0 Gm. of chloramphenicol will result in peak serum concentrations of approximately 10 to 15 μg./ml. of serum, respectively, within two to four hours.[231] The antibiotic concentration falls below 50 per cent of the peak concentration by the twelfth hour. When 1.0 Gm. doses are administered at eight hour intervals, sustained levels may be maintained between 10 and 25 μg./ml. of serum. Concentrations of chloramphenicol in extravascular fluids, such as cerebrospinal fluid,[85, 232] bile, and pleural effusions, usually range between one third and one half of the serum concentration (table III). When the afore-mentioned oral dosage regimen is employed, the concentration of chloramphenicol in the urine varies from 150 to 300 μg./ml.

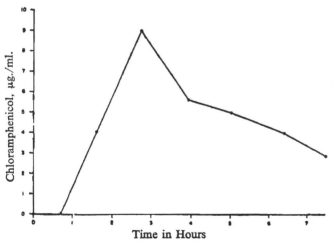

FIG. 4. Chloramphenicol serum concentrations after single 250 mg. oral dose (70 mg./Kg.) of chloramphenicol palmitate in 1 month old boy.

Time in Hours

TABLE IV
Chloramphenicol Serum Concentrations after Intramuscular Administration

Patient	Intramuscular dose, mg./Kg. body weight	Chloramphenicol serum levels, µg./ml.				
		3 hr.	6 hr.	12 hr.	24 hr.	48 hr.
1	150	20.8	24.2	29.2	15.8	3.9
2	150	16.2	24.0	20.4	10.7	0.0
3	300	34.5	37.8	50.1	77.0	33.2

(Modified with permission from Ross et al.[233])

In the pediatric age group, adequate serum concentrations of chloramphenicol are best ensured by employing 100 to 150 mg./Kg. of body weight for patients weighing 10 Kg. or more. It has been our practice not to give less than 750 mg. of chloramphenicol daily to infants, regardless of weight. This is particularly true of chloramphenicol palmitate, with which therapeutically adequate levels of antibiotic may not be achieved with lower dosage schedules. As shown in figure 4, administration of a single oral dose of 250 mg. of chloramphenicol palmitate to an infant weighing 4 Kg. resulted in a peak concentration of 9.0 µg./ml. of serum by the third hour. Serum concentrations after multiple doses of the palmitate ester vary between 5 and 30 µg. when it is given at the rate of 150 mg./Kg. body weight per day.

Intramuscular administration of chloramphenicol results in adequate serum concentrations for 24 hours when 100 to 150 mg./Kg. body weight are employed.[231] Because of this repository effect, intramuscular chloramphenicol may be given at 12 hour intervals if adequate amounts are employed. Table IV presents the results of studies conducted by Ross and his associates[233] with this preparation. These authors, as well as Schoenbach et al,[234] have demonstrated that cerebrospinal fluid concentrations of chloramphenicol using the intramuscular form are comparable to those obtained after oral admininstration of the antibiotic.

Serum concentrations of chloramphenicol after intravenous administration are illustrated in table V. Single intravenous doses of 0.5 and 1.0 Gm. result in peak concentrations of about 5 and 10 µg./ml., respectively. Adequate concentrations can usually be demonstrated in serum six to eight hours after

TABLE V
Chloramphenicol Concentrations after Intravenous Administration

Patient	Weight, Kg.	Intravenous dose, Gm.	Chloramphenicol serum concentration, µg./ml.				
			1 hr.	2 hr.	3 hr.	4 hr.	5 hr.
1	80	0.5	5.4	5.5	4.8	4.3	3.4
2	60	0.5	13.0	10.0	5.9	5.7	—
3	70	0.5	9.0	6.3	5.9	6.0	4.8

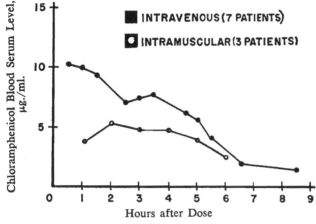

FIG. 5. Chloramphenicol blood serum concentrations after single 1.0 Gm. doses of chloramphenicol acid succinate.

administration of 0.5 or 1.0 Gm. doses. As in the case of other preparations, diffusion into extravascular body fluids is rapid and in a high percentage of the amount given.

Parenteral administration of chloramphenicol has been attended by certain difficulties related to its solubility, absorption, and ease of administration. It has been necessary to employ two forms of the antibiotic for intramuscular and intravenous use. The advantages of a highly soluble, nonirritating form of chloramphenicol for parenteral use are obvious. A new ester, chloramphenicol acid succinate, has been under study recently and it appears that these prerequisites have been met without any loss of antimicrobial activity. One Gm. of this preparation is readily soluble in 2 to 3 ml. of sterile water, physiological saline, or glucose solution. It may be injected intravenously in this volume without untoward effect. Adequate serum concentrations of chloramphenicol are found after the intramuscular or intravenous injection of the chloramphenicol acid succinate, and there is rapid diffusion of chloramphenicol into extravascular body fluids (figure 5) when it is employed in the amounts suggested for other forms of this antibiotic.

Chloramphenicol acid succinate has been used as the sole form of therapy in a variety of acute infectious diseases,[235, 236] and the results suggest that this preparation will be of great value in those instances where parenteral therapy is indicated.

| Chapter V | # Side Effects of Chloramphenicol Therapy |

Before administering a chemotherapeutic agent, the practitioner should consider the proper choice of antibiotic, the route and duration of therapy, the range of action, and the potential patterns of resistance between the microbe and the agent. A decisive factor concerns toxic action on the part of the administered drug. Florey[237] was cognizant of this last criterion when he listed the desirable properties of an antibiotic:

A substance must possess little toxicity to the intact animal body and the less of this the better. Not only must it lack toxicity to the intact body, but also to individual cells such as the leukocyte. It must not damage the kidneys if it is excreted and possibly concentrated by them, and its toxicity must not only be low following a single dose, but it must not cause any changes in the body when given in frequent doses for a considerable length of time.

Chemotherapeutic agents of all types, including the antibiotics, have provoked reactions in man both mild and serious, and the expected therapeutic benefits of an antibiotic must be weighed against its potential undesirable side effects. The undesirable reactions in man ascribed to chloramphenicol may be grouped as in table VI.

GASTROINTESTINAL REACTIONS

A variety of gastrointestinal reactions, such as nausea and unpleasant taste, occasionally accompany the oral administration of chloramphenicol capsules. After several days of therapy, the tongue may become red, the papillae smooth and glistening with slight macroglossia. Stomatitis is usually mild, consisting of congestion and tenderness of the buccal mucosa.[25, 238, 239] Rarely, ulceration and cheilosis ensue with occasional progression to widespread oral lesions of the thrush type. This form of stomatitis is ordinarily caused by superimposed infection to *Candida albicans*[240, 241] and is an indication for stopping the antibiotic.[238] Diarrhea and irritation of the perianal tissues

24

TABLE VI

Grouping of Undesirable Reactions in Man Ascribed to Chloramphenicol

Gastrointestinal reactions	Allergic or hypersensitivity reactions	Blood dyscrasias
Nausea and vomiting	Angioneurotic edema	Aplastic anemia
Stomatitis, glossitis	Vesicular and macular dermatitis	Thrombocytopenia
Diarrhea	Jarisch-Herxheimer reaction	Pancytopenia
Pruritus ani		Leukopenia
Pseudomembranous enterocolitis	Pyrexia	Hypoplastic anemia

may occur after prolonged administration of chloramphenicol or in patients who have received the antibiotic previously. Occasionally diarrhea and pruritus ani may be protracted, although gastrointestinal sequelae are usually minor and regress when antibiotic treatment is stopped.[238, 240-244] Severe diarrhea is more common after the tetracycline antibiotics than after chloramphenicol.[242]

The normal human intestinal flora may be altered appreciably after antibiotic administration. *C. albicans* and other yeasts are prominent among the resistant group of microbes that may ensue. Finland and Weinstein[242] observed that the organisms most frequently increased during antibiotic therapy were *Proteus vulgaris, Ps. aeruginosa, Staphylococcus aureus,* and *C. albicans.* Although fungi of the *Candida* group may be cultivated readily from the intestinal and respiratory tracts after the administration of tetracycline antibiotics and, to a lesser extent, chloramphenicol, significant tissue changes due to these fungi are not common.[243, 244] Chloramphenicol is less antiseptic for the intestinal flora. The lowered incidence of diarrhea may be due to the rapid absorption of the antibiotic from the gut and prompt inactivation of that remaining in the intestine.

Although pseudomembranous inflammation of the intestine has been recognized for more than a century, there appears to be a recent increase in incidence. The pathogenesis is unclear, yet the organism most commonly implicated is *Staph. aureus.* This severe reaction occurs in patients who are already ill with diseases such as pneumonia or peritonitis, or it may follow operative procedures.[245, 246] Pseudomembranous enterocolitis was reported in 5 patients who received chlortetracycline or chloramphenicol or both.[247] The emergence of antibiotic-resistant staphylococci, producing enteritis, is not limited to the use of chlortetracycline, oxytetracycline, or chloramphenicol. In 1948, Kramer[248] reported a fatal case after oral streptomycin therapy. Erythromycin is effective in treatment of staphylococcic enteritis, although this antibiotic may cause gastrointestinal irritation[249] and drug resistance may develop.[250]

Fatty infiltration of the liver has not been a troublesome clinical problem with chloramphenicol.

Experimentally mild anemia may occur when chloromphenicol is administered to dogs in high dosages for long periods.[251] Moreover, large dosages of chloramphenicol given to dogs resulted in inanition, high mortality, and marrow hypocellularity.[252] These authors reported the development of fatty changes in the livers of dogs given synthetic chloramphenicol.[252] These studies were conducted with small numbers of dogs given excessive doses of chloramphenicol, i.e., 250 mg./Kg. body weight. Reutner and his associates[253] confirmed these findings in a suitably controlled study. They attributed the hemopoietic changes to the malnutritional effects secondary to the anorexia produced by large doses of the antibiotic and not to the antibiotic action per se, since similar changes could be produced with other antibiotics if the animals' nutritional intake were limited to that of the animals on chloramphenicol. Some animals received the synthetic and some the fermentive type of drug.

There have been attempts to determine the granulocytopenic properties of chloramphenicol and other antibiotics by utilizing intermittent dosage regimens in dogs.[254] The regimens employed led to granulocyte depression after seven days although the daily doses used were high, i.e., 250 mg./Kg. body weight.

Alterations of the flora of the upper respiratory passages and moniliasis involving the lung parenchyma have been ascribed to antibiotic therapy.[255, 256]

ALLERGIC OR HYPERSENSITIVITY REACTIONS

Various allergic side reactions result from hypersensitivity of the host to the drug. Allergic skin reactions consisting of angioneurotic edema and vesicular and maculopapular types of dermatitis have been reported in patients sensitive to chloramphenicol.[25, 238, 239, 256-258] We have observed urticaria and vesicular lesions after chloramphenicol treatment. The dermal lesions, usually mild, subside when the drug is stopped.

The Jarisch-Herxheimer reaction, regarded initially as a sequel to the antitreponemal action of arsphenamine and penicillin, has been reported after chloramphenicol therapy of patients with syphilis, brucellosis, and probably typhoid fever. Romansky et al [259] noted a mild Herxheimer reaction in syphilitic patients treated with chloramphenicol. A similar exacerbation of symptoms has been reported in brucellosis by Knight.[260] Among approximately 20 patients acutely ill with brucellosis, moderately severe febrile toxic reactions occurred twice.[261] In each patient, demonstration of bacteremia for *Brucella abortus* and *Brucella suis* confirmed the clinical impression. Note in figure 6 that the febrile component of the Herxheimer reaction occurred approximately six

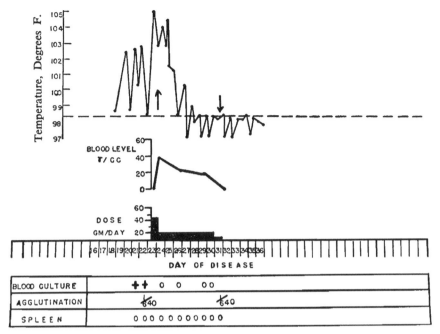

Fig. 6. Brucellosis. Course of illness in 29 year old man (120 lb.) with *Br. abortus* infection. Note febrile reaction after chloramphenicol administration.

hours after the administration of chloramphenicol. The reaction consisted of a pyrexia of 105.5 F. and exacerbation of all clinical manifestations of brucellosis. This reaction subsided in approximately 36 hours, after which time the course was favorable.

Another patient developed a similar reaction beginning 12 hours after chloramphenicol therapy was instituted. After an acute phase lasting approximately 36 hours, recovery rapidly ensued.

Several investigators have been impressed with a "shock-type reaction" characterized by circulatory collapse in typhoid patients treated with chloramphenicol.[262, 263] This has been ascribed to a sudden release of typhoidal endotoxin, which "overwhelms the resistance of an already weakened patient." [262] Unlike the Herxheimer reaction of brucellosis, the temperature is usually depressed. Exacerbation of fever has been reported.[264] The accentuation of symptoms appears usually within 24 hours of the start of chloramphenicol therapy and persists for 24 to 48 hours. The toxic crisis is said to occur in severely ill patients.[238] Conceivably, it represents an enhancement of the typhoid toxemia due to liberation of endotoxin from killed organisms.[264] The point is unproved.

We have not observed these reactions of toxemia or circulatory collapse in approximately 200 chloramphenicol-treated typhoid fever cases but regard each as a phenomenon that should be carefully evaluated. Since these reactions are uncommon in typhoid patients receiving chloramphenicol and rare in other febrile illnesses treated with chloramphenicol, it is illogical to ascribe them to a specific toxic action of this antibiotic.[265]

The toxic crises might be prevented by administering small initial doses of chloramphenicol to very "toxic" patients, increasing the dosage gradually as the infection is brought under control. Farinaud and Portes[266] advocated this program. Cortisone is antitoxemic for patients with typhoid fever, and although we do not advocate the routine use of hormones, untoward toxic manifestations may be controlled.[267-269]

The nature of the Herxheimer reaction is obscure and further work is needed to clarify its pathogenesis.

PYREXIAL REACTIONS

Pyrexia resulting from host sensitivity to chloramphenicol occurs as with other antimicrobial drugs. Marmion[238] reported delayed fever in 7 per cent of typhoid patients treated with chloramphenicol. The temperature rise usually occurred at the end of the drug course. In 4 of 20 patients, urticaria occurred concurrently. Systemic manifestations accompanying the fever are mild and subside two to five days after cessation of treatment.

NEUROLOGICAL SEQUELAE

Blurring of vision, optic neuritis, and digital paresthesia, considered to be manifestations of a toxic polyneuritis, occurred in a patient with ulcerative colitis who received chloramphenicol for five months.[270] Vertigo and convulsions mentioned by one author may have resulted from the tissue changes of typhoid fever rather than as a specific reaction to chloramphenicol.[238] In a patient with staphylococcal endocarditis treated with chlortetracycline and chloramphenicol, peripheral and optic neuritis associated with prothrombin deficiency and gastrointestinal bleeding occurred.[271] Neurological sequelae have not been unduly troublesome.

BLOOD DYSCRASIAS

Soon after the initial clinical trials with chloramphenicol in 1948, it was apparent that the antibiotic was well tolerated. Subsequently, as the other broad-spectrum antibiotics became available, chloramphenicol appeared to be the least toxic in terms of gastrointestinal and other undesirable sequelae. Because of this apparent freedom from important side reactions, the antibiotic attained wide and often unwise therapeutic application.

TABLE VII

Blood Disorders: Results of 1952 Survey

	Group A (chlor- amphenicol alone)		Group B (chloramphenicol plus other drugs)		Group C (chloramphenicol not involved)	
	No. cases	No. deaths	No. cases	No. deaths	No. cases	No. deaths
Aplastic anemia	44	23	95	73	157	97
Pancytopenia	2	—	5	—	15	7
Granulocytopenia	4	—	14	3	80	24
Thrombocytopenia	—	—	10	5	18	5
Anemia, other types	5	—	18	—	30	10
Miscellaneous	—	—	1	1	41	12
Total	55	23	143	82	341	155

(Reprinted with permission from Lewis et al.[284])

Adverse blood reactions attributable to chloramphenicol first appeared in the medical literature in 1950, and additional alarming reports in various periodicals alerted the profession to the potential hazard of this effective antibiotic.[272-283] As a sequel to these distressing reports, the results of a survey on the relationship of chloramphenicol to blood dyscrasia with observations on other drugs was reported in December, 1952, by investigators of the Food and Drug Administration.[284] It was concluded that on rare occasions and in certain susceptible individuals, chloramphenicol was associated with blood dyscrasias including aplastic anemia, thrombocytopenia, purpura, granu-'ocytopenia, and pancytopenia.

Although this report pointed out that the incidence of blood dyscrasias could not be shown to have increased since the introduction of chloramphenicol, the possibility of toxic side effects due to the existence of an obscure sensitization phenomenon was suggested. There were 539 case records from 37 states collected in this survey. In 55 cases chloramphenicol was the only drug known to have been administered since it had first become available in 1949 (see table VII). Forty-four (80 per cent) of these cases were diagnosed as aplastic anemia. Of 143 persons who had been treated with chloramphenicol plus other drugs including broad-spectrum antibiotics, anticonvulsants, antipyretics, and antihistaminics, 95 cases (66 per cent) were ascribed to aplastic anemia. There were 341 cases of blood dyscrasia in which chloramphenicol was not involved. Of these, 157 (46 per cent) were diagnosed as aplastic anemia. Fifty-four cases (15 per cent) in the latter group were associated with the antecedent use of drugs other than chloramphenicol. Those remaining were considered idiopathic.[284]

Based on these and other data, the National Research Council in 1952 recommended that the following statement be required on the labels of all

TABLE VIII

Chloramphenicol: 1953 Survey of Blood Dyscrasias

	Total cases	Aplastic anemia
A. Chloramphenicol only known drug administered	29	26
B. Chloramphenicol and other drugs administered	88	54
C. Chloramphenicol not involved	1050	137
Discarded*	281	
Total cases reviewed	1448	217

(Reprinted with permission from Welch et al.[285])
* Two hundred eighty-one cases discarded because of lack of information or no evidence of actual blood dyscrasia.

formulations for chloramphenicol for systemic use: "Blood dyscrasia may be associated with the intermittent or prolonged use. It is essential that adequate blood studies be made." In the medical literature describing chloramphenicol, the following statement was also recommended: "Certain blood dyscrasias (aplastic anemia, thrombocytopenic purpura, granulocytopenia and pancytopenia) have been associated with the administration of chloromycetin. It is essential that adequate blood studies be made when prolonged or intermitten administration of this drug is required. Chloromycetin should not be used indiscriminately or for minor infections."

As was anticipated, the publicity and required warnings were immediately reflected by a reduction in the use of this antibiotic, and the quantities of chloramphenicol certified by the United States Government after August 1952 showed a precipitous drop. The use of chloramphenicol as an antimicrobial agent was limited by many for a time to treatment of the salmonelloses, including typhoid fever, and to illnesses in which other antibiotics were ineffective. Gradually, it became apparent that chloramphenicol was vitally needed for management of many acute infectious diseases. Moreover, the unjustified use of this drug, so noticeable in the early months of its trials, appeared to have been eliminated as judged by a subsequent survey conducted and completed in 1954 (table VIII).

A total of 1448 case reports of various blood dyscrasias were collected and analyzed, the investigation including all major medical centers in each state.[285] There were 29 cases (category A) in which chloramphenicol was the only drug known to have been used prior to the onset of the dyscrasia. Of this group, 26 (89 per cent) had aplastic anemia. There were 88 instances (category B) in which the dyscrasia developed during the use of chloramphenicol in addition to another drug or drugs administered concurrently or simultaneously. Of these, 54 (61 per cent) had aplastic anemia. The drugs other than chloramphenicol included many that are commonly prescribed, i.e., coal tar analgesics, salicylates, sulfonamides, antihistaminics, barbiturates, and antibiotics other than chloramphenicol (chlortetracycline, oxytetracycline, streptomycin, and dihydrostreptomycin). In many cases, two drugs were used simultaneously or in sequence.

There were 1050 patients (category C) in whom chloramphenicol was not used, but a variety of the afore-mentioned drugs was involved. There were 269 cases (25 per cent) of aplastic anemia of which 137 (13 per cent) were considered idiopathic. Of the remaining 132 patients, 27 received antibiotics other than chloramphenicol. Other types of blood dyscrasia and incidence of occurrence in this category were: hypoplastic anemia or pancytopenia, 126; thrombocytopenic purpura, 499; granulocytopenia, 79; and other types.

The authors concluded that some cases of aplastic anemia and other dyscrasias attributed to chloramphenicol or other drugs may represent idiopathic cases and that the association of any drug in an individual case may be coincidental. Nevertheless, the medical profession was rightfully alerted to the potential hazards involved when chloramphenicol or other drugs were prescribed. Furthermore, the decision to employ chloramphenicol for a given clinical syndrome was placed on the physician, where it properly belonged.[285, 286]

We have used chloramphenicol as specific treatment for patients with epidemic, scrub, and murine typhus fever, Rocky Mountain spotted fever, typhoid fever, the pyogenic meningitides, brucellosis, tularemia, plague, peritonitis, gonococcal infections, and a variety of other microbial diseases. Observations on the hemopoietic status of the patients were made prior to, during, and after antibiotic administration. Adverse blood reactions directly attributable to chloramphenicol were not encountered. Leukopenia was observed in some patients with typhoid fever, scrub typhus, Rocky Mountain spotted fever, and brucellosis, a finding not unusual in the disease naturally. Blood leukocyte counts as low as 1200/cu. mm. occurred in some typhoid patients. In none was there evidence of destruction of bone marrow formation, and on recovery, the white blood cell count returned to normal. One author treated 122 typhoidal children with chloramphenicol (50 mg./Kg. body weight per day) and observed no instances of aplastic anemia.[287] In these patients the hemoglobin, erythrocytes, and leukocytes tended to decrease when the drug was administered, while all of the elements increased after cessation of specific therapy. Moderate anemia was encountered in some of our patients, but this was attributed to the acute infection. In no instance was it necessary to discontinue the antibiotic because of a dyscrasia.

In 632 consecutive patients treated with chloramphenicol, a mean daily dose of 95.0 mg./Kg./day was given for an average of 16.5 days.[288] There were no instances of hematopoietic depression nor were there any deaths traced to toxic depression of the bone marrow. Adverse hematological reactions were not observed in 23 patients given chloramphenicol in the dosage of 1.0 Gm. intramuscularly five times weekly for a total of 120 Gm.[289]

It must be assumed that a small but definite calculated risk attends the administration of chloramphenicol as well as other antimicrobial agents. The use of all drugs should be restricted to instances in which there is a definite need. Chloramphenicol, like all curative medications, should be used only after careful consideration of the patient's problem and should be withdrawn at the earliest sign of a toxic reaction.

In our experience, chloramphenicol has been well tolerated and there has been no need to discontinue it because of alterations in the hematological picture or other side reactions indicative of renal or hepatic damage. In 200 typhoid patients and approximately 1500 additional patients with varied infectious disorders treated with this antibiotic, these reactions were not encountered.[269]

SUMMARY

Most of the side reactions that occasionally occur in human beings as the result of chloramphenicol administration are mild and regress after cessation of the drug. Toxic manifestations may be conveniently grouped in three categories: gastrointestinal, allergic or hypersensitivity, and blood dyscrasias. These complications are rare and not restricted to chloramphenicol alone, but serve as a forceful reminder that the administration of chemotherapeutic agents of all types, including the antibiotics in particular, should be restricted · to instances where there is specific need. They should not be employed as therapeutic panaceas for minor, nondescript ailments.

Chapter VI | The Rickettsial Diseases

The human rickettsioses consist of a variety of clinical entities caused by microorganisms of the family *Rickettsiaceae*. Rickettsiae are pleomorphic coccobacillary organisms but are equal in size to some of the smaller bacteria and are characterized by obligate intracellular parasitism. The majority of the rickettsiae are maintained in nature in a cycle that involves an arthropod reservoir or vector and some mammalian reservoir. Infection of man is incidental in this cycle. Each of the rickettsiae pathogenic for human beings is transmitted to man by arthropods except in the case of Q fever, in which the tick reservoir probably is important in human disease only because of man's inhalation of the tick's infected feces.

The rickettsial diseases are characterized by sudden onset, headache, chills, malaise, prostration, continuous fever, and, except in Q fever, a characteristic exanthem that appears on the trunk and extremities on about the fourth day of disease. This rash, like other anatomical manifestations of the disease, stems from focal areas of endangiitis scattered throughout the body. Delirium, shock, and renal failure occur in the severely ill, i.e., those with epidemic typhus and Rocky Mountain spotted fever. Agglutinins for the *Proteus* organisms when they occur and specific complement-fixing antibodies appear in the patient's serum during the second or third week of disease.

The rickettsial diseases, particularly epidemic typhus, rank among the foremost afflictions as a cause of human suffering and death. Early colonial America, particularly the urban areas of Boston, New York, and Philadelphia, experienced louse-borne epidemics of high mortality. The number of deaths attributed to classic typhus fever during this century in the Balkan countries and in Poland and Russia is astounding. Typhus ravaged Russia and Poland from 1915 to 1920 infecting 30,000,000 of the inhabitants and causing an estimated 3,000,000 deaths. This disease occurs naturally only under conditions that favor the propagation of the body louse. Hence, the most widespread epidemics have been intimately identified with wars, famines, and other human catastrophes of all kinds. Alone, it has been the decisive factor in the outcome of many military campaigns.

33

TABLE IX
Effect of Specific Antibiotics on the Course of the Major Rickettsioses

	Untreated		Treated	
Disease	Average duration fever, days	Mortality, per cent	Average duration fever after treatment, days	Mortality, per cent
Rocky Mountain spotted fever	16	21	3	0
Epidemic typhus	14	30	2	0
Murine typhus	12	2	2	0
Scrub typhus	14	15	1	0

(Reprinted with permission from Woodward and Smadel.[321])

The past two decades have witnessed the development of amazing therapeutic agents for treatment of the rickettsioses of man. Chloramphenicol enjoys the distinction of being the first of the potent broad-spectrum antibiotics with antirickettsial properties[141] that, when administered to man, result in rapid amelioration of the clinical manifestations of illness and arrest of the clinical disease.[211, 290-293] Indeed, mortality has been virtually eliminated—a fitting reward for the painstaking studies that led to chloramphenicol's development and ultimate clinical application.

Several groups of human rickettsial diseases are well established: (1) typhus group: endemic (murine), epidemic, Brill's disease (recrudescent); (2) spotted fever group: Rocky Mountain spotted fever, rickettsialpox, boutonneuse fever, African tick fever; (3) tsutsugamushi (scrub typhus) group; and (4) Q fever.

CLINICAL RESULTS

Information pertaining to the duration of disease and mortality in the major rickettsioses prior to and since the introduction of specific antibiotic therapy is summarized in table IX.

With the advent of chloramphenicol and the other broad-spectrum antibiotics, treatment has been drastically simplified. Specific therapy with chloramphenicol or other antirickettsial antibiotics is most effective when initiated during the early stages of disease either before or coincident with the appearance of the rash. When therapy is delayed until the rash has become hemorrhagic or widespread, the clinical response is less dramatic. Nevertheless, even when treatment has been delayed until the later stages, the antibiotic often demonstrates dramatic effectiveness in ameliorating the toxic manifestations, and although the temperature response may be less striking, recovery is the rule.

Typhus Group: Epidemic and Murine Typhus and Brill's Disease. When chloramphenicol was tested under in vivo conditions, its antirickettsial prop-

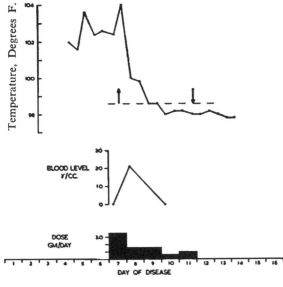

FIG. 7. Murine typhus. Clinical response of a 35 year old man (110 lb.) to chloramphenicol therapy. Diagnosis confirmed by positive Weil-Felix and rickettsial agglutination tests. (Reprinted with permission from Woodward.[322])

WF OX-19		128	512
WF OX-K		40	40
RICK AGGLN	MURINE	160	640
	EPIDEMIC	0	80

erties became apparent.[141] Initial clinical trials demonstrated the merit of chloramphenicol in patients ill with epidemic and murine typhus.[290, 291, 293] Twenty-six patients with classic louse-borne typhus fever were treated by Payne[290] and Smadel[291] and their associates. After initiation of therapy with chloramphenicol, the length of the febrile period averaged from two to four days. Other investigators have confirmed the therapeutic efficacy in epidemic typhus with prompt recovery, without relapse or serious sequelae being the rule.[294, 295]

Murine or endemic typhus fever is generally mild in character although it can lead to death in the elderly or debilitated subject. Ley and his colleagues[293] and Ruiz-Sanchez[296] successfully employed chloramphenicol in 17 patients and noted that the temperature reached normal levels within three days after beginning therapy. Figure 7 summarizes the findings in a moderately ill 35 year old patient with murine typhus in whom chloramphenicol therapy was initiated on the seventh day of disease.

Chloramphenicol has been employed in recrudescent typhus fever (Brill's disease) and it produced defervescence in approximately four days.[297, 298]

Scrub Typhus. Scrub typhus is an acute febrile rickettsial disease resembling the other typhus infections in clinical character. It is caused by .R.

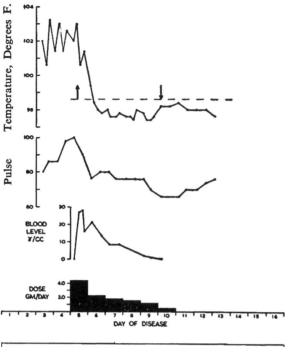

FIG. 8. Clinical course of scrub typhus patient (26 year old man, 120 lb.) treated with chloramphenicol from the fifth to tenth days of disease. (Reprinted with permission from Smadel et al.[211])

tsutsugamushi, which is transmitted to man by larval mites. The disease is usually associated with an ulcerative lesion at the site of attachment of the vector.

The initial clinical success of chloramphenicol against epidemic typhus was soon followed by dramatically successful results with this same antibiotic in the treatment of scrub typhus.[211, 299] Scrub typhus responds so promptly to specific therapy that it is probably the most readily controlled of the important rickettsial diseases of man. Ninety-four patients treated with chloramphenicol experienced defervescence at an average of 30 hours after institution of therapy. Without exception, the response in all treated patients was uniformly favorable. The findings of additional studies by other investigators have been confirmatory.[300]

Shown in figure 8 is the graphic record of one of the early scrub typhus patients treated with chloramphenicol in 1948. The antibiotic, first administered on the fifth day of disease, resulted in prompt amelioration of the toxic signs of illness and return of temperature to normal levels within 20 hours from onset of treatment.

When a short course of specific therapy, i.e., 48 hours, is initiated prior to the third or fourth day of disease, relapse may ensue after antibiotic treatment is stopped, as noted by others,[301, 302] and usually occurs in the nonimmune within approximately eight days after the drug is stopped. In those patients treated early, relapse may be anticipated and prevented by giving more drug on the fifth or sixth day after the initial course.[301, 302] Rickettsiae do not develop resistance to chloramphenicol. The relapse, when it occurs, uniformerly responds to re-treatment. The relapse tendency of the rickettsial disease patient treated with chloramphenicol in the first three or four days of illness attests to the rickettsiostatic rather than the rickettsicidal properties of the antibotic.

The isolation of viable rickettsiae several years after active infection from scrub typhus and Rocky Mountain spotted fever patients who received rickettsiostatic antibiotics[303, 304] lends further confirmation that the mode of action of these antibiotics is suppressive rather than killing. The occurrence in animals of nonapparent infections and the evidence that viable rickettsiae may remain in convalescent scrub typhus and Rocky Mountain spotted fever patients point to the possibility that latent forms of all the rickettsioses, such as Brill's disease, may occur.

Spotted Fever Group. ROCKY MOUNTAIN SPOTTED FEVER. This major rickettsial disease is an acute febrile disorder resulting from the transmission of *Rickettsia rickettsii* to man by ticks. Headache, chills, and fever occur early; a rash appears on about the fourth day, and in the untreated, the active illness may persist for about two and a half weeks. Before the advent of antibiotics, fatality was approximately 20 per cent. The illness is one of the most virulent of the rickettsioses, simulating epidemic typhus in duration, severity, complications, and mortality.

When tested in experimental laboratory infections, chloramphenicol was shown to possess potent antirickettsial properties,[20, 141] and subsequent appraisal has emphasized its rickettsiostatic mode of action. The initial clinical trials confirmed the early favorable prophecies and demonstrated the dramatic effectiveness of chloramphenicol in patients with Rocky Mountain spotted fever.[292]

In moderately ill patients treated early in disease, until about the eighth febrile day, there is rapid amelioration of the clinical signs of illness with abatement of headache, malaise, and general toxicity in about 36 to 48 hours and return of temperature to normal levels in 72 hours. Shown in figure 9 is the graphic record of a 44 year old man first treated with chloramphenicol on the sixth febrile day. The response was rapid.

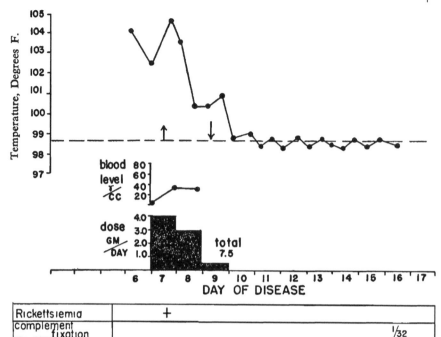

Fig. 9. Rocky Mountain spotted fever. Clinical course in a moderately ill 44 year old man (180 lb.) who was treated with chloramphenicol. (Reprinted with permission from Parker et al.[305])

In seriously ill patients, particularly when therapy is not initiated until after about the eighth day, the clinical response may be less dramatic. Under these conditions, when there has been extensive endovasiculitis with associated hemorrhage and necrosis in the tissues, the febrile response may be prolonged and the general manifestations of toxemia may abate only slowly. In spite of these natural limitations of antibiotic treatment, recovery ensues. Shown in figure 10 is the graphic record of a seriously ill 5 year old boy who was comatose on the eighth day of disease. The rash was purpuric in type. In spite of the widespread tissue reaction, the temperature reached normal levels in about seven days and recovery was complete.

It is to be emphasized that antibiotic treatment of Rocky Mountain spotted fever and other rickettsioses is one of two necessary therapeutic expedients. The other is adequate symptomatic care with particular emphasis on support of the circulation.

In a series of 37 patients with Rocky Mountain spotted fever first treated on an average on the sixth day of illness, there were no fatalities. On the average, the temperature reached normal levels approximately three days after beginning treatment.[292] The experience with this antibiotic in Rocky Mountain spotted fever has been uniformly favorable when employed by various investigators.[305-309] Noteworthy is the reversibility of the illness regardless of its severity or the stage at which treatment is instituted. Temperature response is less dramatic in patients with advanced changes, such as extensive hemorrhages of the skin and parenchymatous tissues. Nevertheless, with appropriate antibiotic and supportive treatment, toxicity is diminished, circulatory, hepatic, and renal damage gradually regresses, and recovery is the rule.

RICKETTSIALPOX. This nonfatal acute febrile illness, caused by *Rickettsia akari* and transmitted to man by mites, is characterized by abrupt onset, severe frontal headache, anorexia, malaise, fever, and chills. The febrile disease rarely exceeds 10 to 12 days. There is usually a small papule at the site

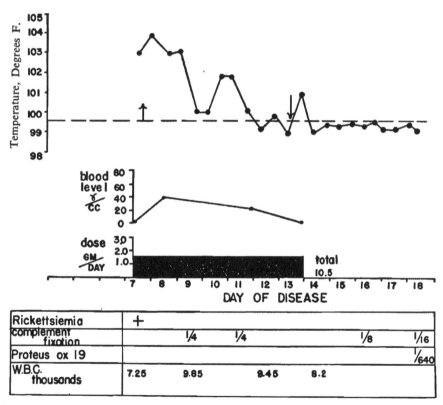

Rickettsiemia	+					
complement fixation		1/4	1/4		1/8	1/16
Proteus ox 19						1/640
W.B.C. thousands	7.25	9.85	9.45	8.2		

FIG. 10. Rocky Mountain spotted fever. Clinical course of a severely ill, semicomatose 5 year old boy (35 lb.) who received energetic supportive therapy as well as chloramphenicol. Convalescence was uncomplicated. (Reprinted with permission from Parker et al.[305])

of attachment of the mite vector, which is subsequently followed by a general-ized cutaneous eruption consisting of erythematous papules and papulo-vesicular lesions on the trunk and extremities. Splenomegaly may occur. Deaths are rare.

Chloramphenicol is an effective agent in this mild disorder. The tempera-ture falls to normal levels usually within 20 hours after instituting specific treatment.[310, 311] Therapy may be discontinued after the temperature has re-mained at normal levels for approximately 24 hours.

SOUTH AFRICAN TICK FEVER AND FIEVRE BOUTONNEUSE. Each of these rickettsial diseases, both similar to Rocky Mountain spotted fever in clinical manifestations, has yielded to chloramphenicol treatment. Investigations con-ducted abroad have demonstrated that patients with South African tick bite fever and fièvre boutonneuse responded in a uniformly favorable pattern.[312-314]

Q. Fever. This disease is a relatively mild rickettsial disease caused by *Rickettsia burneti.* The agent is widely distributed by nature in ticks and in wild and domesticated animals. Man usually becomes infected by inhalation of rickettsiae-laden dusts, which may arise from dry, infected tick feces con-taminating hides of animals or from infected animals. Milk from infected cows may be a source of disease for man. Clinical illness resembles atypical or virus pneumonia, and serological tests are necessary to differentiate it from these conditions. The onset is abrupt, with headache, malaise, chills, fever, and a cough that may be severe. Prostration may be present for some weeks. Unlike the other rickettsioses, a rash does not occur. Recovery is the rule.

Chloramphenicol is indisputably efficacious in the treatment of experi-mentally induced infections in animals.[315] Other broad-spectrum antibiotics have been used more extensively in treatment of the human disease. Zara-fonetis and Bates[316] reported the results of therapy with chloramphenicol in a physician who contracted a laboratory infection of Q fever. The results were gratifying. Chloramphenicol has been employed in approximately 24 patients by various authors who noted defervescence in about three days.[316-319] Oc-casionally some patients fail to respond as uniformly as others, and there is a tendency to relapse after cessation of treatment.

THERAPEUTIC REGIMEN OF CHLORAMPHENICOL IN RICKETTSIOSES

In most of the severe clinical rickettsioses, the initial oral dose is cal-culated on the basis of 50 mg./Kg. body weight and subsequent doses are 1.0 Gm. every eight hours or 0.5 Gm. every four hours for adults. The daily requirement for children is calculated on the basis of 75 mg./Kg. body weight per day. Chloramphenicol powder obtained from the gelatin-sealed capsules may be suspended in saline or distilled water for administration by stomach tube. See chapter IV for details pertaining to parenteral forms of therapy.

SUPPLEMENTAL STEROID TREATMENT

Cortisone provides an ancillary form of therapy for rapid amelioration of the toxic manifestations of certain rickettsioses. Steroids, administered in conjunction with the specifically acting antibiotics, have demonstrated significant antitoxemic properties, provoking often dramatic response in patients with scrub typhus [320] and Rocky Mountain spotted fever.[309] Lacking any direct antirickettsial properties, cortisone or its analogues are regarded only as supplemental aids in certain selected patients with profound toxic signs. Their routine use is ill advised and unnecessary.

SUMMARY OF RESULTS IN RICKETTSIOSES

Without exception, patients with epidemic and murine typhus fever, Brill's disease, scrub typhus, Rocky Mountain spotted fever, rickettsialpox, Q fever, and other rickettsioses respond to chloramphenicol treatment. The dramatic beneficial effects against this family of infectious diseases are the result of chloramphenicol's suppressive rather than rickettsicidal action. Mortality in each of these diseases has been virtually eliminated and the course of disease drastically shortened. The chloramphenicol regimen must be augmented by suitable supportive measures in order to ensure optimal results (see standard texts for details of these ancillary measures). Therapeutic response in patients first treated late in the course of rickettsial disease is usually favorable, although less dramatic than in patients treated early. Relapse of the disease is uncommon except in patients treated prior to the fourth day of illness. Here relapse can be anticipated and prevented by an appropriate therapeutic regimen.

Chapter VII | Therapy of Viral Diseases

Viruses are smaller than ordinary bacteria and are obligate intracellular parasites that require susceptible host cells for multiplication and growth. They vary from the infinitesimal size of the virus poliomyelitis to the larger elementary body of the psittacosis-lymphogranuloma group. The latter are slightly smaller than the rickettsiae.

In viral diseases, action by drugs solely against the extracellular microbes does not lead to rapid recovery; hence the attack must be directed toward modifying the intracellular reproduction of these parasites.[323] Specific antibody, although effective against extracellular viruses, is a relatively helpless therapeutic weapon because of its failure to alter microbial growth within the cell.[324] In order to attack the virus, a chemotherapeutic substance must affect some intracellular process that is either especially required for virus reproduction or it must be used at a more rapid rate by the virus than by the infected tissue cell.[323] Moreover, the hypothetical drug must not injure the host cell. Favorable progress has been made in the laboratory; the reader is urged to consult the symposium on the subject published in 1953.[325]

There is no antibiotic presently available for the patient that effectively suppresses virus growth. Several antibiotics effectively control clinical infections caused by certain obligate intracellular parasites, including the rickettsiae and the psittacosis-lymphogranuloma group of microorganisms. Utilization of the broad-spectrum antibiotics in therapeutically safe doses has not led to tissue concentrations sufficient for total inactivation of microorganisms on which they are effective. These drugs presumably suppress microbial multiplication and kill indirectly.[326] Nonetheless, a number of diseases have been treated successfully with antimicrobial drugs that are primarily bacteriostatic or rickettsiostatic, and it is not too optimistic to expect viral diseases to yield ultimately as the rickettsiae have.

CLINICAL RESULTS IN VIRAL INFECTIONS

Modern antibiotic regimens have enabled the physician to attack certain

42

of the larger viral agents directly rather than to rely solely on the older method of "symptomatic care." The psittacosis-lymphogranuloma group of agents are intermediate in relation to small viruses and rickettsiae and possess certain clinical and biological characteristics of each.

Psittacosis-Lymphogranuloma Group. Penicillin is not devoid of therapeutic efficacy in patients with psittacosis[327, 328] and lymphogranuloma venereum.[329,330] Nevertheless, the value of penicillin is limited, and unless it is administered extremely early in the disease, its contribution is essentially that of controlling the secondary infection. Each of the three broad-spectrum antibiotics showed value against the psittacosis-lymphogranuloma viruses when tested in the laboratory, and fulfillment of this promise is slowly being achieved clinically.[322, 329-337]

PSITTACOSIS. The diagnosis of psittacosis or ornithosis is usually suggested when there is a history of association with parrots, parakeets, or pigeons and when the clinical manifestations resemble nonspecific pneumonitis, "influenza," or "atypical pneumonia." The onset of illness is usually sudden with chilly sensations, fever, anorexia, photophobia, malaise, and severe headache. Occasionally the disease begins insidiously. Epistaxis may occur in 25 per cent of cases. A dry, nonproductive cough develops in the early stages and may be severe. Abnormal physical signs of pulmonary involvement are usually scant in contrast to the roentgenological findings, which reveal patchy areas of consolidation over one or both lungs. The temperature may fall slowly to normal in 7 to 10 days in some cases, but in the more severe forms, the temperature remains elevated for two to three weeks followed by defervescence by lysis. The diagnosis is confirmed by recovery of the virus from the patient's sputum or by the complement fixation test. The case fatality rate prior to 1930 was estimated to be 18 per cent; with the introduction of penicillin, it dropped to about 10 per cent, and with the advent of the newer antibiotics, therapy improved even more.[338, 339]

When tested under laboratory conditions, chloramphenicol seems to be less active than the tetracycline drugs against the psittacosis-lymphogranuloma viruses.[143, 155, 157] There is a paucity of human cases of psittacosis treated with chloramphenicol. Fagin and Mandiberg[334] successfully treated a diabetic woman with chloramphenicol who had psittacosis after failure of this patient to respond to penicillin. Chloramphenicol was administered in the dosage of 3.0 Gm. initially and 0.5 Gm. every four hours for four days. There was improvement within 48 hours after this form of therapy was instituted.

LYMPHOGRANULOMA VENEREUM. Lymphogranuloma venereum is ordinarily transmitted by venereal contact. The clinical illness is protean in character and characterized by acute and protracted tissue changes in the inguinal and anorectal regions. The first clinical manifestation is usually a primary sore that appears on the penis in males and on the labia, vagina, and cervix or anal regions of women. The initial lesion may be transient and herpetiform, it may appear as an ulcer, or it may escape detection altogether. The primary sore persists for several days, after which the characteristic adenitis appears. Pain in the groin and enlargement of lymph glands may be the only subjective symptoms. In approximately 50 per cent of cases, large tender inflammatory masses in the inguinal nodes progress to suppuration. In women, the nodes of the posterior pelvic group are involved. The tertiary stage presents the readily recognized chronic granulomatous lesions of the vulva and anorectal area, consisting of fistulas, chronic ulceration, elephantiasis of the penis, and chronic rectal stricture. Constitutional symptoms of fever and headache are often present during the early stages, and the disease may spread to involve the bones, joints, liver, and central nervous system. Ocular syndromes including keratitis, iritis, and uveitis have been reported.

The sulfonamides are more effective in treatment of the early stages of lymphogranuloma venereum than of the late complications such as elephantiasis, ulcerative lesions, and multiple draining sinuses.[340] Penicillin has proved ineffective as a specific drug in treating the disease in human beings. In experimental mouse infections, chloramphenicol has shown varying degrees of effectiveness.[157, 341] Chloramphenicol, when employed in treatment of human cases of lymphogranuloma venereum, has produced variable but promising results on dosage schedules providing approximately 1.0 Gm. every eight hours for three weeks. The experience with chloramphenicol in this disease is extremely limited. Based on the available information, it would appear that the broad-spectrum antibiotics are of value in treatment of this disease. Beneficial effects can be anticipated in both the acute and chronic stages of infection and against secondary bacterial invaders. The drugs do not obviate the need for surgical correction of the anatomical alterations of tissues that the disease often causes.

See chapters IX and XIV for additional details pertaining to therapeutic results in patients with psittacosis and lymphogranuloma venereum.

Trachoma and Inclusion Blennorrhea. Progress has been made in treatment of trachoma, which is caused by a virus similar to that of the psittacosis–lymphogranuloma venereum group. Sulfonamides and penicillin given systemically or locally have been very helpful.[342, 343] Chloramphenicol and the tetracycline antibiotics have all shown antitrachomatous activity.[344] After oral administration their effect has been comparable to that of sulfonamides, but when applied topically the antibiotics appear to be more efficacious than sulfonamides administered locally.

Two independent groups of investigators[345, 346] have reported favorable results in approximately 20 patients with trachoma. Best results were obtained in treatment of the acute form, and in the chronic form to a lesser extent, provided therapy with chloramphenicol was continued for several months.

Inclusion blennorrhea is an acute form of viral conjunctivitis that is common in the newborn infant as well as in adults. Sulfonamides,[347] penicillin,[348] and chlortetracycline[349] are said to be effective when applied topically or when administered systemically, although the effects of penicillin are not uniformly favorable.

Primary Atypical Pneumonia. Primary atypical pneumonia, a disease of protean clinical and pulmonary manifestations, is loosely called "virus pneumonia" although no virus has been definitely identified as the etiological agent in the majority of cases. Treatment prior to the availability of the antibiotics was mainly symptomatic. With currently available drugs it is generally accepted that chlortetracycline,[350] oxytetracycline,[351] and chloramphenicol[240, 352] alleviate some of the acute manifestations and shorten the febrile course. Infiltration of the lung as shown by roentgen examination is little altered by these antibiotics, and the disease tends to run a more protracted course than pneumococcal lobar pneumonia. One investigator, in studying a large series of cases of virus pneumonia under controlled conditions, concluded that the antibiotics have no definitely helpful effect when administered to patients with this disease.[353]

Other Viral Diseases. There is a group of viral infections in which the chemotherapeutic and antibiotic agents exert no direct action on the causative agent per se but rather benefit the patient through treatment of the secondary or superimposed bacterial infection. Antibiotic therapy of measles, variola, varicella, epidemic influenza, and pemphigus are examples. Indirect helpful action may be observed in cases of herpes zoster, infectious hepatitis, and epidemic parotitis, in which there is no known antiviral action of the antibiotics.

SUMMARY

Recent years have witnessed the partial conquest of the viruses by chemotherapeutic agents, and continued investigation in this field makes it reasonable to predict the eventual inclusion of these microbes in the realm of diseases for which there is specific treatment.

Chapter VIII

Typhoid Fever, Other Salmonelloses, and Dysentery Disorders

TYPHOID FEVER

Typhoid fever has ravaged mankind since the days of Hippocrates and undoubtedly prior to that era. It is an acute febrile illness of several weeks' duration caused by *S. typhosa* and characterized by a sustained and subsequent remittent fever, headache, cough, toxemia, apathy of varying intensity, and a sparse maculopapular exanthem. Bacteremia, leukopenia, and agglutinins for flagellar (H) and somatic (O) antigens characteristically are demonstrated in the patients' blood.

Enlightened preventive medical measures have failed to eradicate typhoid fever in this country and abroad, and it is unlikely that this serious enteric disease will disappear spontaneously or artificially in the next few decades.

Paradoxically, many antimicrobial agents possess potent inhibitory actions against *S. typhosa* when tested in vitro, yet only chloramphenicol has proved of practical value in the treatment of typhoid fever. Despite the obvious therapeutic benefits of chloramphenicol in this disease, several important problems await solution. (1) Relapses occur in an appreciable proportion of treated cases; (2) *S. typhosa* may persist in the biliary tract and feces for variable periods; (3) the typhoid carrier state is not cleared permanently by chloramphenicol; and (4) the important complications of intestinal hemorrhage and perforation continue to occur. Experience gained by all observers has confirmed the early impressions that, in the human being, chloramphenicol is primarily bacteriostatic rather than bactericidal in action and that this antibiotic fails to eradicate *S. typhosa* from the host promptly.

For proper understanding of the efficacy and limitation of chloramphenicol therapy in patients with typhoid fever, an awareness of two basic factors is vital: the anatomical alterations in the intestine and other areas invoked by the bacteria or their poison, and the noxious action of the typhoid bacillus and the toxic products of the ulcerative lesion upon the host.

Current concepts appear to confirm older theories of pathogenesis; namely, that ingested *S. typhosa* gain access to the small intestine after passing the acid barrier of the stomach. The alkaline environment in the small bowel favors bacterial multiplication, and in the susceptible victim, bacilli penetrate the intestinal wall primarily via the Peyer patches and lymph follicles, entering the mesenteric lymph glands and ultimately the liver and spleen, where they multiply readily. Upon entering the thoracic duct, bacilli reach the general circulation for eventual dispersal to all elements of the body, including the reticuloendothelial system. From the liver, organisms are excreted to the intestine and feces. Multiplication in the renal pelvis may lead to their urinary exit. Typhoid bacilli are readily isolated from the blood, rose spots, feces, and occasionally from the urine. The common complications of typhoid fever include intestinal hemorrhage and perforation, pneumonia, osteomyelitis, periostitis, chondritis, phlebitis, orchitis, cholecystitis (later cholelithiasis), meningitis, arthritis, endocarditis, and perisplenitis.

A typical patient with untreated typhoid fever shows, in the absence of complications, gradual temperature elevation that reaches a maximum in 8 to 12 days, falling by lysis at the end of three to six weeks. Rose spots on the upper abdomen and lower chest appear usually during the second week. Headache and apathy typify the first week, and delirium and stupor ensue during the second to fourth weeks. Intestinal hemorrhage and perforation usually appear during the third week. Confirmation of the clinical diagnosis by isolation of typhoid bacilli from the blood, feces, or urine at appropriate times is usually easy, and agglutinins for the typhoid O antigen confirm the diagnosis during the later days.

Clinical Results. EFFECT ON PYREXIA AND TOXEMIA. The classic descriptions of typhoid fever should be read in standard texts, particularly the writings of Osler. Although the abatement of toxic signs and fever is variable, the usual total duration in uncomplicated cases in adults who receive only supportive care ranges from 30 to 40 days.[354] In 58 cases of typhoid fever treated with chloramphenicol, the temperature returned to normal levels in an average of four days irrespective of age, severity of illness, or stage of disease when specific treatment was instituted.[21, 226, 355, 856]

Usually, amelioration of the recognized signs of toxemia antedates the defervescence. Nevertheless, this uniform consistency of a three to five day febrile-toxic period has been observed in several hundred reported cases.[226, 355-361] The response to chloramphenicol is uniform in most instances. After three days of therapy there is general improvement, with the pulse rate returning to normal. Headache along with the toxemia is relieved, and the patient is more alert and usually regains appetite. Abdominal discomfort is appreciably

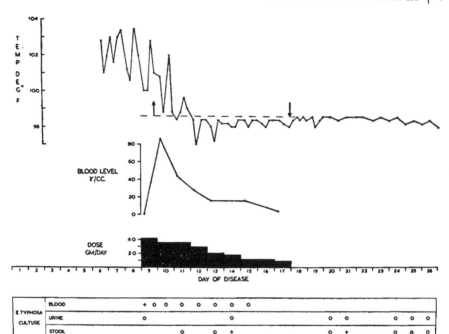

Fig. 11. Typical course of typhoid fever in a 24 year old woman (108 lb.) first treated with chloramphenicol on the ninth day of illness. (Reprinted with permission from Woodward et al.[21])

relieved at this time and continues to improve except in the instances of perforation. In 398 typhoid patients treated with varying regimens, the average duration of fever after beginning chloramphenicol was three and seven-tenths days, and the mean time lag for abatement of the toxic manifestations, approximately three days.[361]

Figure 11 is a graphic presentation of the findings in a representative case of typhoid fever treated with chloramphenicol. This case was one of the original series in which chloramphenicol was shown to be effective in this disease.[21] This 24 year old woman initially received the antibiotic on the ninth day of illness. There was no abatement of pyrexia or toxemia in the first 24 hours of therapy, but during the third day these signs decreased and the general condition was greatly improved. The patient became afebrile between the third and fourth days after initiation of therapy. Bacteremia was demonstrated on the ninth day of disease, and the organism was recovered from the feces on the fourteenth and twenty-first days of disease. Subsequent cultures of blood and feces were negative for typhoid bacilli and the convalescent course was uneventful.

An explanation of the three to five day lag period of fever and toxemia is not readily apparent. Bacteremia is controlled usually within several hours after initiating therapy.[226] Conceivably, this reaction is dependent on the host response to the results of absorption of foreign protein from lysed bacteria (endotoxin) and toxic products from the intestinal ulcer and other tissues.[267] Further reduction of these toxic manifestations by ancillary hormonal therapy will be discussed subsequently. In several series of chloramphenicol-treated typhoid fever patients, there were instances of continuation of toxic signs and failure of the temperature to reach normal levels within the first week.[287, 358] Fortunately, such instances are unusual, and under these conditions super-imposed or localized infections should be suspected.

EFFECTS OF CHLORAMPHENICOL ON S. TYPHOSA IN THE HOST. Usually *S. typhosa* is demonstrable in the patient's blood for no more than several hours after chloramphenicol has been administered. Of 58 cases, typhoid bacilli were demonstrated in 3 during the first 24 hours after institution of treatment, and in 2 other patients positive cultures were noted after 48 hours.[21, 226, 355, 356] Other investigators have isolated typhoid bacilli during the first 24 hours after beginning chloramphenicol.[238, 357] In spite of the lack of an available method for inactivating the antibiotic in culture media, the occasional positive results make it probable that the negative results generally indicate absence of bacteremia.

In 22 of 58 cases, *S. typhosa* could not be cultured from the feces at any time during therapy and convalescence, although 18 of these patients had typhoid bacilli in the stool prior to treatment.[21, 226, 355, 356] The persistence of *S. typhosa* in 36 cases was extremely variable, ranging from 6 to 50 days. None of these patients developed the carrier state during the period of observation. Marmion noted typhoid bacilli to disappear from feces during chloramphenicol treatment, but not invariably so.[238] Persistent excretion often heralds relapse, according to some authors.[362, 363] In a series of 300 cases treated with chloramphenicol by variable regimens, several patients continued to excrete sal-monellae. In only 3 did this continue for 90 days or more.[238] There were no permanent carriers. The tissues of 2 chloramphenicol-treated patients pro-duced *S. typhosa* on culture of material obtained at post-mortem examination. There is general agreement that the urinary excretion of typhoid bacilli is less common than fecal elimination and that chloramphenicol therapy does not free the urinary tract of *S. typhosa.*[226, 238, 269, 356, 361]

THE PROBLEM OF RELAPSE. Recrudescence, signifying a return of the toxic manifestations and demonstrable bacteremia for *S. typhosa,* varies in untreated cases from 5 to 15 per cent. Utilizing data obtained from 27,057 cases recorded in the American and European literature in 1907, McCrae noted a relapse rate of 8.8 per cent.[354] Among more than 400 patients treated with chloramphenicol by various investigators[21, 226, 355-360, 364-366] and reviewed in recent years,[269] an over-all relapse rate of 18.3 per cent resulted. The initial experience with chloramphenicol regimens of approximately eight days resulted in numerous relapses, but when therapy was given for two to three weeks, there were fewer recurrences.[355, 367] The incidence of relapse observed by most investigators has been essentially similar, roughly 20 per cent, with drug regimens of 10 days or less,[359, 360, 364, 366] although Good and MacKenzie[366] and others, in reporting the results of smaller series, observed a relapse rate of 50 per cent. In a series of 272 cases, Marmion noted 76 relapses or 28 per cent.[238]

The mean day of disease on which therapy was begun in 436 cases was 15.3, with an average of 22 Gm. of chloramphenicol being given over a period of 13 days.[21, 226, 355-360, 364-366] There was uniformity of the time when relapse occurred, i.e., 15 days after antibiotic therapy was stopped or usually during the sixth week of disease. In one series of 122 children, there was a relapse rate of 13 per cent.[287] A relationship between relapse and the stage of disease at which chloramphenicol treatment was initiated impressed this author; i.e., the per cent of relapse with respect to beginning treatment during the first, second, and third weeks of illness was 40, 14, and 5 per cent, respectively.[287]

The relationship between early treatment and incidence of relapses is unsettled, but experience suggests that those typhoid patients treated early tend to relapse more often. In Marmion's experience[238] with 272 patients for whom reliable data were available, the relapse rate for those treated in the first, second, and third weeks of illness was 36, 25.5, and 19.7 per cent, respectively. Longchampt and Carbonel[368] consider this factor significant, whereas El Ramli, in a series of 200 cases, reported relapse rates of 16.7, 25.5, and 37.5 per cent when treatment was instituted during the first, second, and third weeks, respectively.[358]

A relationship between the duration of therapy and relapse has been proposed with the suggestion that treatment be administered for four to six weeks continuously or throughout the anticipated course of the disease.[369] Contrary to this viewpoint are the following pertinent observations. In an 8 year old typhoid patient, continuous daily suppressive therapy with chloramphenicol from the third to the sixty-third days of disease failed to eradicate *S. typhosa* from the host in spite of apparent cure, and a relapse with typhoidal bacteremia occurred 15 days after cessation of antibiotic administration (the seventy-eighth day from the onset of illness).[269]

An explanation of relapse in previously treated typhoid patients presents an intriguing problem. In the naturally occurring disease unaltered by antibiotic suppression, a relapse rate of 8 to 10 per cent is usual. Furthermore, although repetitive attacks of typhoid fever are said to be uncommon, Marmion et al described two large outbreaks in the same community, within five months, which produced 11 examples of second attacks.[370] In these outbreaks different phage types of *S. typhosa* were responsible for the outbreak.

Based on the data available, the authors concluded that an attack of typhoid fever does not confer more than a moderate degree of specific immunity. Hence, in nature, immunity in a strict sense often fails, and chloramphenicol, lacking direct bactericidal properties, might occasionally influence those instances where the host resistance is low or fails to develop during a course of therapy.

Regardless of the concentration of chloramphenicol obtained in the body fluids, only bacteriostatic action is achieved. No appreciable bactericidal effect on *S. typhosa* is noted. Concentrations of 80 μg. or more per ml. in the bile have failed to free the host of *S. typhosa*.[226] It appears that, although the clinical disease may be ameliorated by therapy, patients may harbor within plasma cells and monocytes viable organisms that re-emerge when the antibiotic effect is lost, causing recrudescent disease in the absence of sufficient immunity. Permanent recovery is dependent on the development of immunity, yet such immunity cannot be satisfactorily gauged by serological or immunological tests presently available.[269]

The problem of relapse is not unique to antibiotic-treated typhoid patients. An analogy may be sought in the antibiotic-treated scrub typhus cases where there usually is a relapse in many patients receiving specific therapy within the first several days of disease. (see chapter VI on Rickettsial Diseases, page 37). Moreover, based on experimental tests in man, complete suppression of growth of *Rickettsia orientalis* with chloramphenicol, beginning with the day of infection and continued through the fourth week, is effected to the extent that no immune response is elicited. Viable rickettsiae remain in the host under these conditions, and when prophylaxis is withdrawn, full-blown disease develops. In scrub typhus, intermittent prophylaxis with weekly doses of chloramphenicol allows multiplication of organisms so that subclinical disease as well as immunity occurs. With such phenomena in mind, the concept of intermittent therapy in typhoid fever was given study.

A study designed by Marmion provided for an intermittent regimen of chloramphenicol, consisting of an initial course of not less than five days, an interval of seven days, and a second course of approximately seven days.[238] A control series received chloramphenicol for approximately 12 days. Of 97 patients receiving an intermittent regimen, 42 per cent relapsed in contrast to a relapse rate of 18 per cent of 47 patients given a continuous course. Over a period of three years our group treated approximately 20 typhoid patients on a schedule providing an initial course of chloramphenicol for five days, a rest period for five days, and a second therapeutic course of five days. There was one instance of relapse.[269] These findings vary from those of Marmion but are hardly comparable to his because of the smallness of our series.

Another means of providing added antigenic stimulus to prevent relapse was explored by the administration of typhoid vaccine during early convales-

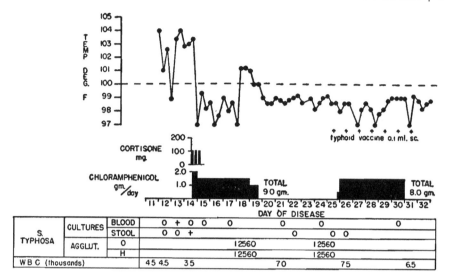

Fig. 12. Clinical response in a 6 year old boy with typhoid fever treated with chloramphenicol administered on an intermittent schedule. Typhoid vaccine administered during convalescence. (Reprinted with permission from Woodward et al.[269])

cence. Before chloramphenicol was available, Italian investigators utilized typhoid vaccine in treatment of the active disease. Rapellini and DiNola encountered two relapses in 24 patients treated with combined chloramphenicol-vaccine, whereas they observed eight relapses in 28 patients treated with chloramphenicol alone for approximately 10 days.[371] Our observations with this combined treatment method have accumulated slowly over the past five years, no relapse having been encountered among 6 patients.

Shown in figure 12 is the graphic record of a 6 year old patient first treated with chloramphenicol on the fourteenth day of disease. Abatement of the fever and toxemia occurred within the first day of treatment, aided in part by supplemental steroid administration. The patient received 0.1 ml. of killed typhoid vaccine subcutaneously each day for seven days beginning 11 days after defervescence. Relapse did not ensue. In the small series of vaccine-treated cases, significant general reactions to vaccine were not encountered.

In Marmion's studies a relapse rate of 17.6 per cent was noted in 34 patients treated with chloramphenicol on a continuous daily schedule and with 0.02 ml. T.A.B. vaccine injected subcutaneously on each of the first 10 days.[238] Conversely, with an intermittent drug regimen supplemented with vaccine, a relapse rate of 4.8 per cent was noted in 21 cases. Although these findings suggest that combined chemovaccine therapy with the antibiotic administered on an intermittent basis is more effective in preventing relapses than any other presently known regimen, the point is not proved. Inherent qualities of the infecting organisms and the variable host factors must be appraised. The problem merits further investigation, and the application of these principles during a typhoid epidemic with appropriate control observations is needed to determine the optimal regimen. In a disease of such protean features, conclusions pertaining to incidence of relapse, duration of illness, and hemorrhage must be based on observations made on a large series of cases under carefully controlled conditions.

INTESTINAL PERFORATION. Antibiotic therapy of typhoid fever has not reduced appreciably the incidence of perforation of the typhoid ulcer. The incidence of perforation in untreated cases varied from 3.1 per cent in Mc-Crae's 34,916 reported cases[354] to 1.9 per cent in 360 patients observed in recent years by Stuart and Pullen.[372] An incidence of 5.1 per cent of 58 patients treated with chloramphenicol was reported in our initial studies,[21, 226, 355, 356] although the complication occurred in 1 instance prior to administration of the antibiotic. In the 2 remaining cases, perforation occurred three and four days, respectively, after first administration of the antimicrobial drug. In two series of 200 and 300 cases of typhoid fever, perforation occurred in 3.5 and 0.7 per cent, respectively.[238, 358] Regardless of the type of therapy, the damaged intestine would require an appreciable time for healing. Hence, the danger of perforation or hemorrhage exists after therapy is instituted even though the patient becomes afebrile.

The question of optimal therapy for the typhoid patient with intestinal perforation and peritonitis cannot be settled definitely from the evidence available. Management of this condition has changed radically since the introduction of chloramphenicol and other antibiotics. It has been demonstrated that medical therapy may be surprisingly effective and surgical intervention may be avoided or deferred in some instances with reliance placed on the control of the spreading peritoneal infection by antibiotics and well-established supportive measures. Seven of 11 typhoid patients with intestinal perforation recovered on medical management alone.[226, 355-358, 373-375] Our group treated 5 patients by medical regimens, with 1 fatality. Death in this patient was caused by toxemia rather than by peritoneal infection, which was found to be well localized at post-mortem examination.[355]

At the moment, it seems that treatment should be primarily antibiotic and supportive, with surgery serving as an adjunct in selected instances at the opportune time agreed upon by the internist and surgeon.

INTESTINAL HEMORRHAGE. Gross bleeding from the typhoidal ulcer of the ileum is one of the common complications encountered in patients with this disease. In McCrae's series of 23,271 patients,[354] intestinal hemorrhage occurred in 7 per cent, whereas Stuart and Pullen[372] noted this complication in 21 per cent of 360 cases. In our series of 58 cases, gross bleeding was noted in 13.8 per cent. Complications first appeared, on an average, on the fifteenth day of disease, which coincides with the observed time of this complication in untreated cases. In this series, bleeding was noted in 3 instances prior to institution of chloramphenicol therapy, and in 5 instances, bleeding occurred on an average of four and four-tenths days after the antibiotic was started. In 32 patients treated with combined chloramphenicol and cortisone, the incidence of intestinal hemorrhage was less than 10 per cent.[267, 268, 320]

It would appear, therefore, that the incidence of gross intestinal hemorrhage is not increased in treated cases. This impression is substantiated by the observations of Knight and his associates,[357] El Ramli,[358] Meneghello et al,[360] and Marmion,[238] who found it occurring in 7.7, 3, 2, and 1 per cent, respectively. It should be emphasized that, in treated patients in whom the febrile courses are shortened, this complication may occur in early convalescence, a fact that would militate against the use of vigorous enemas, too early ambulation, and too free liberalization of diet.

FATALITY RATE IN TREATED CASES. The mortality rate in typhoid fever in the United States prior to the introduction of specific antibiotic therapy was about 13 per cent.[372] As data accumulated on the effect of modern regimens on mortality, a significant reduction was apparent. In 58 cases there was 1 death (1.7 per cent).[21, 226, 355, 356] El Ramli noted a fatality rate of 6.5 per cent among 200 cases in a hospital whose usual rate was about double this.[358] In Marmion's series of 272 typhoid cases, there were 3 deaths or approximately 1 per cent.[238] One patient died as a result of circulatory failure, 1 of intestinal perforation, and a third was treated late and failed to respond.

Despite the efficacy of chloramphenicol in the therapy of typhoid fever, a certain number of fatalities are to be expected, especially in patients with serious complications. Early diagnosis and adequate prompt treatment instituted before extensive lesions develop should reduce this fatality rate to a minimum.

COMBINED TREATMENT WITH CHLORAMPHENICOL AND CORTISONE. Earlier it has been emphasized that, despite the obvious benefits of chloramphenicol in typhoid fever, a period of three to five days is required after therapy is instituted before pyrexia and toxemia abate. The protective action of cortisone against the shocking action of typhoidal toxin in adrenalectomized rats was clearly demonstrated by Lewis and Page.[376] This concept has been applied clinically with the demonstration that cortisone administered in combination with chloramphenicol apparently shortens the febrile-toxic interval in typhoid patients in whom improvement is delayed. In 32 patients who received combined therapy, those on intramuscular cortisone became afebrile on an average of 15 hours after beginning treatment, and when oral cortisone was given, on an average of six hours. Constitutional symptoms regressed *pari passu* with the fever.[267, 268, 320]

Figure 12 is a graphic presentation of the response in a 6 year old boy, seriously ill with typhoid fever, who received 300 mg. of cortisone during two days in combination with 17 Gm. chloramphenicol administered on an intermittent schedule. Specific treatment and hormonal therapy were instituted on the fourteenth day of disease. Abatement of fever and toxemia occurred in 18 hours. Within 12 hours after treatment was begun, there were striking changes in the clinical condition and the temperature reached normal levels rapidly. Convalescence was uneventful (see figure 12).

Occasionally a precipitous drop in temperature to subnormal levels ensued after large doses of cortisone.[267, 320] This could be prevented by giving a smaller initial dose of cortisone. The initial studies demonstrated that the febrile toxic state returned approximately 12 hours after the hormone was discontinued. This was avoided by continuing cortisone for three or four days. In this manner the suppressive effect of the hormone on the fever and toxemia was maintained until the antibiotic effect was fully manifest.[267, 269, 320] While treatment of typhoid fever with cortisone is of considerable theoretical interest, its use as a routine supplement to chloramphenicol is not advised. However, there are instances in which severe toxemia and pyrexia might be justifiably brought under control as promptly as possible by the judicious administration of cortisone with chloramphenicol. Moreover, cortisone may readily avert the "toxic crises" or Herxheimer-like reactions that have been reported in seriously ill typhoid patients who have been treated with chloramphenicol. (See chapter V, page 26.)

THERAPEUTIC REGIMENS OF CHLORAMPHENICOL IN TYPHOID FEVER. A number of investigators have employed schedules providing treatment intervals of 2, 4, 8, and 12 hours.[21, 226, 267, 355, 356, 358] It has been our practice to administer a large initial dose of chloramphenicol of approximately 50 mg./Kg. body weight followed by a daily maintenance dose of 50 mg./Kg. given in divided doses at eight hour intervals.[21, 226, 355, 358] This regimen provides blood levels ranging from 5 to 40 μg./ml., usually within an hour after the loading dose, and results in the maintenance of a therapeutically effective concentration. Initial studies prescribed a continuous daily course of the antibiotic for periods ranging from 7 to 21 days.[21, 226] Other investigators have avoided the initial "loading" dose and reported equally favorable results.[287, 358, 361] "Priming" doses of chloramphenicol have been regarded as harmful by virtue of the excessive liberation of endotoxin and attendant enhancement of toxemia.[266, 287, 377] We have been fortunate in not observing this reaction but regard it as a phenomenon that should be carefully appraised. Avoidance of excessive antibiotic dosage is mandatory.

Present recommended regimens provide an initial course of chloramphenicol for five days as described, and after an eight day rest period, a second course of 50 mg./Kg./day for five days is given. The reasons for adoption of an intermittent therapeutic regimen have been discussed.

OTHER SALMONELLA INFECTIONS

Salmonella infections, caused by a group of gram-negative motile bacilli readily distinguishable from *S. typhosa* by their ability to ferment carbohydrates and produce gas in ordinary culture media, are diseases of man similar to, but readily distinguishable from, typhoid fever. Transmitted to man by ingestion of contaminated food or drink, the salmonellae cause clinical diseases of several clinical types: (1) *Salmonella* or paratyphoid fever, which is essentially a typhoidal type of bacteremia, (2) gastroenteritis or *Salmonella* food poisoning, which usually occurs in epidemics and accounts for the highest percentage of *Salmonella* infections, (3) septicemic *Salmonella* infection, which may produce localized inflammatory lesions such as cholecystitis, peritonitis, appendicitis, pneumonia, osteomyelitis, periostitis, endocarditis, arthritis, purulent meningitis, and abscesses in various parts of the body. *Salmonella* gastroenteritis and food poisoning are characterized by sudden onset after a short incubation, nausea, vomiting, colicky abdominal pain with diarrhea, and fever usually persisting for three to five days. Clinical recovery is the rule. Certain of the *Salmonella* infections are primarily bacteremic in type. Illness due to *Salmonella choleraesuis* is particularly characteristic of this group, causing sporadic disease manifested by signs of toxemia and bacteremia with and without focal signs of disease. Fatality rates in *S. choleraesuis* infection may reach 15 to 20 per cent, in contrast to a low rate of about 5 per cent for *Salmonella* diseases as a group.

Clinical Results. In spite of the in vitro sensitivity of various *Salmonella* strains to chloramphenicol and other antibiotics, the clinical manifestations and response to therapy may be variable and frequently unpredictable. A lack of demonstrable antimicrobial effect is frequently observed in the instance of "carriers." As a rule, there is a definite ameliorative effect on typhoidal and localized *Salmonella* infections after chloramphenicol treatment. Other chemotherapeutic drugs, including the sulfonamides, streptomycin, the tetracyclines, and polymyxin, are usually ineffective clinically.[378]

Reinman and Lian reported very favorable therapeutic benefits with chloramphenicol in 52 adult patients with paratyphoid A infections.[379] With chloramphenicol therapy, the average duration of fever after beginning the drug was five days, regardless of whether specific treatment was begun on the tenth febrile day or before. The average duration of fever for the 52 patients was 16 days as compared to 23.7 days in a controlled series of 53 untreated patients. Therapy did not appear to alter the incidence of relapse, which was 18 per cent. Although paratyphoid A infection is ordinarily less severe than typhoid fever, with a death rate in the untreated of about 1 per cent, the effectiveness of chloramphenicol is less striking than one would desire. In approximately 50 cases of paratyphoid A infection in infants and children, a favorable clinical result with respect to febrile response and general improvement was reported.[361] In this series chloramphenicol was administered in the dosage of 12.5 mg./Kg. every 12 hours and an initial "loading dose" was not employed.

Marmion studied a series of 46 patients with paratyphoid fever, types A and B, simultaneously with a larger group of cases of typhoid fever.[238] Thirty of the paratyphoid patients received chloramphenicol, and the author reported no difference in the mode of response between typhoid fever and paratyphoid fever types A and B. Many of the cases of paratyphoid were mild in severity, rendering the appraisal of chloramphenicol's effects less significant.

Christie employed chloramphenicol in 8 children with paratyphoid fever. Seven responded favorably and 1 died.[381] In a total of 13 cases of paratyphoid fever treated by various authors, the majority being caused by group B salmonellae, there was satisfactory clinical response with return of temperature to normal and amelioration of clinical signs within 48 hours after beginning chloramphenicol.[258, 382-384] Of 4 patients who were not treated, 2 died and 2 recovered after long illnesses.[258] In 6 patients with paratyphoid B infection, the clinical response to chloramphenicol was favorable.[361]

In a small series of 9 patients with enteritis caused by various strains of salmonellae reported by Ross et al, there was some favorable therapeutic benefit with chloramphenicol.[378] In spite of achieving blood levels of the antibiotic in excess of the demonstrated in vitro sensitivity, 7 of the 9 patients exhibited salmonellae in the stools for 5 to 40 days after stopping chloramphenicol. In some there was a clinical relapse.

Chloramphenicol's therapeutic effect on the salmonelloses other than typhoid is irregular and not uniformly favorable. In a patient with *S. choleraesuis* endocarditis, the infection was uncontrollable and death ensued in spite of intensive chloramphenicol and other antibiotic therapy.[385] In another patient with meningitis due to *S. choleraesuis* and a small infected membranous sac in communication with the subarachnoid space, chloramphenicol and massive penicillin therapy failed to eradicate the infection.[386] There is sufficient evidence that chloramphenicol has no fundamental beneficial effect on the *Salmonella* carrier state, including *S. typhosa*.[226, 378, 380, 387, 388] In a hospital outbreak of 57 infections caused by *Salmonella newington,* many patients recovered without antibiotic therapy.[387] In 7 patients, chloramphenicol was given because of more severe gastrointestinal symptoms or persistence of salmonellae in the feces. In 4 of these 7 cases the organism was eliminated, and in the remaining 3, *S. newington* persisted in the feces for variable periods. The authors administered oxytetracycline to these patients, and although bacteriological clearance resulted, the data were considered insufficient for proper evaluation.[387] Hewitt considers that chloramphenicol, chlortetracycline, and oxytetracycline are disappointing in the clinical treatment of the salmonelloses and emphasized that, although antibiotic treatment may assist in controlling the acute symptoms and improve the nutritional status of the patient, the course of disease in this group of infections may be mild and self-limiting, and specific therapy leaves much to be desired.[388] Moreover, chemotherapy has not effectively cleared salmonellae from the feces, and bacteriological relapse remains a problem.

During an epidemic of *Salmonella typhimurium* infection arising from the ingestion of contaminated meat, the effectiveness of various antibiotics was tested.[389] The diagnosis was verified in 654 patients by positive bacteriological or serological tests. Clinical symptoms were unaffected whether or not antibiotics were given, and antibiotics did not hasten freedom from bacilli. In repeated in vitro tests, *S. typhimurium* bacilli were sensitive to chloramphenicol, chlortetracycline, and oxytetracycline. Although the dosages of the antibiotics employed were comparatively small, the broad-spectrum antibiotics appeared to be relatively valueless in the treatment of *S. typhimurium* infection.

DOSAGE SCHEDULES. The recommended dosage of chloramphenicol for the salmonelloses is gauged in general on the regimens found useful in the therapy of typhoid fever (see "Typhoid Fever"). As a rule, the antibiotic is administered on the basis of 50 mg./Kg. body weight per day given in equally divided doses at intervals of six to eight hours. Therapy should be continued until the temperature has been normal for approximately five days, the total therapeutic course being about 10 days. There are no suitable data with respect to interrupted regimens.

BACILLARY DYSENTERY

Bacillary dysentery is recognized as an epidemic scourge, and although its incidence has been reduced drastically, it does cause disease when hygienic conditions are of low order and when a population group may be susceptible by virtue of malnutrition, misery, and privation. The acute infection is caused by microorganisms of the genus *Shigella* and is characterized by fever, abdominal pain, and diarrhea. The causative shigellae that are most important from the clinical standpoint are *Shigella dysenteriae* (Shiga), *Shigella flexneri*, *Shigella boydii*, and *Sh. sonnei*. Most of the cases of bacillary dysentery occurring in the United States are caused by strains of the *Sh. flexneri* or *Sh. sonnei* groups. All members of the genus *Shigella* possess an endotoxin, although the clinical implications with respect to this toxin are undefined. Frequent bloody stools are common. In untreated patients the disease may persist for two weeks, and an occasional patient may lapse into a chronic phase marked by periods of remission and exacerbation. Dystenery organisms are isolated readily from the stool utilizing various selective media.

Clinical Results. A carefully controlled clinical study was designed to test the comparative efficacy of various chemotherapeutic agents. The observations were made by a Joint Dysentery Unit in Korea under auspices of the Armed Forces Epidemiological Board.[390] A team of American physicians working with Korean prisoners performed this investigation in 1951. Patients shown to have active bacillary dysentery, confirmed by isolation of the specific microorganisms, were treated in rotation with chlortetracycline, chloramphenicol, oxytetracycline, sulfadiazine, and nonspecific medication. Suitable data were obtained in 339 cases proved by culture. Therapeutic schedules varied, from seven, four, and one day of treatment. In one group, a single dose of 2.0 Gm. of the respective antibiotic was given. A wide variety of *Shigella* infections were reported, although those of the *Sh. flexneri* type predominated. Chlortetracycline, chloramphenicol, and oxytetracycline were all effective chemotherapeutic agents, and the authors stated that any one drug may be recommended for routine use or in sulfonamide-resistant infections.

In 84 patients, chloramphenicol produced highly satisfactory results. Patients who received either the single 2.0 Gm. dose or a total of 4.0 Gm. in seven days responded less satisfactorily than those treated with larger dosages. On clinical grounds, the authors recommended an initial 2.0 Gm. dose with 1.0 Gm. at 12 and 24 hour intervals thereafter. Based on studies reported by Cheever of cases of *Shigella* dysentery treated in Korea, chlortetracycline, oxytetracycline, and chloramphenicol proved to be very effective and prompt clinical recovery was the general rule.[391] Twelve patients treated with chloramphenicol on a dosage schedule of 4.0 Gm. given over two days responded satisfactorily. In 35 infants and children ill with *Sh. sonnei* and *Sh. flexneri* dysentery, satisfactory and prompt recovery followed chloramphenicol treatment.[380] In this series, therapeutic regimens ranged from 6 to 11 days and the average antibiotic dosage was 250 mg. every four hours. Three patients with persistent dysentery bacilli in the feces were regarded as treatment failures when sulfadiazine and polymyxin B were used. Bacteriological cure followed chloramphenicol treatment.

By contrast, Lieberman and Jawetz, in a small series of cases with chronic dysenteric symptoms, observed less encouraging results with chloramphenicol and chlortetracycline.[392] In a chronic carrier of *Sh. flexneri* bacilli, previously shown to be resistant to various sulfonamides, bacteriological clearance followed 10 days' treatment with chloramphenicol.[393]

AMEBIASIS AND AMEBIC DYSENTERY

The term "amebiasis" is applied to the disease caused by *Endamoeba histolytica* and in which there may or may not be associated gastrointestinal and constitutional symptoms. Amebic dysentery refers to infection with this same protozoan and characterized by diarrhea and associated blood or mucus in the stools. Most patients infested with *E. histolytica* do not have dysentery, and the symptoms in these subjects may be varied and numerous. The disease affects the colon primarily, although extraintestinal involvement of the liver, lungs, brain, and other organs may ensue.

Confirmation of the clinical diagnosis by laboratory means can be made only by identification of the trophozoites or cysts of *E. histolytica* in tissues or in fecal or other discharges of the host. A laboratory diagnosis of amebic infection requires the services of a trained and competent observer. Hepatic manifestations of the disease may take two forms: (1) amebic hepatitis, in which the response to appropriate therapy is dramatic, and (2) amebic abscess of the liver.

Clinical Results. The best opportunity to assess the therapeutic value of the new antibiotics in treatment of acute amebic dysentery occurred in Korea in the spring of 1951 during an outbreak of acute diarrheal diseases among prisoners of war held in South Korea. The Joint Dysentery Unit previously referred to conducted the clinical and laboratory studies. The observations were complete in every detail, and the volume of cases studied permitted an adequate therapeutic comparison of the conventional versus the newer types of specific treatment. The therapeutic response in 538 cases of amebic dysentery to various regimens was assessed at the end of six weeks. Standard amebicides were employed individually, in combination with each other, and also concurrently with antibiotics.[394] Standard amebicides used individually were declared inadequate agents in this group of cases, whereas combinations were found to be more effective.

The results obtained with the broad-spectrum antibiotics seemed quite clear-cut and indicate that chloramphenicol plays a minor role, if any, in treatment of this disease. The authors report that oxytetracycline proved to be the most effective of the antibiotics. A total of 104 patients were treated with this drug in varying dosages (usually 2.0 Gm. initially and 0.5 Gm. every six hours for 10 days), and all responded clinically. Six patients relapsed, 3 early in the follow-up period and 3 later. One of these had amebic hepatitis clinically. The remaining 98 patients were well and free of evidence of recurrent infection at the end of six weeks. Chlortetracycline also produced a good initial response in all but 3 of 41 patients treated. At six weeks, 7 of the remaining 38 patients had *E. histolytica* in the stools and 4 of these were symptomatic.

Chloramphenicol was regarded as ineffective in treatment of this disease. Only 11 of 41 patients treated responded satisfactorily. Most of the patients designated as treatment failures continued to shed *E. histolytica* in the feces until re-treatment with another drug.

Oxytetracycline administered in combination with standard amebicides proved to be effective therapeutically. Based on studies of 66 patients followed without specific therapy, the authors concluded that spontaneous recovery does occur and must be given consideration in the evaluation of any specific therapy. This statement is not adapted peculiarly to dysenteric disorders.

NONSPECIFIC ULCERATIVE COLITIS

The role of chloramphenicol in the therapeutic regimen of patients with chronic ulcerative colitis is a relatively minor one. No specific microbe has been incriminated unmistakably as the cause of this disorder; hence results with chemotherapeutic agents have been disappointing. Most clinicians have employed antimicrobial drugs for a temporary palliative action rather than as a cure. The intestinal flora may be reduced appreciably after chloramphenicol administration, although resistant bacteria and various strains of fungi may become the dominant inhabitants (see chapter V on Side Effects).

From the years 1949 to 1953, Bercovitz administered chloramphenicol to 67 patients with chronic nonspecific ulcerative colitis.[395] According to this investigator, 67 per cent of the patients improved, whereas 33 per cent showed no essential change. Other investigators have reported similar equivocal results when chloramphenicol and other antibiotics have been employed for treatment of nonspecific ulcerative colitis, a disease variable in its clinical manifestations and response. We have been unable to recognize significant specific beneficial effect in severely ill patients with this disease. In a group of 8 patients who received chloramphenicol and subsequent tetracycline therapy, there was no sustained improvement attributable to the antibiotics.[385] In spite of the supplemental measures, colostomy was required in 4 of these cases.

Palliation may follow judicious antimicrobial therapy in nonspecific colitis, but as a rule antibiotics are not helpful, and the hazard of sequelae such as glossitis, diarrhea, pruritus ani, and other side effects may actually worsen the clinical dilemma presented by these troublesome and often pathetic patients.

SUMMARY OF RESULTS

Typhoid Fever. A summary of the general experiences accumulated the world over in the treatment of typhoid fever with chloramphenicol has established the drug as the only practical therapeutic agent currently available for this disease. Despite the regularly foreshortened course of fever and toxemia in the treated case, however, complications of intestinal hemorrhage, intestinal perforation, and relapse remain distinct problems in the management of typhoid fever.

Cortisone in appropriate dosage may serve as a useful adjunct to chloramphenicol therapy since it shortens to a matter of hours the toxic febrile period. This may be useful in selected seriously ill patients and may help in ameliorating the reported "toxic crises."

Intelligent application of modern antimicrobial drugs and supportive measures in the typhoid patient with intestinal perforation shows promise of shifting the emphasis in this complication from surgical intervention primarily to medical management, with surgery serving in an ancillary capacity in selected instances.

It has been postulated that permanent recovery or relapse is related in large measure to the extent of the immune response in the patient. Accordingly, the principle exemplified by a regimen of intermittent chloramphenicol administration supplemented with typhoid vaccine during convalescence serves as a possible means of providing the prolonged antigenic stimulus apparently needed to produce the degree of immunity necessary to assure permanent recovery. Several investigators are convinced of the value of this combined regimen. Critical evaluation of the results of treatment of larger numbers of patients under carefully controlled conditions will be necessary to establish the optimal regimen.

Salmonelloses. Chloramphenicol is useful as a therapeutic agent in ameliorating and shortening the clinical course of *Salmonella* infections. The results of therapy with this antibiotic, although distinctly better than with other available antimicrobial drugs, are variable and unpredictable and lack the uniformity of favorable response observed in typhoid fever patients treated with chloramphenicol. There is little benefit with respect to clearance of *Salmonella* carriers. It should be re-emphasized that the clinical course in most of the *Salmonella* diseases is variable, ranging from mild to severe and often fatal infections, particularly in the *S. choleraesuis* group.

Bacillary Dysentery. Chloramphenicol is very often effective for treatment of patients with acute bacillary dysentery. A therapeutic regimen of approximately one week is recommended. Results in chronic cases are less striking.

Amebiasis and Amebic Dysentery. Based largely on the knowledge gained from the available limited but clear-cut clinical experience, it may be concluded that chloramphenicol has no place in therapeutic regimens for treatment of amebiasis, amebic dysentery, hepatic amebiasis, or other amebic infections in so far as specific action on *E. histolytica* itself is concerned. Oxytetracycline is the drug of choice in acute amebic dysentery. A relapse rate of 5 to 10 per cent may be anticipated. Emetine hydrochloride is effective in controlling symptoms within two to three days. Other amebicides are effective in the treatment of intestinal amebiasis. For amebic hepatitis, or liver abscess, chloroquine is preferred. Emetine hydrochloride is also effective in the hepatic form of *E. histolytica* infections. Consult standard texts for details of specific therapy with respect to dosage, duration of therapy, and ancillary measures.

Nonspecific Ulcerative Colitis. Chloramphenicol and other antibiotics are helpful in controlling the bacterial sequelae of patients with nonspecific ulcerative colitis. Temporary palliation may follow judicious antimicrobial therapy, but it provides no specific curative action.

Chapter IX

Therapy of Infections of the Respiratory Tract

The broad antimicrobial spectrum of chloramphenicol has placed this drug in a unique position in the therapy of infections of the respiratory tract because it is effective against many of the gram-positive and gram-negative bacteria, the rickettsiae, and some of the viruses that cause specific respiratory infections. It also serves as a useful adjunct in the management of chronic mixed pulmonary infections. The role of chloramphenicol in the treatment of some of the more common respiratory infections is discussed in this chapter.

PNEUMOCOCCIC LOBAR PNEUMONIA

Lobar pneumonia is an acute infectious disease, usually caused by *Diplococcus pneumoniae,* whose dominant clinical features characteristically are: an abrupt onset of chill and fever, pain in the chest, cough, and the expectoration of rusty sputum. The disease is characterized by an extensive inflammatory reaction involving one or more lobes of the lungs. In the uncomplicated and untreated case, fever usually lasts between 5 and 10 days, often terminating in a sharp decline in temperature to or below normal.

Lobar pneumonia has been displaced from an affliction described as one of the most serious to which man is heir, having an over-all mortality of 30 per cent or more, to a disease of only moderate concern, with an over-all mortality rate of about 5 per cent. Chloramphenicol has taken a place alongside an increasing number of chemotherapeutic agents that shorten the course of this disease.

Clinical Results. Chloramphenicol, penicillin, and the tetracyclines are stated to be of approximately equal value in the treatment of pneumococcal lobar pneumonia.[58, 240, 396-404, 406-408] Chloramphenicol, administered according to regimens that vary from a single 1 Gm. dose per day to a total of 3 to 6 Gm. a day given in divided dosage, causes a prompt return of the temperature

63

TABLE X
Response of Pneumococcal Lobar Pneumonia to Chloramphenicol and to
Other Forms of Therapy

Therapy	No. cases	Mortality, %	Delayed resolution, %	Atelectasis, %	Bacterial complications, %							
					Abscess	Empyema	Sterile effusion	Arthritis	Meningitis	Endocarditis	Pericarditis	Peritonitis
None[405]		32.8	4.0		0.5	5.1	4.6	0.6	1.8	0.4	0.5	0.2
Serum[406]	889	16.9										
Sulfonamides[406]	1274	12.3	2.6		0.8	1.9	1.6	0.1	0.6	0.6	0.4	
Penicillin[407]	686	5.2	3.9			0.7	1.6					
Antibiotics[406]	920	5.1	3.8		0.1	0.7	1.1	0.1	0.4	0.1	0.1	
Antibiotics[404]	358	3.5	17	3.0	1.0	2.0						
Chloramphenicol[240, 396-401]	147	5.4	2.7	0.4	0.9		5.0		0.4			

to normal within 48 hours in 75 to 80 per cent of the cases, in some even within 24 hours. As with other chemotherapeutic agents, resolution of the inflammatory reaction with complete radiological clearing does not occur with the same rapidity as defervescence; however, resolution usually takes place well within the conventional three week dividing line between normal and delayed resolution.

Regardless of the antibiotic employed or the regimen by which it is administered, a minimum of 3 to 5 per cent of patients with pneumococcal pneumonia still die. This situation is not attributable to resistance of the pneumococcus to the antibiotic but, rather, is influenced mainly by host factors and the state or extent of the infection at the time therapy is begun. Thus, in an analysis of 358 patients treated with penicillin, chlortetracycline, or chloramphenicol, van Metre[404] found that increasing age, concomitant disease other than pneumonia, chronic alcoholism, multilobar involvement, pneumococcal bacteremia, leukopenia, and infections due to type 2 or type 3 pneumococci were associated with increased mortality or slow recovery and with an increased incidence of suppurative complications in the nonfatal cases. Hence, is would seem that special emphasis must be placed on management of the associated condition of the patient and on enlightened general supportive measures whenever possible if the mortality rate is to be reduced further.

Patients with lobar pneumonia treated with chloramphenicol develop approximately the same types of complications and in the same proportion as do patients treated with other effective antibiotics. Table X summarizes some of the results obtained by different groups with chloramphenicol and compares them with the results obtained with other forms of therapy. Since the number of reported cases treated with this drug is relatively small, the manner of reporting by the various authors is not uniform, and criteria for the proof of the etiology of the pneumonitis varies considerably, the figures in this table must be regarded as rather rough approximations. The series reported by Ebeling et al [400] comparing chloramphenicol with penicillin deserves special mention because the laboratory evidence given in support of the etiology is particularly detailed. Despite these variations in reporting, the figures do support the general impression that no great over-all difference in response exists between patients treated with chloramphenicol and those treated with other effective antibiotics. Kirby,[738] however, has pointed out that the superiority of penicillin may not be manifest except in particularly severe cases of pneumococcic pneumonia.

The choice of drug, then, for the treatment of pneumococcic lobar pneumonia would seem to rest heavily on considerations other than the relative efficacy of the available antibiotics. Indeed, on theoretical and economic grounds, penicillin would probably be regarded as the treatment of choice, provided that an accurate bacteriological diagnosis of pneumococcic pneumonia is made; with reasonable effort, this is usually possible. When, for some reason, the use of penicillin is not desirable, chloramphenicol or the tetracyclines may be employed with assurance of an essentially comparable response.

While there is no basis for believing that antibiotic combinations are particularly desirable in the treatment of lobar pneumonia, it is of interest to note that the use of chloramphenicol in combination with other antibiotics in this disease is not complicated by observable antagonistic effects.[402, 403]

FRIEDLÄNDER'S BACILLUS PNEUMONIA

The pneumonia caused by *K. pneumoniae* deserves special mention even though it accounts for only a relatively small proportion of all cases of pneumonia because: it is likely to be a serious infection progressing rapidly to death or to widespread destruction of lung tissue unless proper therapy is instituted early and, when first seen, it is often confused on clinical grounds with pneumococcic lobar pneumonia and may be treated as such with penicillin, which is ineffective, while irreparable damage takes place. Hence, the possibility of its occurrence should always be borne in mind and certain features, when present, should automatically arouse suspicion of the possibility of Friedländer's bacillus pneumonia.[409-412] Classically, this disease occurs most frequently in malnourished or debilitated middle-aged and elderly men, such as chronic alcoholics and morphine addicts. Infections, however, may occur in all age groups. About one fourth of the patients produce a characteristic bloody, sticky or highly viscous, and tenacious sputum. Right upper lobe and multiple lobe involvement is not infrequent. The roentgenogram may reveal early cavitation and downward bulging of adjacent fissures. Severe toxicity, confusion or delirium, and circulatory collapse are common features. The white cell count may be elevated, but in severe infections it may be in the normal range or distinctly depressed. A low white blood cell count and bacteremia signify a poor prognosis. Infections have been classified into the following three categories: [413] acute primary Friedländer's pneumonia, acute mixed or secondary infections, and chronic Friedländer's pneumonia.

Because of the rapidly progressive nature of the acute forms of the disease, early diagnosis is paramount. Here, examination of a gram-stained smear of the sputum is invaluable. While *K. pneumoniae* cannot be differentiated from other gram-negative organisms on a morphological basis alone, the finding of gram-negative bacilli in the sputum immediately alerts the physician to the fact that he is not dealing with ordinary lobar pneumonia. *K. pneumoniae* may be the predominant organism in the smear; however, it is not uncommon to find it present along with pneumococci or other organisms. Final identification of the organism is made from sputum cultures where *K. pneumoniae* presents no special problems in cultivation.

Bacteriologically, *K. pneumoniae* is essentially indistinguishable from *Aerobacter aerogenes*. The current trend among bacteriologists is toward combining the two genera. A multitude of strains of this new *Klebsiella-Aerobacter* group, designated by arabic numerals, can be distinguished on the basis of the antigenic structures of the capsule.[414, 415] In a recent study, Weiss et al [416] found that types 1, 2, and 4 were associated with about one third of their cases of Friedländer's pneumonia in which there was destructive disease of the lungs. The higher types, seldom found in such patients, were often isolated from patients who had been treated with penicillin but in whom the bacteria only occasionally gave rise to superinfection. Hence, it would appear that virulence may be closely associated with certain antigenic types.

In vitro antibiotic sensitivity tests indicate that a high proportion of strains of *K. pneumoniae* are sensitive to chloramphenicol, streptomycin, and the tetracyclines.[416-418]

Clinical Results. Prior to the advent of streptomycin, the mortality rate of the acute forms of Friedländer's pneumonia ranged in different series from about 50 per cent to about 95 per cent.[412, 418] Even with modern antibiotic therapy, the mortality rate remains disturbingly high (20 per cent to 53 per cent). Delays in seeking medical aid, in diagnosis, and in application of specific therapy, the generally debilitated state of patients usually acquiring this infection, and the fulminating nature of the disease all contribute to the continued high mortality rate.

Chloramphenicol, 3 to 4 Gm./day, has been employed successfully as the antimicrobial component in the therapy of Friedländer's pneumonia. Indeed, chloramphenicol and streptomycin have been recommended by some as the drugs of choice, although successful therapy has been reported with the tetracyclines.[398, 409, 411, 412, 416, 418-425] Jervey and Hamburger[418] recommend treatment in every case with a combination of a sulfonamide, streptomycin, and a tetracycline. However, the total number of patients treated with the different antibiotics and reported in the literature is too small to permit a conclusive statement on the relative merits on any one drug in actual clinical trials or on the desirability of combined therapy. All treatments are associated with an unsatisfactorily high mortality. General supportive therapy seems to play an especially important role in this disease, although the value of such measures as administration of L-norepinephrine, corticoids, and ACTH remains to be established beyond doubt.[425]

PERTUSSIS

On clinical grounds, the usual course of pertussis has been divided into the catarrhal, paroxysmal, and convalescent stages, a classification that has also gained considerable significance in regard to the efficacy of chemotherapy *(vide infra)*. The pathogenesis of this disease is puzzling and poorly understood. Although *Hemophilus pertussis* is found by cultural methods with somewhat variable regularity in the respiratory tract of untreated patients during the catarrhal stage, the frequency with which it is isolated tends to decrease as the paroxysmal stage develops and progresses. This and other features suggest that the persistence of the respiratory symptoms results from tissue reactions that, once initiated, depend to a diminishing degree on the continued and simultaneous presence of *H. pertussis* as the paroxysmal stage evolves and passes into its later phases. Hence, the influence on the course of the disease of chemotherapy specifically directed against this organism might also be expected to diminish in the later stages of the uncomplicated disease. On the other hand, pneumonitis of diverse etiology, an important complication of pertussis, may be influenced favorably by antibacterial therapy.

Clinical Results. Chloramphenicol, like streptomycin and the tetracycline antibiotics, inhibits the growth of *H. pertussis* in low concentration in vitro and may be lethal to it. [68, 186, 426] Yet, very divergent claims have appeared regarding the efficacy of antimicrobial therapy in pertussis.[427-444] Despite the fact that the organism often disappears from the respiratory tract within a few days after therapy is begun, paroxysms usually continue for some time. The results recorded in larger controlled studies explain in part the contradictory reports, because they indicate that the efficacy of antimicrobial therapy in reducing the symptoms of the uncomplicated case of pertussis is greatly influenced by the stage that the disease has attained at the time chemotherapy is instituted. Thus, the most pronounced beneficial effect is observed when the treatment is begun early in the course of the disease, especially in the catarrhal stage. And the demonstrable effect of antibiotic therapy lessens when it is initiated after onset of the paroxysmal stage and tends more or less to diminish or disappear as this phase runs its course. Since most cases of pertussis are not recognized until the paroxysmal stage has set in, the usual effect of chloramphenicol and the other antibiotics may not be very striking. However, it is the opinion of several groups that, when instituted in the early paroxysmal stage, chloramphenicol therapy has resulted in some reduction in the severity and frequency of paroxysms, a shortening of the average duration of the disease, and a lowered mortality rate.

In contrast to the relatively undramatic effect of antimicrobial agents on the course of uncomplicated pertussis in its later stages, the use of antibiotics for the treatment of complicating pneumonitis, caused either by *H. pertussis* or by other bacteria, is more gratifying and may be lifesaving. Here, depending on the kind of offending organism, chloramphenicol may exert a decidedly beneficial action.

Chloramphenicol and other forms of antimicrobial therapy might be expected to exhibit a beneficial action most clearly among infants under the age of 2 years, in whom the mortality rate is the highest and death is often the result of superimposed pneumonitis. Indeed, the majority of studies bear out the impression that the broad-spectrum antibiotics do reduce the mortality in this young age group. The recent report of Williams[443] from Australia illustrates this by revealing the following trends there over the years in mortality rate from pertussis among children under the age of 2 years: no chemotherapy, 18.5 per cent; sulfonamides, 17.0 per cent; penicillin and streptomycin, 9.4 per cent; and broad-spectrum antibiotics, 1.2 per cent.

Opinion is fairly widespread that young infants with pertussis might benefit from antibiotic therapy; on the other hand, there is less general agreement as to the advisability and efficacy of the routine administration of these drugs to older children, in whom the disease tends to be relatively mild. For those to be treated, the daily dosage and duration of therapy recommended by different observers have varied between 50 to 100 mg. chloramphenicol per Kg./day for a period of 7 to 10 days. The higher dosage (i.e., 100 mg./Kg./day) has been advocated for optimal effects. Chloramphenicol palmitate, which tends to give lower blood levels, has been reported to be inadequate.[445] Infectious complications require specific therapy according to their nature and etiology. The disturbing experiences of Weinstein[446] with respect to chemoprophylaxis and superinfections in pertussis point to the need for limiting the duration of antibiotic administration. Moreover, the failure of antimicrobial therapy to influence significantly the later stages of the disease has redirected attention to the possibility of attempting to modify the tissue reactions and responses of the patient as well as to control bacterial growth.[447] This concept, which is attractive, has not had adequate development or trial and requires further exploration. None of these measures supplants the need for superior nursing care, refeeding, and close attention to maintenance of clear respiratory passages, which have played such an important role in the management of pertussis in the past.

VIRUS PNEUMONIA: PRIMARY ATYPICAL PNEUMONIA

Viral, or presumably viral, agents are prominent among the causes of nonbacterial pneumonias.[448-451] The terms "virus pneumonia" and "primary atypical pneumonia" have come into rather common use in the past decade or two in connection with this group of disorders. When chemotherapy is evaluated, it is very important to bear in mind that these terms have not been applied uniformly to a single disease entity caused by one specific organism. Instead, they refer to a clinical syndrome that is usually characterized by fever, constitutional symptoms, cough often with sputum, pneumonic infiltration best demonstrated by roentgenographic examination, absence of any regular association with pathogenic bacteria in the respiratory tract, and often a normal to low total white blood cell count. A clinical picture of this kind may be produced at different times by any one of a number of known viral agents (see table XI), as well as by an undetermined number of unidentified agents, some of which may be viral in nature.[448-454]

Laboratory diagnostic methods are available for many of the known viral agents. These make it possible to assign a specific etiological diagnosis to a portion of the cases, thereby removing them from the category of primary atypical pneumonia, etiology undetermined. However, even with maximal application of the diagnostic methods currently available, many cases of the virus pneumonia syndrome remain in which the causative agent has not been established beyond reasonable doubt. While these probably form a heterogeneous group from the etiological standpoint, those cases that are accompanied by the appearance of cold hemagglutinins or *Streptococcus* MG agglutinins are considered by some as a distinct entity to which the name

TABLE XI

**Susceptibility to Chemotherapy of Some Specific Viral,
or Presumably Viral, Diseases
that May Cause "Virus" Pneumonia Syndrome**

Viral agent	Response to therapy with			
	Sulfon-amides	Penicillin	Tetra-cyclines	Chloram-phenicol
Influenza A and B	0	0	0	0
Adenoviruses	0	0	0	0
Sendai virus	0	0	0	0
Psittacosis-ornithosis	0	+	+	+
Q fever	0	0	+	+
Smallpox	0	0	0	0
Vaccinia	0	0	0	0
Rubeola	0	0	0	0
Varicella	0	0	0	0
Lymphocytic choriomeningitis	0	0	0	0
Infectious mononucleosis	0	0	0	0

"primary atypical pneumonia" should be restricted. The etiological agent of this disease, presumed to be a virus because it has been transmitted to human volunteers through bacteria-free filtrates of respiratory secretions, is still undecided.[153, 448, 452, 455]

Clinical Results. Because of the heterogeneous nature of the agents that may cause the atypical pneumonia syndrome and because diagnostic tests have been limited in many of the studies reported, it is particularly difficult to assess the results of chemotherapy. In fact, the variable results obtained by different groups may stem in part from the fact that in many instances the diseases studied were not of the same etiology. The known agents vary considerably in their susceptibility to the antibiotics and sulfonamides (see table XI). Very few studies have excluded all of these agents. Nevertheless, there is more or less general agreement that what has been commonly called primary atypical pneumonia by different groups of investigators does not respond to sulfonamides or penicillin. In contrast, a wide divergence of opinion exists as to the efficacy of the broad-spectrum antibiotics. The early reports, particularly, suggested a favorable response, while more recent studies have reported either a beneficial effect only in the more seriously ill patients or no beneficial action at all. Studies with chloramphenicol, though more limited in number, have been equally contradictory.[240, 350, 352, 353, 456-463] Despite the fact that a number of these studies dealt with cases that were associated with the formation of cold hemagglutinins, the possibility remains that different etiological agents with divergent susceptibilities to the antibiotics were encountered among the several studies and, indeed, at different times within a single study. It is likely that a satisfactory evaluation of chemotherapy in this syndrome must await further elucidation of the etiological agents and the development of specific diagnostic methods. Only then will it be possible to ascertain the action of the antibiotics in cases with a single known cause in controlled studies. Meanwhile, some clinicians continue to give one of the broad-spectrum antibiotics a therapeutic trial on empirical grounds in cases of this syndrome coming under their care.

PSITTACOSIS

The microbial agents that cause psittacosis and ornithosis are usually classified among the large viruses, but they resemble the rickettsiae in some ways, especially in their susceptibility to chemotherapeutic agents currently available. Strain variations in virulence for man and animals are pronounced. Hence, the clinical manifestations of infection may vary from an inapparent disease to a fulminating, highly fatal one. The variations in the clinical picture have been re-emphasized recently by Seibert et al.[464]

Clinical Results. Studies of chloramphenicol in the treatment of experimental infections by viruses of the psittacosis-lymphogranuloma group in embryonated eggs and animals indicate that this antibiotic is less effective than the tetracycline group of antibiotics.[143, 155, 157] Reported human cases treated with chloramphenicol are few indeed and these are contradictory. It was the opinion of Fagin and Mandiberg,[384] Chapman,[465] and Bacon[466] that the patients observed by them responded favorably to chloramphenicol, while Händel and Kühnlein[467] felt that it was of little value. Relapse has been noted when therapy was discontinued prematurely. In view of the variable nature of the disease and the diverse origin of viral strains in the sporadically occurring cases, it is virtually impossible to evaluate accurately the place of chloramphenicol in the therapy of psittacosis on the basis of these limited observations. Moreover, comparison is even more difficult since the clinical observations on the effect of other antibiotics are also limited and irregular.

INFECTIOUS CROUP (NONDIPHTHERITIC)

"Infectious croup" is a term applied to acute infections of the respiratory tract associated with respiratory obstruction to which the anatomical diagnoses of laryngitis, laryngotracheitis, laryngotracheobronchitis, and laryngotracheo-bronchopneumonitis also have been applied, depending on the extent of involvement of the respiratory tree. Obstruction to air passage is an outstanding feature of the disease. Edema and inflammatory reaction of the mucous membranes with abundant mucopurulent exudation and, at times, crust formation are prominent immediate causes of interference with air flow. This condition is a cause of grave concern, often constituting an acute emergency, in young children, although deaths have been reported in adults. Systemic reaction with fever, severe prostration, pale cyanosis, and a shocklike state often accompanies the signs and symptoms referable to the respiratory tract. Death is usually the result of suffocation.[468-475]

It is likely that infectious croup is a disease syndrome or symptom complex that can be elicited by different agents, either singly or in combination. This concept has an important bearing on the success of antimicrobial chemotherapy. Rabe[476-478] suggested that infectious nondiptheritic croup could be classified etiologically into (1) croup caused by *H. influenzae* type B and (2) croup of "virus" origin. The former is a well-defined disease characterized by supraglottic edema with little or no involvement of the lower respiratory tract. It is now a well-recognized entity that can be differentiated fairly well from other forms of croup on clinical grounds by the marked edema of the epiglottis and by minimal signs in the lower respiratory tract.[478, 479] The latter, i.e., the "virus" croup, included cases of all degrees of involvement of the respiratory tract from which specific bacterial pathogens peculiar to this disease could not be isolated. Hence, the appellation "virus" croup originally came about more or less by default. Nevertheless, the recent virological studies of Chanock[480] indicate that viral agents may well be associated with some forms of croup. Other authors have stressed, often without presenting a critical analysis of the bacteriological data, the probable role of the *Streptococcus,* pneumococcus, *Staphylococcus,* and other bacteria as primary causative agents of acute obstructive laryngotracheobronchitis. It is difficult to assess the validity of these claims because the organisms mentioned are very frequently inhabitants of the respiratory tract, even in healthy subjects, and their mere presence cannot automatically be assumed to indicate a causal relationship to the disease.[468, 472, 476, 481] While their role as primary instigators is still not definitely proved, it is not improbable that they may serve at times as secondary invaders, perhaps superimposed on a primary viral infection, and thereby contribute to the disease process. Indeed, Everett's claim of an 80 per cent reduction in mortality rate from noninfluenzal croup after the institution of antimicrobial therapy suggests that bacteria may frequently play a significant role.[475]

Clinical Results. Because of the probability that the causes of croup are varied, the reports in the literature on the efficacy of antibiotic agents in the treatment of this syndrome may actually be records of the responses of several different etiological entities. Moreover, some patients die of acute respiratory insufficiency so rapidly that antimicrobial agents have little time to act. As a consequence, impressions of the value of antibiotic therapy have ranged from glowing acceptance to recommendations against their use. However, most authorities now emphasize the importance of antibiotics, especially their early use in an attempt to forestall the development of the serious emergency of severe respiratory obstruction. The variety caused by *H. influenzae* definitely seems to respond to chemotherapy. Chloramphenicol, which is active against this and virtually all other bacteria that have been implicated, has been used by several different observers in the treatment of infectious croup with the same general responses that have been attributed to other antibiotic agents.[456, 482-487] The dosage of chloramphenicol recommended is between 50 and 100 mg./Kg. body weight per day. The higher range is preferred in *H. influenzae* infections. As in atypical pneumonia, the definite role of chemotherapy will probably remain somewhat obscure until controlled studies have been performed on large series of cases where etiology is carefully defined.

Chemotherapy of the infection is only one facet in the management of obstructive laryngotracheobronchitis. The use of oxygen, cool moist atmosphere, wetting agents, tracheotomy when indicated, and other procedures to reduce respiratory obstruction are beyond the scope of this discussion.

BRONCHIECTASIS

Bronchiectasis is an irreversible process that involves the bronchial tree to varying degrees. The dilatation of the bronchi characteristic of this disease interferes with the normal expulsion of secretions and microbial agents from the lung. This, in turn, fosters puddling of secretions and growth of the micro-organisms. Some of these microbial agents may cause varying degrees of infection of the peribronchial and adjacent lung tissue from time to time. The flora is usually mixed, having aerobic and anaerobic bacterial, spirochetal, and, at times, fungal components.

Surgical resection of the diseased tissue is currently accepted as the most satisfactory method of treatment. However, many patients are not suitable candidates for definitive surgical therapy and, hence, must be cared for by medical means. This usually entails general supportive measures, efforts to drain the sputum and to reduce it in amount, and management of infection when indicated.

Clinical Results. Penicillin has been the most widely used antibiotic for the management of infection in bronchiectasis and is administered both by parenteral routes and by aerosol inhalation. Other antibiotics have also been employed with comparable results. Shifts in microbial flora toward strains or species resistant to the particular antibiotic being administered are common-place.[488] If superinfection presents a problem and makes further antibiotic therapy necessary, a careful bacteriological study with sensitivity determinations and the selection of an appropriate drug are indicated. However, successive changes in the kind of antibiotic are frequently followed by parallel shifts in resistant flora. Therefore, antibiotics are logically reserved in so far as possible for the short-term treatment of acute intercurrent infections.

Chloramphenicol has been employed in the management of bronchiec-tasis.[488-492] It is not surprising that good results, within the limitations of antibiotic therapy, have been seen because the broad spectrum of this antibiotic encompasses a high proportion of the bacteria commonly encountered in bronchiectatic lungs. In some instances, reduction in the amount of sputum was striking and was maintained for a considerable period of time. As might be expected, recurrence usually followed discontinuation of the suppressive treatment.[492]

Chapter X | Therapy of Meningeal Infections

Within the past two decades there have been rapid strides in the therapeutic conquests of bacterial meningitis. Despite the antibiotics now available for treatment of these acute meningeal infections, fatalities still occur in significant degree, i.e., (1) *Neisseria intracellularis* meningitis, 5 per cent or less, (2) *Hemophilus influenzae* meningitis, 10 per cent, and (3) *D. pneumoniae* meningitis, approximately 30 per cent.

Fatalities and irreversible residual changes in patients with pyogenic meningitis are attributable in most instances to delay in making a prompt, accurate bacteriological diagnosis and to delay in instituting optimal therapy, i.e., the proper drug in sufficient dosage to obtain enough concentration in the tissues. For the most part, failures do not result from ineffective antibiotic action or development of resistance by the causative microbe, but from inability of the antibiotic to reach the point of inflammation before unabated progression to infiltration, localization, and often overwhelming invasion have occurred. The invasiveness of the infectious process in the susceptible host may damage the meninges, the blood vessels, and the brain so rapidly as to outdistance the favorable action of ordinarily effective therapy.

Chloramphenicol, because of its ease of administration, its therapeutic concentration in the blood and spinal fluid, its wide range of antibacterial effectiveness, is a valuable therapeutic agent in meningitis.

CLINICAL RESULTS

H. influenzae *Meningitis.* Meningeal infections due to *H. influenzae* usually occur in children less than 3 years of age. In addition to meningitis, *H. influenzae* may cause arthritis, pneumonia, laryngitis, conjunctivitis, and, rarely, endocarditis. After an upper respiratory infection, the onset may be insidious or abrupt, and when the meningtis is full-blown, the gram-negative organism may appear in the spinal fluid as a rod or coccobacillus. The organism is sensitive to chloramphenicol in the concentration of 0.1 to 5.0 μg./ml., as shown by in vitro testing.[20, 186, 493]

74

Numerous investigators consider chloramphenicol the drug of choice in *H. influenzae* meningitis.[64, 232, 234, 494-496] Almost all strains of the microorganism are sensitive to this antibiotic, and it traverses the blood-brain barrier in sufficient therapeutic concentration. In a series of 15 consecutive unselected cases of *H. influenzae,* type B, meningitis, Prather and Smith[497] reported recovery in all patients. The disease in this series was of average severity, and the striking feature was the rapidity with which the cerebrospinal fluid cultures became negative after the start of chloramphenicol. In 35 patients treated in the author's experience,[495] there were 3 instances of subdural collection of fluid and 3 deaths (8.5 per cent). Ross et al,[494] in a series of 15 patients treated with chloramphenicol, reported recovery in 13 and death in 2 patients first treated on the ninth and tenth days, respectively. Schoenbach et al,[234] Scott and Walcher,[498] and others[499] have confirmed the highly favorable results of the early reports.

Combined therapeutic regimens utilizing streptomycin in combination with broad-spectrum antibiotics have provided equally excellent results,[500] although the need for combination therapy instead of treatment with chloramphenicol alone has not been definitely established.

THERAPEUTIC REGIMEN. An effective regimen for *H. influenzae* meningitis consists of the initial administration of intravenous chloramphenicol in dosages calculated on the basis of 5 to 10 mg./Kg. of body weight. Chloramphenicol should be administered orally in capsular form in dosages calculated on the basis of 100 to 125 mg./Kg. of body weight per day. Chloramphenicol palmitate is less rapidly absorbed from the gastrointestinal tract than is the capsular form, and for this reason, capsular material is preferred during the period of acute illness. When capsules cannot be taken readily by mouth, the antibiotic powder may be suspended in distilled water or saline and administered by stomach tube. Simultaneous administration of an intravenous and an oral dose by stomach tube initially seems advisable. Subsequent doses may be given on a six to eight hour schedule.

Meningococcal Infections. Meningococci may invade the blood stream and attack the leptomeninges with such rapidity as to outdistance therapy, and at the other extreme may be so subtle in their invasiveness as to elude diagnosis. The route of invasion for this group of microorganisms is from the pharynx to the blood stream and ultimately to the meninges. The onset of meningitis is generally sudden, beginning with severe occipital headache, vomiting, chills, fever, stiffness of the neck, mental confusion, delirium, or any combination of these. A characteristic exanthem occurs in approximately 70 per cent of cases and consists of scattered petechiae of the mucous membranes and skin involving principally the trunk, extremities, and oral and conjunctival membranes. During the course of systemic meningococcal infections, the rash may be macular, maculopapular, vesicular, petechial, and, in many virulent cases, ecchymotic. The combination of sudden onset, high fever, delirium, widespread skin rash, and circulatory collapse constitutes the syndrome of fulminant meningococcemia. Precision of diagnosis is mandatory for correct therapy. Utilizing modern therapy, fatality in uncomplicated forms of meningococcal meningitis is less than 5 per cent, whereas the syndrome of acute fulminant meningococcemia may prove fatal within a few hours of onset with little or no clinical evidence of meningitis.

Sulfonamides remain the drugs of choice in the treatment of meningococcal meningitis. When they are combined with adequate supportive care with respect to nutrition, fluid balance, sedation, and adequate nursing care, meningococcal meningitis is readily amenable to control, and acute meningococcemia may be abated if treated prior to irreversible changes in the adrenal glands and vascular system. Penicillin is effective in treatment, although it is ineffective in meningeal infections unless administered in sufficiently high dosage.

Chloramphenicol has been successfully employed in treatment of 48 of 49 patients with meningococcal meningitis and meningococcemia.[495] The febrile response averaged 2.9 days after initiation of treatment, which was given for an average of 7.5 days. A subdural collection of fluid was noted in 1 infant aged 3 months. This complication cleared without residual signs. One patient, a 53 year old housewife, failed to recover. This patient was hospitalized on the second day of illness when clinical signs of fulminant meningococcemia (confluent hemorrhages, confusion, vascular collapse) and meningitis were present. In spite of energetic treatment including chloramphenicol, adrenocortical extract, and cortisone, death occurred after four days of hospitalization. At autopsy, bilateral confluent adrenal hemorrhages were found, but cultures of the blood and adrenal tissues at necropsy failed to reveal *N. intracellularis*.

Shown in table XII are the pertinent data for the 49 patients with meningococcal meningitis who were treated exclusively with chloramphenicol.

TABLE XII

Therapeutic Results with Chloramphenicol in 49 Patients with Meningococcal Meningitis

	No. cases	Treatment days	Duration fever after treatment started, days	Subdural effusion	Deaths
McCrumb et al, 1951[85]	30	6.0	2.7	0	0
Deane et al, 1953[232]	8	11.5	1.5	1	0
Menon et al, 1954[501]	9	9.1	5.0	0	1
Other, 1954	2	8.0	2.5	0	0
Total	49	7.5(av.)	2.9(av.)	1	1(2%)

(Reprinted with permission from Parker et al.[495])

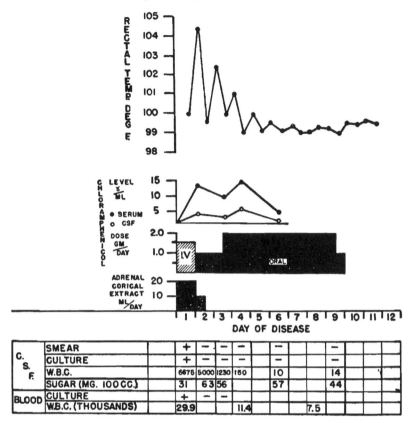

FIG. 13. Meningococcemia, meningococcal meningitis. Course of illness in a 7 year old boy (20 Kg.) treated exclusively with chloramphenicol. Recovery was prompt without sequelae. (Reprinted with permission from McCrumb et al.[85])

A representative example of the efficacy of chloramphenicol in meningococcal meningitis and meningococcemia is shown in figure 13. The patient, a 7 year old boy, received chloramphenicol on the first day of illness. There was rapid abatement of the systemic manifestations of illness with return of the temperature to normal levels in approximately three days.

Other investigators have reported the successful treatment of meningococcal meningitis with chloramphenicol.[502, 503] Knight and Collins[502] noted rapid improvement with chloramphenicol in a 39 year old man with chronic meningococcemia. A 19 month old patient with acute meningococcal meningitis made a prompt recovery after the administration of chloramphenicol given by the intramuscular route.[503] The antibiotic was given in the dosage of 0.25 Gm. three times daily for five days and subsequent smaller doses for a total of 26 days.

Chloramphenicol is efficacious in the treatment of patients with meningitis caused by *N. intracellularis.* The antibiotic diffuses into the central nervous system, and satisfactory spinal fluid levels are readily demonstrated. Thus, in the occasional acutely ill, confused patient showing extensive purpuric skin lesions compatible with a diagnosis of Rocky Mountain spotted fever (late second week) or meningococcemia, the therapist, in administering chloramphenicol, may feel confident that either condition would yield to therapy. The authors have encountered this clinical dilemma on several occasions. Sulfadiazine is the therapeutic agent of choice for a given case of meningococcal disease but is devoid of benefit in any of the rickettsioses. Its concurrent use with chloramphenicol in this rare situation would not be contraindicated for infection caused by *N. intracellularis.* For either syndrome, energetic conventional supportive measures are mandatory.

Pneumococcal Meningitis. Pneumococci may invade the leptomeninges very quickly, provoke exudate on the brain surface, and damage the blood vessels and cerebral parenchyma, leading ultimately to irreversible changes. Fatality and irreversible residuals in patients with pyogenic meningitis, particularly when caused by *D. pneumoniae,* are attributable to delay in instituting optimal therapy early in the course of infection.

Prior to the chemotherapeutic era, pneumococcal meningitis ended invariably in death. Despite the numerous effective drugs specifically active against *D. pneumoniae,* adult patients with this form of meningitis do not all recover; indeed, the fatality rate approximates 30 per cent. The outcome is likely to be unfavorable unless effective treatment is instituted early. As in meningococcal meningitis, drugs other than chloramphenicol are considered to be of choice in therapy. Penicillin given intramuscularly in dosages not less than 10,000,000 units/day (1,000,000 units intramuscularly every two hours) is the therapy of choice, and most clinicians feel that sulfonamides are of supplemental value or at least are not antagonistic.[504] Some laboratory and clinical evidence suggests that commonly used broad-spectrum antibiotics should not be combined with penicillin in treatment of this virulent infectious process.[125, 505, 506] Although the conclusion has been drawn that penicillin and chlortetracycline are mutually antagonistic when employed simultaneously in the treatment of pneumococcic meningitis,[505] this has not been proved.

The therapeutic experience with chloramphenicol in patients with pneumococcal meningitis is not extensive. Three patients with meningitis resulting from *D. pneumoniae,* types 12, 18, and 29, respectively, recovered after chloramphenicol therapy.[232] The spinal fluid in these patients became sterile after three days of treatment. One patient developed a subdural collection of fluid. In another series of 17 patients with bacteriologically proved *D. pneumoniae* meningitis, chloramphenicol was employed as the initial form of treatment.[495] Among 12 in whom chloramphenicol was used exclusively for treatment, there was 1 death. This occurred in a 65 year old man first treated on the fourth day of disease. After an initial satisfactory response, death occurred on the sixteenth day of disease as a result of a superimposed staphylococcal infection.

In 5 additional patients, chloramphenicol was supplemented with penicillin and sulfadiazine in 4, and with penicillin and chlortetracycline in the fifth. Two of these 5 patients died. In 1 of the fatal cases, a child aged 2, chloramphenicol therapy was instituted on the fourth day of disease. Penicillin and sulfisoxazole were used subsequently, as was trypsin. Death occurred on the twenty-fourth day of disease as a result of irreversible brain damage and subdural effusion. An adult, aged 51, with a prior history of alcoholism, succumbed to meningitis and an associated pneumonia. This patient died on the fourth day of meningitis. Regardless of the limitations invoked by alcoholism and pneumonia in 1 instance and delay in instituting treatment until the fourth day in another, these 2 patients represent chloramphenicol failures. For the 17 patients with pneumococcal meningitis who were treated, the duration of fever, after treatment was instituted, was 4.8 days; therapy was given for an average of 12.1 days. There were 2 instances of subdural collection of fluid and 3 deaths.

ILLUSTRATIVE CASE REPORT. A fulminant case of *D. pneumoniae* meningitis showing rapid response to chloramphenicol is presented as a representative

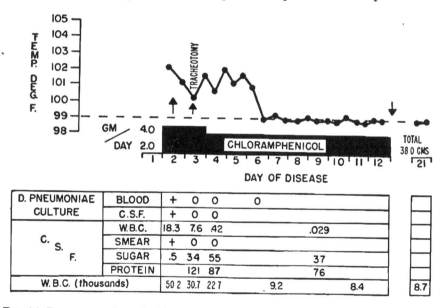

FIG. 14. Pneumococcal meningitis. Course of illness in a 29 year old man treated with chloramphenicol. Treatment instituted on the second day of illness. Recovery complete without sequelae. (Reprinted with permission from Parker et al.[495])

example of the ability of chloramphenicol to control such infections, provided therapy is instituted early in the course (see figure 14).

The patient, a 29 year old man, became ill suddenly with headache and fever at 10:00 P.M. After having a restless night, the patient was hospitalized in an extremely disoriented and agitated condition, approximately 12 hours after onset of illness. Conventional signs of meningitis were apparent, and a right facial paralysis was noted. The spinal fluid was turbid and contained 18,300 cells/cu. mm. Immediate intravenous chloramphenicol therapy was given, and chloramphenicol suspended in saline was administered by stomach tube. A tracheotomy was performed on the second hospital day because of upper respiratory obstruction resulting from inspissated mucus and crusting in the pharynx and trachea. The patient's infection was rapidly brought under control and recovery was ultimately complete. Pertinent clinical features are presented in figure 14.

Streptococcal Meningitis. Beta hemolytic streptococcal infection may primarily involve the meninges or develop as a sequel to otitis media, mastoiditis, sinusitis, or infection elsewhere in the body. The symptoms and clinical manifestations resemble those in the other pyogenic forms of meningitis with the characteristic findings in the cerebrospinal fluid. Best results are obtained with aqueous penicillin administered intramuscularly in doses of 1.0 million units every two hours. The simultaneous administration of sulfadiazine in conventional dosages is probably advisable.

CLINICAL RESULTS WITH CHLORAMPHENICOL. Very few patients with culturally proved streptococcal meningitis have been treated with chloramphenicol exclusively. One 59 year old man with meningitis caused by a nonhemolytic *Str. viridans* type recovered after 10 days of chloramphenicol treatment.[507] In this patient, who had active signs of meningitis and a cerebrospinal fluid pleocytosis of 16,000 white blood cells/cu. mm., there was rapid clinical improvement and return of temperature to normal levels within six days after instituting specific therapy. Another patient with a nonhemolytic streptococcal meningitis promptly recovered on chloramphenicol therapy.[495] In this series, an infant aged 1 week, with meningitis caused by beta hemolytic *Streptococcus,* responded promptly after five days of chloramphenicol therapy. One dose of penicillin had been administered prior to hospitalization, in spite of which the initial smear and culture of the cerebrospinal fluid were positive. The initial spinal fluid cell count was 12,000 white blood cells/cu. mm. Recovery was rapid with return of temperature to normal levels within two days after initiating therapy.

Staphylococcal Meningitis. Fortunately, staphylococcal meningitis is uncommon. Even under favorable conditions the prognosis is poor, since the meningitis is usually a secondary focal infection developing as a sequel to generalized sepsis, and the causative bacteria are frequently resistant to penicillin. Any patient with staphylococcal disease who develops signs or symptoms suggestive of meningeal inflammation merits an adequate diagnostic puncture. *M. pyogenes* is readily identified by direct smear and subsequently by culture.

With early and intensive treatment, recovery occurs in about 50 per cent of cases.

The in vitro sensitivity reaction of the isolated *Staphylococcus* to each of the antibiotics known to be clinically effective should be determined. Single or combination therapy may be indicated. Refer to chapter XII with regard to specific chloramphenicol therapy for staphylococcal infections.

Experience relating to the use of chloramphenicol in staphylococcal meningitis is limited. Anderson and Ellis[508] reported the successful treatment of a 44 year old patient with staphylococcal meningitis after failure with penicillin, streptomycin, and chlortetracycline. Chloramphenicol (crystalline) was given intrathecally in doses varying from 100 to 150 μg. in 1.0 ml. distilled water for 19 days. Oral chloramphenicol was given in doses of 1.0 to 2.0 Gm. every six hours. Another adult patient with *Staph. aureus* meningitis, which developed as a postoperative complication, recovered after the oral and intrathecal administration of chloramphenicol.

Meningitis Due to Gram-Negative Enteric Bacilli. Meningitis caused by enteric bacteria is most common in newborn and older infants, who are particularly susceptible.[496] Various strains of the genus *Salmonella* cause purulent meningitis. Meningitis due to *S. typhosa* is rarely associated with typhoid fever, but as such is an ominous complication. Ramirez et al [509] successfully treated such a patient with chloramphenicol. In another isolated instance of *S. typhosa* meningitis, there was a fatal outcome in spite of chloramphenicol administration beginning on the fifteenth day of disease.[510] It is significant that the local meningeal infection in this patient, measuring 9 by 7 cm., was in the region of the right temporal lobe. The dura mater covering the right temporal fossa was acutely inflamed but appeared normal elsewhere. *S. typhosa* isolated from this localized focus were sensitive to chloramphenicol in the concentration of 5.0 μg./ml. This case demonstrates the failure of an effective antibiotic to eradicate a well-established focal infection. It is presumed that this is an example of subdural empyema, a not uncommon complication of pyogenic meningitis. Ripy[511] reported the failure of 13 month old Negro infant to respond to chloramphenicol, but recovery followed the addition of chlortetracycline to the therapeutic regimen.

S. choleraesuis is notorious for its diversity of clinical manifestations, of which meningitis is an example. Fitzgerald and Snyder[886] successfully controlled the acute meningeal signs of a patient with purulent meningitis due to *S. choleraesuis* by using both chloramphenicol and massive penicillin therapy. Recovery ensued only after the surgical removal of an infected cyst that was in communication with the subarachnoid space. There are other instances of the successful treatment with chloramphenicol of patients with meningitis due to *S. typhimurium*[512] and *Salmonella newport*.[513] A child aged 1 year, with meningitis due to *H. influenzae*, responded to chloramphenicol treatment after initial failure with chlortetracycline. After partial recovery the patient had a second attack of meningitis caused by *Salmonella san diego,* first detected after 59 days of convalescence. The patient failed to respond to chloramphenicol, chlortetracycline, and streptomycin treatment.[64] A 28 year old patient with osteomyelitis of several lumbar vertebrae due to *S. choleraesuis* but without associated meningeal involvement responded favorably to chloramphenicol treatment for four days.[514]

Meningitis caused by shigellae is very unusual. Trindade and Nastari[515] successfully treated a 22 year old patient with meningitis caused by *Shigella paradysenteriae,* which presumably developed as a complication of spinal anesthesia. The meningeal signs failed to improve in spite of antibiotic treatment with penicillin, streptomycin, sulfonamides, and orally administered chloramphenicol for two days. After the installation of 62.5 mg. of chloramphenicol intracisternally, the patient began to improve within 24 hours and recovery ensued.

Organisms of the genus *Proteus* may provoke purulent meningitis usually as a late manifestation of systemic infection by these microorganisms. Despite massive therapy with chloramphenicol, streptomycin, neomycin, and chlortetracycline, the disease continued unabated, to death, in a 31 year old man. The tissues at autopsy revealed extensive focal inflammation due to *P. vulgaris,* which produced otitis media, mastoiditis, purulent meningitis, brain abscess, lateral sinus thrombosis, pneumonitis, mediastinitis, and psoas abscesses.[516] Darnley[517] successfully treated a patient with *Proteus* meningitis by the simultaneous administration of chloramphenicol and streptomycin.

The colon bacillus is an uncommon cause of purulent meningitis in adults, and most of the recorded cases have occurred in newborn and older infants. Before the advent of specific chemotherapy, *E. coli* meningitis was usually fatal. Lepper and his associates[518] treated 2 infants with chloramphenicol. One patient treated on the third day of life made a complete recovery. The other infant received penicillin, streptomycin, and oxytetracycline for six weeks before hospitalization. The spinal fluid was grossly purulent. Chloramphenicol administered intravenously for three days was without effect. The infection was brought under control after the intramuscular and intrathecal administration of polymyxin and the intrathecal and intraventricular inoculation of streptokinase and streptodornase.

Single case reports by Ebsworth and Leys[519] and Fisch[520] describe the successful treatment of colon bacillus meningitis with chloramphenicol. The infants, aged 10 and 13 days, respectively, made complete recovery after the oral and intrathecal administration of the antibiotic. One of the patients[519] received polymyxin and other antibiotics, although chloramphenicol appeared to play the decisive role.

For *E. coli* meningitis, one author[521] recommends the administration of sulfadiazine, chloramphenicol, and streptomycin. This program is advocated by Alexander,[500] who emphasizes that the infecting organism must be eliminated in the shortest possible time. This investigator recommends chemotherapeutic agents working through different mechanisms as preferable, with one drug primarily bactericidal in action. An infant several days old, with septicemia and meningitis due to simultaneous infections with *E. coli* and *Ps. aeruginosa,* recovered on multiple antibiotic therapy consisting of chlortetracycline, chloramphenicol, and oxytetracycline.[522] Colon bacillus meningitis is a serious and often fatal disease for which the optimal therapeutic regimen is as yet unknown.

Miscellaneous Types of Meningitis. The Friedländer bacillus (*K. pneumoniae*) causes virulent disease in man. Pneumonia is the common form of clinical illness, and meningitis may develop as a serious complication or, rarely, as a primary manifestation. Martin and his associates[523] successfully treated a patient with Friedländer's bacillus meningitis that developed postoperatively. The initial course of treatment with streptomycin was unsuccessful. An 8 year old child with meningitis due to *K. pneumoniae* recovered on chloramphenicol therapy.[524] After various therapeutic failures with other antibiotics, another isolated patient with Friedländer meningitis recovered on chloramphenicol.[525]

In 2 adult patients with purulent meningitis caused by *K. pneumoniae,* chloramphenicol seemed to have given the best results of any agent tried and was regarded as responsible for cure.[518] Treatment with penicillin and chlortetracycline failed initially to control the infection in each of these cases.

Listeria monocytogenes, a gram-positive pleomorphic rod occasionally resembling a diphtheroid, is a rare cause of purulent meningitis. Finegold and his associates[526] tested the reaction of six strains of *L. monocytogenes* to seven antibiotics by the tube-dilution method, and the sensitivity of the strains to chloramphenicol ranged from 6.3 to 12.5 μg./ml. Bennett et al [527] and Berry[528] found strains of *Listeria* sensitive to chloramphenicol in concentrations of 3.1 and 0.83 μg./ml., respectively.

A 42 year old woman with signs of acute meningeal infection due to *L. monocytogenes* responded successfully after oral administration of chloramphenicol[495] begun on the third day of illness. The chloramphenicol was continued until the twentieth day, and recovery was complete.

The mortality in *Listeria* meningitis has been reduced in recent years. In most series of reported cases, two or more therapeutic agents have been employed, making definitive appraisal of one specific agent difficult. Bennett and associates[527] reported the recovery of a 15 year old patient who received sulfadiazine, penicillin, chloramphenicol, and oxytetracycline. Line and Appleton[529] successfully treated a premature infant who received sulfonamide, penicillin, dihydrostreptomycin, and each of the broad-spectrum antibiotics. Finegold et al [526] felt that in their series chlortetracycline and oxytetracycline played decisive roles in recovery, although appraisal was difficult because of multiple drug therapy. Based on limited experience, these authors recommended either of these drugs as the treatment of choice in *L. monocytogenes* meningitis. The point is unsettled.

SUMMARY OF RESULTS

A single chemotherapeutic drug suitable for the entire gamut of purulent meningitides is not available, and it is unlikely that a drug fulfilling all the necessary qualifications will ever be a reality. Chloramphenicol possesses remarkable versatility in this field and is readily administered. The authors have been impressed with the effectiveness of chloramphenicol in meningeal infections when it has been administered as a single form of specific treatment. Although primarily effective against meningitis caused by gram-negative bacteria, it possesses commendable action against the gram-positive group.

It should not be inferred that the effectiveness of chloramphenicol in meningococcal meningitis is superior to the action of the sulfonamides nor that chloramphenicol can be placed on a level with massive penicillin therapy in pneumococcal meningitis. A large series of patients, preferably treated during a sizable outbreak, employing rigid controls in drug selection, would be required before definitive statements could be made. Indeed, the optimal therapy in pneumococcal meningitis is not established definitely because of limitations in numbers of cases and variable therapeutic regimens in reported series. However, chloramphenicol is of major value in the therapy of influenzal meningitis.

Chloramphenicol is effective in meningococcal, influenzal, and pneumococcal meningitis when given early in the course of these infections. It fails, as other therapeutic agents have failed, when outdistanced by the microbe at the tissue level. The necessity for administering prompt effective treatment is emphasized. No substitute will be found to eliminate the need for prompt clinical and laboratory diagnosis.

Chapter XI | Brucellosis, Tularemia, Plague

BRUCELLOSIS

Brucellosis, which is caused by *Brucella melitensis, Br. abortus,* or *Br. suis,* has world-wide distribution. The acute disease, protean in clinical character and variable in intensity, has a great tendency to relapse after a spontaneous remission. After several recrudescent episodes, the clinical disease may subside spontaneously or lapse into a chronic form of two or more years' duration. The clinical disease frequently is associated with low-grade fever, indefinite manifestations of weakness, anorexia, weight loss, arthralgia, and myalgia. Fatality is rare in either the acute or chronic forms. Febrile relapses with return of the active manifestations of illness occur in approximately 20 per cent of cases. Chronic brucellosis is common. The infectious agent may multiply in various foci leading to localized disease of the lymph nodes, spleen, bone, joints, meninges, endocardium, gall bladder, testicle, and ovary.

The natural course of brucellosis is extremely variable, making appraisal of specific chemotherapeutic agents difficult. The onset is usually gradual, with weakness, malaise, and drenching sweats characteristic of the acute case. Temperature elevations generally occur in the late afternoon or early evening, and frank chills or chilly sensations are frequent. An undulating febrile course associated with frank remissions is common in the *Br. melitensis* form. The clinical diagnosis of brucellosis is confirmed (1) by the isolation of brucellae in suitable culture media and (2) by the demonstration of agglutinins in significant titer.

Acute Brucellosis. CLINICAL RESULTS. The antibiotics are of demonstrated value in ameliorating the acute manifestations of illness. No specific antibiotic or combination thereof has shown unmistakable evidence of bactericidal action in the human host: that is, eradicative action in the strict sense. Hence, relapes occur in treated patients in about the some relative frequency as in the natural disease. Moreover, therapy in the chronic forms of brucellosis leaves much to be desired. It follows, therefore, that established foci in the aforementioned organs are eliminated with difficulty by antibiotic agents.

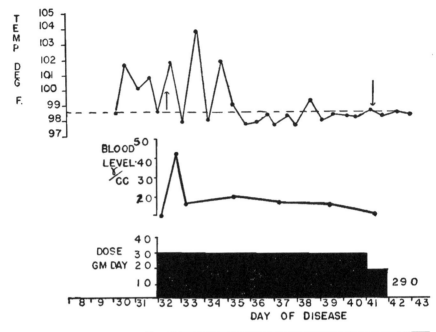

Fig. 15. Course of illness in a 24 year old man (170 lb.) with brucellosis of *Br. abortus* type. (Reprinted with permission from Woodward et al.[530])

Chloramphenicol is of demonstrated value against all species of *Brucella* when tested by in vitro techniques.[20] In the treatment of human brucellosis, rapid defervescence and improvement have occurred. In one series of 9 cases of acute brucellosis,[530] chloramphenicol was administered orally with an initial dose of 50 mg./Kg. of body weight and subsequent doses of 0.25 Gm. every three hours until the temperature had remained at normal levels for five days. In this group the average duration of fever prior to administration of the antibiotic was 30 days. In each patient the temperature became normal in less than three days. Noticeable general improvement occurred within 36 hours in 2 seriously ill patients and during the first 24 hours of treatment in the remaining 7. One patient in this series (see figure 15) relapsed approximately 30 days after chloramphenicol was stopped. Four additional patients with acute brucellosis likewise responded promptly to chloramphenicol treatment, with recurrent disease in 1.[546]

The pertinent clinical aspects of a chloramphenicol-treated patient are presented in figure 15. The temperature of this 24 year old man returned to normal levels approximately 48 hours after treatment was instituted. The diagnosis of a *Br. abortus* infection was confirmed by demonstration of bacteremia and by agglutination tests. Thirty days after cessation of chloramphenicol therapy, a relapse ensued that responded to re-treatment with this antibiotic.

Other groups of patients treated with chloramphenicol showed clinical improvement soon after treatment was instituted and subsequent clinical relapse in periods ranging from one to eight weeks.[531-537] The series of 13 patients treated by Knight et al [532] is particularly representative of this limitation of therapy. In spite of the rather uniform rapid improvement, relapses occurred. The age range in this series was 17 to 67 years, and when therapy was started, 11 patients had been ill for as long as 90 days and 2 for 7 and 10 months, respectively. Dosage regimens of chloramphenicol were similar to those quoted previously. By the third day of treatment, all patients were afebrile and felt greatly improved. Nevertheless, relapse occurred in 6 patients one to eight weeks later. In 3 of these, the recurrent symptoms were mild and the patients recovered without additional therapy, while the other 3, who were acutely ill, recovered after additional treatment. Twelve patients with brucellosis who were treated by McDermott [531] showed satisfactory clinical response. Single cases of brucellosis treated with chloramphenicol have been reported by various investigators[534-536] with satisfactory results.

In a therapeutic study of 35 patients with infection caused by *Br. abortus,* 5 patients were treated with chloramphenicol in dosages of 2.0 Gm. daily for 10 days.[538] The clinical response to therapy was described as satisfactory, with abatement of toxic signs and improvement of fever. This investigator did not continue his studies with the antibiotic because of the potential risk of serious bone marrow suppression. Spink and his associates[539] treated 8 patients with clinically active brucellosis with chloramphenicol regimens of about 10 days. One patient with *Br. melitensis* infection received chloramphenicol for 23 days. Chloramphenicol treatment was without benefit in 1 patient who had been treated previously with chlortetracycline. This patient had a definite psychoneurosis, although active *Brucella* infection was suspected. Prompt and complete recovery occurred in 2 patients without any subsequent relapses or residuals of the infection. One patient had persistent positive blood cultures for *Br. abortus* after completion of 10 days of chloramphenicol therapy. This patient continued to have residual complaints after a subsequent course of therapy with dihydrostreptomycin and chlortetracycline and then with chlortetracycline alone. While no relapses were encountered, there were 4 patients with continued complaints after therapy was stopped. Spink and his collaborators stated that these clinical results coincide with those observed in experimentally infected animals, i.e., on a weight-for-weight basis, chlor-tetracycline was more effective than chloramphenicol against brucellosis.[135, 539] These investigators, who have had extensive experience in the clinical and laboratory aspects of brucellosis, state that one of the most difficult problems is the proper evaluation of subjective complaints and that objective data indicative of active infection are often lacking.[539] The earlier observations with antibiotics used singly in therapy of brucellosis, although recognized as an advancement in therapy, led this group and others to favor regimens with combinations of dihydrostreptomycin and the tetracycline antibiotics.[136, 137, 539, 540] Studies of treatment of the clinical disease with combinations have been made and would appear to favor their use as a first choice in acutely ill patients and in those with the localized form of brucellosis.[541]

This point is at present unsettled, and according to a recent opinion expressed by Spink,[555] the prolonged administration of one of the tetracycline antibiotics alone is the regimen of choice. See page 26 for a discussion of the Herxheimer reaction.

DOSAGE. The daily dosage of chloramphenicol is usually calculated on the basis of 50 mg./Kg. of body weight given in divided dosage at six hour intervals. This is continued for approximately 10 days or until the temperature has remained at normal levels for about a week. After defervescence the daily dosage may be halved (25 mg./Kg. body weight).

Chronic Brucellosis. The clinical results in patients with chronic brucellosis attest to the amelioration of systemic signs but failure to prevent the return of symptoms or active relapse. McDougal [542] reported improvement with chloramphenicol in 4 chronic cases. Clinical relapses occurred in 2 patients after six weeks and four months, respectively. Ralston and Payne[543] used regimens of chloramphenicol lasting for 7 to 10 days in 55 chronic cases. These observers reported partial to complete relief in approximately 90 per cent of patients. Harris[533] observed a favorable effect of chloramphenicol therapy in 46 acute and chronic cases. In 20 patients diagnosed as having chronic brucellosis or probable chronic brucellosis, chloramphenicol regimens of an average of 22 days resulted in clinical improvement in about 50 per cent of cases.[544] The improvement was reported to be of short duration, lasting from several weeks to a few months. Several patients reported unusual improvement.

Brucellae as intracellular parasites cause disease in man with a natural tendency to recur and provoke chronic illness. The ability of these microorganisms to parasitize cells of the reticuloendothelial system and to reside within the host cell for long periods undoubtedly contributes to this tendency.[545] In view of the failure of antibiotics used singly or in combinations to eradicate brucellae effectively from the host cell and prevent chronic manifestation of illness, another regimen has been explored. For several years a series of patients with acute brucellosis and some with the chronic form have received antibiotics on a regimen providing an initial course of 10 days and short intermittent courses extending over two years.[546] Every three months the patients received three days' treatment (50 mg./Kg./day in equally divided doses every eight hours), regardless of the presence or absence of active signs. This regimen made use of the bacteriostatic properties of the antibiotic and was in no sense designed to eradicate the infectious agent per se. Observations in approximately 25 patients treated with chloramphenicol or a tetracycline antibiotic indicated a favorable response with this intermittent regimen.[546] These patients, in most instances, adhered to the three day treatment courses during asymptomatic periods, and the antibiotic did not provoke adverse ill effects, including reactions of the Herxheimer type. In several instances active manifestations occurred during intervals between treatment. Precise evaluation is impossible since the series is small and, under natural conditions, patients with acute brucellosis will lapse into the chronic form extending one or more years.[547] Antibiotic treatment, in spite of its ameliorating effect on acute manifestations, has not significantly altered the incidence of chronic disease.[539] There are no acceptable data indicating that the intermittent program has made a significant therapeutic advance.

Combined Treatment with Steroids. Corticoids have been shown to exert a favorable antitoxemic action in experimental brucellosis and in the treatment of human beings.[545] Relapse rates appear to be slightly higher in patients receiving cortisone for one to three weeks as compared to those who received it up to four days.[548] Although the use of cortisone during the first three or four days of antibiotic therapy evokes a rapid and often dramatic clinical response, steroid administration in brucellosis should be reserved for use in acutely toxic cases,[548] if at all. Conceivably, corticoids might serve as palliative agents to guard against the Herxheimer reaction in very ill patients.

TULAREMIA

Pasteurella tularensis, the cause of human tularemia, is acquired by man by handling the carcasses of infected animals, chiefly wild rabbits, and by blood-sucking arthropods, chiefly ticks and deer flies. All clinical types may be characterized by headache, chills, nausea, vomiting, fever, weakness and sweats. Most cases are of the ulceroglandular type, and in addition to formation of an ulcer, usually on a finger, adjacent lymph glands become enlarged and painful, and occasionally ulcerate. Enteric symptoms characterize the typhoidal type, and a severe pleuropneumonia may complicate any of the clinical forms. Pneumonia also may occur as a primary infection. Tularemic pneumonia is a serious manifestation of the disease and requires prompt detection and appropriate effective therapy in order to prevent unwanted sequelae, such as pulmonary abscess and a chronic form of pleuritis with effusion.

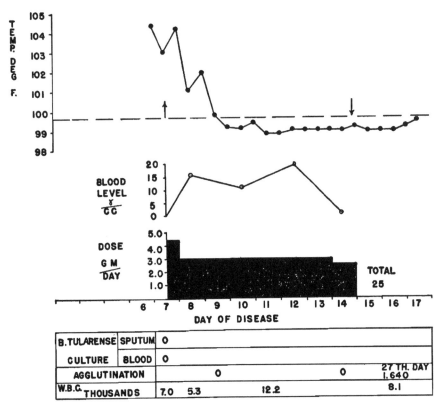

FIG. 16. Clinical course of a 53 year old man with ulceroglandular tularemia and pleuropneumonia. Treatment with chloramphenicol instituted on seventh febrile day.

Clinical Results. Chloramphenicol has demonstrated antibacterial action against *Past. tularensis* when tested under in vitro and in vivo conditions.[24, 549] In a series of 6 tularemic patients,[24] chloramphenicol was of demonstrated value, leading to prompt amelioration of the systemic signs of disease. In this group, 2 patients had an associated pleuropneumonia, and in 1 the disease was of the primary pneumonic type. The clinical response was dramatic in all with return of temperature to normal levels within 48 hours after instituting treatment. Two patients, treated initially within the first week of illness, relapsed but responded rapidly to a second course of antibiotic.

Shown in figure 16 is the graphic record of a 53 year old man with ulceroglandular tularemia and a complicating pleuropneumonia. The temperature returned to normal levels within approximately 36 hours after chloramphenicol treatment was instituted, and the systemic manifestations of the illness rapidly abated. There was no recrudescence in this patient.

Two patients with tularemia who were treated with chloramphenicol by a European observer[550] responded within 24 hours. Both patients were treated for a short time, i.e., two days. A relapse ensued in 1 with prompt recovery on re-treatment. Recent observations in patients with experimentally induced infections have demonstrated that chloramphenicol is effective in arresting the acute manifestations of ulceroglandular tularemia.[551] In these patients, the action of chloramphenicol was apparently bacteriostatic, whereas streptomycin appeared to provoke a bactericidal effect.

Dosage Schedule. With the background of experience pertaining to chloramphenicol therapy in acute infections and based on these limited clinical data in treatment of tularemia, a schedule providing an initial dose of 3.0 Gm. followed by 1.0 Gm. every eight hours for five to seven days is regarded as effective.

After a rest period without antibiotics for about four days, a second five-day treatment course may be given. In patients with tularemia first treated during the first week of illness, the aforementioned interrupted regimen seems worthy of trial. In patients treated later in the illness, an interrupted regimen is not recommended. There are insufficient clinical data available on which to base recommendations for optimal therapy with chloramphenicol. Streptomycin is dramatically effective in human tularemic infections and is regarded as the antibiotic of choice.

PLAGUE

Plague, a disease of antiquity and one of the great scourges of mankind, is endemic in many parts of the modern world and ever ready to strike when public health safeguards are lowered. The disease, caused by *Pasteurella pestis,* provokes three principal types of clinical disease, i.e., bubonic, septicemic, and pneumonic plague. The Black Death of the Middle Ages probably resulted from septicemia and pneumonia. All clinical types are prevalent today, with the bubonic form responsible for the highest percentage of cases. In bubonic plague, fatality in the untreated rarely exceeds 30 per cent, in contrast to the uniformly fatal outcome in the septicemic and pneumonic types. Indeed, the toxemia displayed by the latter types is overwhelming. At the height of the fever in these clinical types, vomiting, diarrhea, convulsions, delirium, and vascular collapse are commonly encountered. In addition to these manifestations, the pneumonic patient develops cough, dyspnea, and hemoptysis of frothy, bloody sputum associated with some chest pain in the early stages. In the untreated patient, pneumonic plague is invariably fatal within 48 to 72 hours. Modern antibiotic therapy has drastically altered this unfavorable situation with recovery in all forms of the disease—a dramatic testimony to the impact of antimicrobial treatment.

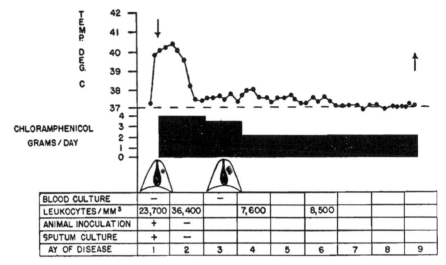

Fig. 17. Course of pneumonic plague in a 42 year old man treated with chloramphenicol. (Reprinted with permission from McCrumb et al.[554])

Clinical Results. In experimental plague infections, Meyer et al [150, 552] found chloramphenicol, other broad-spectrum antibiotics, and dihydrostreptomycin effective and deserving of clinical trial. After an initial trial in a small series of cases, chloramphenicol was shown to be beneficial in patients with bubonic and septicemic plague.[553] A 4 year old patient with septicemic plague recovered promptly after an initial intravenous dose of chloramphenicol and subsequent oral administration of this antibiotic.

McCrumb and has associates,[554] working in collaboration with French investigators in Tananarive, Madagascar, reported the successful treatment of 13 patients with the pneumonic form of plague. Six patients received chloramphenicol. Clinical response was prompt and complete without evidence of significant residuals. In figure 17, it is noted that the adult patient with confirmed pulmonic plague responded dramatically to chloramphenicol treatment, which was initiated on the first day of illness. The febrile response was prompt and the ultimate course was uneventful.

From this series it was concluded that recovery in pneumonic plague is dependent on prompt administration of an effective antibiotic in sufficient dosage. Should therapy be delayed beyond the twentieth hour after onset of illness, a favorable outcome with any known antibiotic is unlikely. In 2 such patients, cortisone acetate, administered as an antitoxemic agent concurrently with the antibiotic, failed to cure.[554]

Dosage Schedule. Chloramphenicol has been employed on the following schedule: an initial dose of 2.0 to 3.0 Gm. and subsequent daily doses of

4.0 Gm. equally divided at six hour intervals for adults during the acute phase of illness. After improvement, the daily dose may be reduced to 3.0 and 2.0 Gm. later in the course. Treatment should be continued for approximately eight days.

SUMMARY OF RESULTS

Brucellosis. Chloramphenicol is effective as a therapeutic agent in reducing the fever and general manifestations of acute brucellosis and in chronic brucellosis to a lesser extent. The antibiotic serves as a bacteriostatic agent and fails to prevent relapse in either the acute or chronic forms of brucellosis. Therapeutic regimens in either type should be carried out for approximately 10 to 14 days.

Tularemia. The acute manifestations of ulceroglandular, typhoidal, and pneumonic forms of tularemia respond adequately after chloramphenicol treatment. Clinical results are based on evaluation in small numbers of treated patients.

Plague. Experimentally produced plague infections respond to chloramphenicol. In human patients treated with this antibiotic, the clinical response has been dramatically effective. The available studies are highly encouraging in bubonic, septicemic, and pneumonic forms. Therapy in the pneumonic form, which is characterized by a very short and virulent course in the untreated, must be begun before the twentieth hour of illness in order to effect recovery.

| Staphylococcal Infections

Almost 30 years ago Ryle[556] introduced a discussion about staphylococcal infections with the following statement:

> Staphylococcal infections are at all times prevalent. They are part of the daily material of the general practitioner and the out patient department. They produce complications which fall within the province of the general physician and general surgeon. They provide problems for the dermatologist, the bacteriologist and other specialists. They create important difficulties in differential diagnosis. There is much uncertainty as to the value of the immuno-therapeutic and chemo-therapeutic measures often employed to combat them.

Staphylococcal infections have been, and continue to be, serious problems. To be sure, certain details seem to have changed; some types of infection seem to have increased in incidence and others have decreased; there have been apparent changes in recognized age distribution. Nevertheless, many fundamental aspects of staphylococcal infection are essentially unchanged, and infections with these organisms continue to challenge medical science.

Pathogenic staphylococci elaborate a variety of factors whose properties suggest that some may play important roles in the production of the characteristic infections. Among others, these include coagulase, various hemolysins and leukocidins, enterotoxin, dermonecrotoxin, lethal toxin, and hyaluronidase. While it is generally held that at least some of these factors are more than likely involved in the process of infection, unequivocal proof more often has eluded the investigator.[80, 557-561] Nevertheless, there is a fair degree of correlation between coagulase-production, alpha toxin-production, and pathogenicity;[559, 561, 562] some observations suggest a correlation between the capacity of plasma to react with coagulase and the formation of the characteristic localized lesions.[560, 563-565] Experimental results suggest that antibodies against coagulase may modify somewhat the course of infection although they do not decrease mortality.[566] The enterotoxin reproduces the symptoms of staphylococcal food poisoning, and strains isolated from cases of staphylococcal enterocolitis possess the capacity to produce enterotoxin.[567] Staphylococcal toxins produce profound systemic effects in human beings and

94

on the vascular system of experimental animals;[80, 568-576] antitoxic antibodies have been reported to convert fulminating infections in which general toxemic manifestations predominate into more chronic infections in which metastatic abscess formation is prominent.[574, 575] Some clinical material suggests the possible participation of dermonecrotoxin in occasional infections.[80]

Small colony variants (G variants) of staphylococci; known to bacteriologists for years, have recently received renewed attention. This kind of variant has been induced in vitro by the presence of certain antibiotics and has been isolated from patients who have received antibiotic therapy.[577, 578] Their clinical significance is not clearly defined at present. However, small colony variants have been associated with infection on occasion despite the fact that most are relatively avirulent for mice.[577, 579] Moreover, their relative increase in antibiotic resistance over that of the parent strain, their capacity to remain viable for long periods in the tissue of experimental animals, and their tendency to revert to the large colony forms whose virulence is equal to or greater than that of the parent strain suggest a number of possible roles for the G variants in the natural history of staphylococcal infections.

The great capacity of staphylococci to develop resistance to the antibiotics as each was introduced for general clinical use, while still retaining their virulence, and the tendency for such strains to be concentrated in hospitals have been responsible, in part, for the *staphylococcus* problem currently causing concern in many parts of the world.[75, 114, 189, 557, 580-587] The resistant virulent strains are presumably the product of spontaneous mutation and selection by environment.[589] Development of resistance to chloramphenicol by staphylococci does occur, yet the incidence of resistant strains remains relatively low.[75, 114, 189] The relatively restricted use to which this antibiotic has been held in many centers over a number of years has probably played an important role in curbing the appearance of resistant strains. Indeed, one study reported a significant increase in incidence of chloramphenicol-resistant strains of staphylococci shortly after the drug was introduced into the hospital and enjoyed widespread use. This was subsequently followed by a decrease in the incidence of resistant strains after use of the antibiotic was sharply curtailed.[179] Regardless of the causes of the relatively low proportion of resistant strains, this fact has placed chloramphenicol high on the list of antibiotics currently useful in the treatment of staphylococcal infections. In this regard, it should be borne in mind that the action of this drug on staphylococci at concentrations that are clinically attainable is primarily inhibitory or bacteriostatic, although with some strains it does exhibit a killing or bactericidal effect.[189]

McDermott [590] has recently re-emphasized very clearly the importance of the state of the host's resistance in staphylococcal infections. It has been suggested that infants have a tendency to develop diffuse lesions, i.e., cellulitis, instead of the more classical localized abscess.[560] Debilitated states, pre-existing and associated disease, such as fibrocystic disease, influenza, and neo-plasms, and malnutrition are accompanied by greater susceptibility to staphy-lococcal infection.[557, 590-596] Disturbances in the endocrine system also may lower resistance markedly.[557, 580, 593] Trauma of the skin, whether it be a burn, laceration, surgical wound, or chemical irritant, breaks down an important barrier to the entry of staphylococci. Elek[558] has shown that the presence of a foreign body such as a suture may reduce the number of staphylococci neces-sary to establish a local lesion by as much as ten thousand-fold. It is plain, then, that both local and systemic factors influencing host resistance may upset the balance between the host and the ubiquitous staphylococci and lead to infection of greater or lesser severity. Management of established infection or prevention of infection may at times logically include measures designed to bolster defense mechanisms or correct underlying disease responsible for increased susceptibility.

Although other reactions such as cellulitis may occur, the type of lesion considered to be most characteristic of localized infection by staphylococci is the abscess. Studies of experimental infections in the hamster cheek pouch, maintained under direct microscopic visualization, have revealed that a tran-sient vasoconstriction within the first few hours after injection of staphylococci was followed by vasodilation, edema formation, appearance of petechial hemor-rhages, and accumulation of leukocytes. Later, well-defined abscesses de-veloped at the site of injection. By this time, bacteria could be recovered from the abscesses but had disappeared from the surrounding tissues.[596] The structure of the typical abscess is generally well known. Early, there is fibrin deposition, thrombosis of the small vessels, and localized necrosis of tissue. Leukocytes accumulate within the abscess and staphylococci may remain viable in the abscess contents for considerable periods of time. The exact roles played by the known staphylococcal products (vide supra), on the one hand, and host reactions such as phagocytosis, products of tissue destruction anti-bodies, hypersensitivity, and antibacterial factors of humoral and leukocytic origin,[557, 598-603] on the other, are not all well defined and remain topics for discussion and further study. Nevertheless, the end result is a relatively avascular lesion, which harbors the staphylococci. This structure undoubtedly modifies the ease with which humoral factors of different kinds, i.e., circulating antibacterial substances, specific antibodies, and chemotherapeutic agents, may gain access to the microorganisms and may alter the metabolic state of the microorganisms themselves. Thus, it may explain in part the relative in-effectiveness of immune mechanisms in preventing or curing localized infec-tions and the relative resistance of some staphylococcal infections to chemo-therapy with drugs to which the organism is sensitive according to the usual in vitro tests.

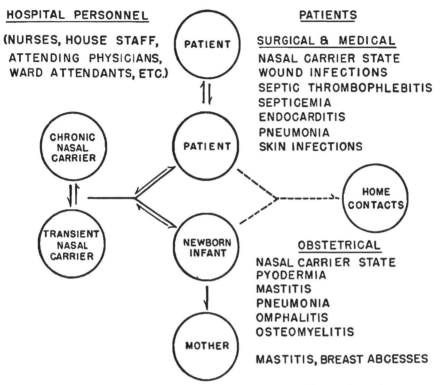

HOSPITAL PERSONNEL

(NURSES, HOUSE STAFF,
ATTENDING PHYSICIANS,
WARD ATTENDANTS, ETC.)

CHRONIC NASAL CARRIER

TRANSIENT NASAL CARRIER

PATIENT

PATIENT

NEWBORN INFANT

MOTHER

PATIENTS

SURGICAL & MEDICAL
NASAL CARRIER STATE
WOUND INFECTIONS
SEPTIC THROMBOPHLEBITIS
SEPTICEMIA
ENDOCARDITIS
PNEUMONIA
SKIN INFECTIONS

HOME CONTACTS

OBSTETRICAL
NASAL CARRIER STATE
PYODERMIA
MASTITIS
PNEUMONIA
OMPHALITIS
OSTEOMYELITIS

MASTITIS, BREAST ABCESSES

FIG. 18. Principal lines of transmission of hospital staphylococci.

Thrombosis of vessels in the vicinity of a localized infection is highly characteristic of lesions produced by staphylococci. When the bacteria traverse the vessel wall to produce a septic thrombophlebitis, heavy seeding of the blood stream with staphylococci is possible. Indeed, careful studies have shown that a very high proportion of systemic staphylococcal infections can be traced to an initial localized infection that was complicated by a septic thrombophlebitis.[604]

Experimental studies in rabbits reveal that staphylococci introduced into the blood stream are quickly phagocytized, either by the fixed reticuloendothelial system or by circulating leukocytes.[607, 608] Within the leukocytes, pathogenic staphylococci not only survive but also continue to circulate in the blood.[605-608] In this intracellular location, the staphylococci may be disseminated widely throughout the body apparently protected from humoral factors (antibodies, antibacterial substances) as well as from some of the antibiotics.[606-610] Thus, the intracellular location might play an important role in the pathogenesis of at least some kinds of staphylococcal infections; it may contribute to the resistance of some infections to therapy with antimicrobial agents to which the staphylococci are sensitive according to in vitro tests; and it may explain in part the apparent ineffectiveness of antibodies.

NASAL CARRIER STATE

Epidemiological studies point to the nasal carrier as playing a key role in the dissemination of pathogenic staphylococci.[80, 557, 580-582, 584, 585, 611-619] The patient's own nose may be the source of the staphylococci that cause recurrent infections of the skin. Of still greater importance is the proved capacity of the nasal carrier to contaminate other persons in his surroundings (see figure 18).

Nasal carriers among hospital personnel have been the subject of considerable concern because of the frequency with which patients acquire serious staphylococcal infections from them. Staphylococci from a healthy carrier may produce overt and serious infection in others in whom local or systemic defense mechanisms are lowered, such as newborn infants, lactating mothers, patients with surgical or traumatic wounds, and persons with various debilitating diseases.

Elimination of the nasal carrier would probably be a major step in reducing the problem of hospital-acquired infections. Hence, increasing consideration is being given to means of controlling this state. Host factors that govern the carrier state are poorly understood, although it is recognized that some persons tend to eliminate staphylococci rapidly while others carry them for long periods of time and that perhaps residence of one strain may hinder the establishment of another strain in this site.[582, 612, 620, 621] Removal of the efficient chronic carriers from vulnerable areas, such as the operating room and nursery, is effective but often causes serious administrative problems. Both masks and ultraviolet light have their limitations.[615, 622-624] Control of the carrier state through the use of antibiotics has been explored in the following three variations.

(1) Oral or parenteral administration of antibiotics to established carriers has not generally been very effective or practical.

(2) Prophylactic oral or parenteral administration of antibiotics, including chloramphenicol, to newborn infants upon their entry into the nursery for the purpose of preventing the establishment of the carrier state in them has been employed with some success during outbreaks of staphylococcal infection.[614, 625-628]

(3) Temporary reduction in nasal carrier rate among personnel has been accomplished by frequent periodical local applications of one or another of various antibiotic-containing ointments or creams to the anterior nares. Chloramphenicol ointment used in this way has been found to reduce the nasal carrier state. Application of this principle for carrier control has been

reported to have been effective in controlling outbreaks of staphylococcal infections.[614, 627-630]

These measures can be regarded as only temporary and suitable only for meeting an acute situation. They are not now generally recommended for long-term use.

STAPHYLOCOCCAL INFECTIONS OF THE SKIN AND SOFT TISSUES

Three categories of skin infection are considered individually because they differ somewhat from one another in the details of epidemiology, clinical manifestations, and measures required for prevention and treatment: (1) the superficial skin infections commonly seen in newborn infants (including the intradermal pustular form and the more extensive pemphigus neonatorum); (2) impetigo contagiosa; and (3) furunculosis.

The occurrence of superficial staphylococcal skin infections in the newborn infant is intimately related to the problem of the spread of pathogenic staphylococci in nurseries of newborn infants (see "Nasal Carrier State"). Preventive measures taken by various groups have been directed toward reducing the interchange of staphylococci between the attendants and environment with the newborn infant, as well as between infants themselves. This may be accomplished either by attempting to reduce the chance of colonization of the infant upon its entry into the nursery through various forms of skin care, isolation techniques, or systemic administration of prophylactic antibiotics, or by diminishing the staphylococci in the environment of the infant by elimination of carriers and by sterilizing the bedclothes, etc.[614, 618-634] Chloramphenicol has been employed successfully as a prophylactic and therapeutic agent when given to infants systemically and for local application to the anterior nares of carriers.[625, 627, 632]

Recent reports have implicated the *Staphylococcus* as an important cause of impetigo contagiosa. Moreover, these reports have also presented evidence to implicate specific strains of *Staph. aureus*, i.e., phage type 71, as a cause of some epidemics of impetigo and other skin infections.[634-637] It has been suggested that the nasal carrier does not seem to play the same key role in the spread of this infection as he does in certain other forms of staphylococcal disease. Therefore, therapeutic and preventive measures have been directed primarily at the organisms in and on the skin. In addition to the time-tested general measures for cleansing the skin and removing the crusts from the lesions, a decision must be made on the basis of the severity of the infection and extent of the lesions as to whether local or systemic antibiotic therapy is to be employed. Chloramphenicol has been employed successfully both locally and systemically in the management of this type of skin infection.[638, 639]

Furuncles, when small, sparse, and uncomplicated, rarely require antibiotic therapy. Large lesions surrounded by more extensive areas of cellulitis may benefit from systemic administration of appropriate antibiotics as an adjunct to therapy. However, with abscess formation, response to antimicrobial therapy alone is often disappointing and viable staphylococci may persist in such avascular lesions for long periods of time, even when antibiotics to which in vitro tests indicate sensitivity are administered continuously (see "Introduction"). Hence, surgical drainage of pus, removal of necrotic tissue, and possibly enzymatic debridement still constitute an important part of the management of large furuncles and abscesses. Occlusive dressings have been recommended to protect the wound from new infection and to minimize dissemination of the organisms causing the lesion. Chloramphenicol has been employed successfully in the management of localized staphylococcal infections of this kind.[638, 640] As with other antibiotics, cellulitis responds more readily than do frank abscesses. Sensitivity tests are useful guides to the selection of an appropriate antibiotic.

Persistent and recurrent severe furunculosis constitutes an especially difficult problem. Intelligent management requires scrupulous attention to the following points: (1) elimination of the reservoir of staphylococci, which is often the nose of the patient himself, by application of an antibiotic ointment (see "Nasal Carrier State"); (2) correction of any underlying skin or systemic disorder that might contribute to perpetuation of the infections; (3) reduction of the number of staphylococci on the skin by shaving hirsute areas and scrubbing with a nonirritating, nonallergenic soap containing hexachlorophene; (4) treatment of the existing active lesions.[640, 641] Howe[640] has suggested that an antibiotic carefully chosen on the basis of sensitivity tests be given systemically and then all active lesions be drained surgically under general anesthesia.

The occurrence of wound infections is often closely associated with the spread of staphylococci within hospitals (see "Nasal Carrier State"). Hence, prevention of wound infections depends on institution of measures to control the spread of staphylococci within surgical units and to prevent their access to surgical wounds.[624, 642, 643] Prophylactic antibiotics given to the patients have not been effective in reducing wound infection; instead, they have actually introduced additional complications.[580, 647] Treatment of established staphylococcal wound infections follows the same general principles outlined previously, namely, surgical drainage and debridement when necessary, local or systemic antibiotic therapy chosen on the basis of sensitivity tests, and the prevention of ingress or egress of organisms by use of strictly aseptic procedures and occlusive dressings.[640, 642-644] Chloramphenicol may often play a very useful role in the treatment of wound infections.[642-646]

STAPHYLOCOCCAL PNEUMONIA AND EMPYEMA

Two broad categories of staphylococcal pneumonia are recognized: (1)

"primary" staphylococcal pneumonia disseminated through the lung tissue by way of the bronchi and (2) secondary staphylococcal pneumonia, which is another manifestation of metastatic infection arising out of hematogenous spread of the organism from a distant primary focus. In cases of the latter type, secondary to staphylococcal sepsis, metastatic suppurative foci may also coexist in other organs (*vide infra*). The characteristic pathological picture consists of infected thrombi surrounded by areas of infarction and abscess formation.[648-654]

The clinical course of primary staphylococcal pneumonia may range from a fulminating form with death occurring within a few hours after onset, through a continuous series of gradations to an insidious and prolonged illness. Suppuration plays a minor role in the fulminating cases. In these, the lesion is hemorrhagic and edematous, low in leukocytic reaction, and exhibits various degrees of necrosis of the respiratory epithelium and lung parenchyma. Patients who survive longer, i.e., a few days or more, show multiple abscess formation clustered about the bronchioles and distributed segmentally or diffusely toward the periphery of the lung, often involving the pleura. As suppuration advances, several lesions may coalesce to form large abscesses that may rupture into a bronchus or through the pleura. Empyema and pyopneumothorax are common complications.[648-654]

Primary staphylococcal pneumonia is seen frequently in infants or as a terminal event in debilitated or aged persons. Chronic pre-existing disease, such as fibrocystic disease, chronic pulmonary disease, or blood dyscrasias, predisposes to staphylococcal infections of the respiratory tract.[655-661] Moreover, there is growing evidence that some viral infection of the respiratory tract may pave the way for the entrance and bronchogenic spread of staphylococcal infection, even in young adults.[648, 649, 651, 654, 658, 662-668] Indeed, staphylococcal pneumonia was recognized as an important cause of death during the influenza epidemic of 1918-1919, and influenza virus has been isolated with increasing frequency from the lungs of patients dying of staphylococcal pneumonia in both local outbreaks and sporadic cases in more recent times. It is likely that some such predisposing respiratory infection often accounts for the occurrence of primary staphylococcal pneumonia in otherwise healthy young adults.

The rapid course of the fulminant or catastrophic form gives very little opportunity for specific antibacterial drugs to act. If chemotherapy is to be effective, it must be instituted without delay and in adequate dosage. Even with large dosages of antibiotics, the mortality rate is very high.[656, 657, 670, 671] The appearance of the lesions as well as the condition of the patient as a whole suggests that staphylococcal toxins play a predominant role in the pathogenesis of this form of the disease, and hence, toxin already formed might continue to act unabated even in the presence of an antibiotic that is capable of destroying the organism. It has been suggested, but not yet tested, that staphylococcal antitoxin might provide a useful adjunct to antimicrobial and supportive therapy.[656, 666]

When the course is more prolonged, antibiotics have more time to exert their effects. However, the formation of abscesses introduces additional difficulties in management. Prolonged administration of an appropriate antibiotic, i.e., for a minimum of three to four weeks, may be necessary to eliminate the staphylococci from such lesions and to prevent relapse.[659] Even under the most favorable circumstances, the mortality rate remains high. Moreover, the strain of *Staphylococcus* causing the infection may exhibit a broad range of antibiotic resistance. Despite this, however, a high proportion of strains causing pneumonia are still found to be sensitive to chloramphenicol by in vitro tests.[657, 659, 660, 668-670] In the hands of some, chloramphenicol has been found to exert a favorable or curative action on the disease,[660, 669] while others have not observed strikingly beneficial effects.[657, 668, 670] Indeed, some authors have lamented the relative ineffectiveness of broad-spectrum antibiotics generally in this disease, especially after abscess formation is advanced, despite encouraging results in in vitro sensitivity tests; consequently, various combinations of antibiotics have been given therapeutic trial.[655, 657, 679]

When large abscesses are present, surgical drainage may become a necessary adjunct to specific chemotherapy. Removal of the exudate from the pleural cavity remains an important part of the therapy of staphylococcal empyema and continues to find application in conjunction with antibiotic therapy. The techniques of repeated aspiration and of closed drainage both have their advocates.[651, 655, 657, 669]

STAPHYLOCOCCAL SEPTICEMIA AND ENDOCARDITIS

Staphylococcal septicemia, with or without associated endocarditis, remains a grave disease attended by a high mortality rate. The clinical course varies from the acute fulminating case, which gives the impression of a severe toxemia and in which metastatic abscesses are not prominent, to the more prolonged "septicopyemia" of the older literature, in which metastatic abscesses throughout the body are common and contribute significantly to the course of the disease. In a large proportion of cases, the origin of the septicemia can be traced to some primary localized infection; it often complicates a surgical procedure or is associated with some serious underlying disease.[573, 595, 604, 672, 673] Introduction of antibiotic therapy has not caused a lasting dramatic reduction in morality rate from staphylococcal sepsis. Increasing resistance of the staphylococci to the antibiotics has contributed much to the perpetuation of this problem. Nevertheless, patients still die of staphylococcal sepsis and endocarditis all too frequently, even when an antibiotic is administered to which the organism has been shown to be sensitive by in vitro tests. The factors contributing to this problem are probably very complex (see page 94).

A review of the experiences of several groups with staphylococcal sepsis and endocarditis emphasizes several principles that seem especially important for achieving best therapeutic results in infections of this kind.[580, 595, 673-675]

(1) Response to therapy is best if it is begun early in the course of the disease and, therefore, should be instituted without delay when the diagnosis is made. The initial choice of drugs may be made empirically, choosing those that experience has shown most likely to be effective at the specific time and place. Sensitivity tests guide the final choice of drugs as soon as results of these are available.

(2) Intensive and prolonged antibiotic therapy is often required for complete recovery.

(3) Results seem to be better if it is possible to employ a drug or combination of drugs that is capable of killing the staphylococci in in vitro tests. Bacteriostatic drugs have tended to be less effective.

(4) Recovery is facilitated if all accessible suppurative and necrotic foci are drained.

(5) Careful attention to nutrition, general supportive measures, and correction of underlying disorders contribute to recovery. These last two measures were well-established principles of therapy long before the introduction of antibiotics and remain essential components of the therapeutic regimen.

Strains of penicillin-resistant staphylococci causing sepsis are at present often found to be sensitive to chloramphenicol by the usual in vitro tests. Experience has shown, however, that although chloramphenicol alone occasionally brings about cures, it has often failed to control the infection.[676-680] Reports from several centers suggest that considerably better results may be obtained when this drug is employed in combination with another antibiotic, such as bacitracin or erythromycin,[595, 673-675] an observation that has kept chloramphenicol high on the list of drugs to be considered for therapy of this difficult type of infection. The variable course of the disease, the variable resistance of the organism, and the small numbers of patients treated with any single combination preclude drawing firm conclusions about the optimal specific regimen. Nevertheless, the general objective of a drug with bactericidal action penetrating in effective amounts into all the reaches and recesses wherein staphylococci may reside is sound, regardless of whether it must be achieved by a single agent or a combination chosen on the basis of reliable clinical experience and laboratory data.

OSTEOMYELITIS

In many respects, antibiotics have revolutionized the management of acute hematogenous osteomyelitis, for they have provided specific means for the treatment of both the generalized infection (see "Staphylococcal Septicemia and Endocarditis") and the localized process in the bone. Early, accurate, and complete diagnosis is essential for best results, since antibiotic therapy is most effective when it is initiated prior to the occurrence of bone destruction and the development of a relatively avascular lesion.[681] Prolonged therapy is usually required to eradicate the infectious process and to prevent relapse. Chemotherapy must be integrated properly with any surgical procedure that is contemplated. The general objectives of surgical intervention now include eradication of walled-off or persistent foci, increased contact of the therapeutic agent with the affected area, and prevention of damage to important structures.[681-684] Penicillin has been the drug of choice for the treatment of osteomyelitis caused by staphylococci. However, the frequent occurrence of penicillin-resistant strains of this organism has necessitated the evaluation of other antimicrobial agents. In a number of centers, chloramphenicol has yielded good therapeutic results[683-685] despite the fact that one report indicates that bacteriostatic agents generally, including chloramphenicol, are less effective than penicillin and their use is more likely to be complicated by relapse.[686]

SUMMARY

Pathogenic staphylococci are ubiquitous in human beings, spread readily from person to person, develop resistance to most antibiotics with relative ease, and produce infections that may be serious and difficult to manage. Antibiotics, chosen on the basis of sensitivity tests, constitute an important, though not always dramatic, part of the therapy of the more serious staphylococcal infections. The response of localized tissue infections to antibiotic therapy is generally more rapid before necrosis and abscess formation have occurred; hence, early therapy is especially important. After abscess formation has occurred, drainage and elimination of necrotic tissue remain integral parts of the therapeutic regimen and speed recovery. In many instances, prolonged antibiotic administration is necessary to eradicate the staphylococci and prevent relapse. Moreover, antimicrobial therapy alone is often not sufficient to alter the rapid course of some fulminating infections in which toxemia predominates.

The incidence of chloramphenicol-resistant strains of staphylococci is currently low; hence, indications for use of this drug are frequent. Superficial and localized infections caused by sensitive organisms tend to respond well to chloramphenicol. On the other hand, when this drug is employed alone for the treatment of staphylococcal septicemia, its effect is often irregular and disappointing. In combination with certain other carefully selected drugs, however, its action in this form of infection compares favorably with that of other drugs in current use.

Chapter XIII

Therapy of Infections of the Genitourinary Tract

The probability is not small that any given individual will develop a urinary tract infection at some time during his life. No precise figures are available on the magnitude of the risk, but this risk is sizable, particularly for females, in whom urinary tract infections are common both in childhood and in pregnancy. It is often stated that urinary tract infections are second in frequency only to upper respiratory infections. Indirect evidence of this frequency comes from reports that histological evidence of active or healed pyelonephritis is found in more than 20 per cent of routine autopsies.[687] The clinical diagnosis of renal infection had not been made in more than two thirds of these cases of pyelonephritis prior to death,[687] emphasizing the difficulty in detecting chronic pyelonephritis in an asymptomatic patient.

Patients with acute upper or lower urinary tract infections may become asymptomatic and on follow-up study have normal urinary findings with negative cultures when their therapy was supportive only and without antibiotic agents. On the other hand, it is certainly true that, in other patients, urinary tract infection may persist in spite of what is currently believed to be adequate and appropriate antibiotic and chemotherapeutic treatment. Chronicity of urinary tract infection appears to be dependent on stasis and obstruction, and the presence of either condition makes effective treatment difficult or impossible. Uncontrolled diabetes, disturbances in bladder innervation, and local areas of infection in proximity to the urinary tract also predispose to persistence of infection.

When these factors are not present or are not demonstrable in a patient, it is difficult to understand the failure of adequate therapy against antibiotic-sensitive organisms, although such failures are disappointingly common. Initially, the responsible bacteria are usually sensitive in vitro to the action of one or more of the antibiotic or chemotherapeutic agents, and when these same organisms cause infections elsewhere in the human body, they usually are susceptible in vivo. Although these comments apply to infections anywhere in the genitourinary tract, they are particularly important in patients with pyelonephritis. The surprisingly poor response of chronic pyelonephritis to antibiotic therapy, even in patients who have no urinary obstruction, has been commented on recently by Beeson.[688] He points out the inadequacy of our knowledge of factors responsible for this poor response and believes that "frequent or continuous seeding of the kidney with fresh supplies of bacteria" is a likely hypothesis for these therapeutic failures. To what degree (1) possible intracellular parasitism, (2) slow bacterial growth rate versus antibiotic effectiveness on bacteria in active multiplication, or (3) relatively ineffective phagocytosis of bacteria in the urine contributes further to therapuetic difficulties is not clear at this time. Then, too, it might be mentioned that although most physicians treat bacterial infections of the kidney with reference to an effective serum (tissue) level of an antibiotic or chemotherapeutic agent, it is not clear how much importance should be attached to urine levels of these same agents. Indwelling catheters and other urological procedures may play a significant role in the introduction of bacteria into the urinary tract and also in the alteration of the flora in a patient already infected. A recent paper[687] reports only a 10 to 15 per cent cure rate in the long-term follow-up of patients with chronic pyelonephritis.

Urinary tract infections frequently are divided, anatomically, into upper and lower tract infections. However, the clinical diagnosis of concomitant pyelonephritis in a patient with lower urinary tract infection may be difficult if that patient has no localizing symptoms pointing to renal involvement. It is felt that the bacteria causing lower urinary tract infections are the same as those that cause pyelonephritis, with the exception of infections caused by *Streptococcus faecalis,* which for the most part are confined to lower portions of the urinary tract.[687]

Therapeutic evaluation of any antibiotic in the management of urinary tract infection should consider the responsible bacteria and their sensitivity to the antibiotic agent, as well as the afore-mentioned factors that predispose to unsatisfactory and equivocal results.

Urinary tract infections may be caused by a single strain of organisms, but mixed infections are common and are found in a little less than 50 per cent of patients. Table XIII lists the organisms in their relative frequency of occurrence in acute and chronic urinary tract infections, and the in vitro sensitivity to chloramphenicol of the majority of the strains of each organism is presented. Most of these organisms are sensitive in vitro to the action of chloramphenicol, although the usual variation in strain sensitivity is encountered with this drug as well as with other antibiotic and chemotherapeutic agents. *Ps. aeruginosa* is particularly likely to be resistant to chloram-

TABLE XIII

**Common Organisms Causing Urinary Tract Infection
and Their Sensitivity to Chloramphenicol**

Oganism	μg./ml. to which majority of strains are sensitive
Escherichia coli	6.0
Staphylococcus	8.0
Aerobacter aerogenes	12.0
Proteus	15.0
Pseudomonas aeruginosa	R*
Enterococcus	5.0
Klebsiella pneumoniae	3.1

*Resistant.

phenicol, and in recent years proportionately more strains of *Proteus* are being found to be resistant.

CLINICAL RESULTS

Chittenden et al [689] used chloramphenicol in the treatment of 50 patients with acute and chronic urinary tract infections; almost half received penicillin, sulfonamides, or both in combination with chloramphenicol. Thirty-eight per cent of these patients became symptom-free with sterile urine cultures. Forty-four per cent were clinically improved but continued to have positive cultures. Of the 9 patients who were unimproved, 8 had either structural abnormality of the urinary tract with obstruction, infection with *Pseudomonas,* or both. The other patient had a clinical diagnosis of viral urethritis. In the group of patients who were improved but not cured, there were fewer patients with evidence of obstruction or infection with *Pseudomonas* than in the unimproved group. Of the 19 patients who were cured, more than half had neither obstruction nor infection with *Pseudomonas.*

Hewitt and Williams[240] reported the use of chloramphenicol as the sole therapeutic agent in the treatment of 93 patients. A good clinical response was observed in 75 per cent and urinary sterilization occurred in 70 per cent. Of those patients with urinary sterilization, 52 were followed for at least one month after treatment, and reappearance of bacilluria was noted in 25 per cent.

There were 23 patients with acute pyelonephritis in Hewitt and Williams' series. Three patients with acute pyelonephritis of pregnancy showed prompt improvement with urinary sterilization. Of 20 additional patients with acute pyelonephritis, 17 showed good clinical response with urinary sterilization in 11. Six patients without urinary sterilization showed either infection with *Ps. aeruginosa,* structural abnormality of the urinary tract, or both.

Fourteen patients with acute infections of the lower urinary tract were treated with good clinical response and urinary sterilization in 12 patients, although 3 of the 12 showed bacteriological relapse after treatment. In both patients who responded poorly, *P. vulgaris* persisted throughout the treatment period.

In Hewitt and Williams' report, 56 patients with chronic urinary tract infections were treated and good clinical results occurred in 36 patients, 35 of whom had urinary sterilization; the other patient continued to have bacilluria with *Ps. aeruginosa*. Bacteriological relapse was observed in 8 patients. Of 20 patients experiencing no clinical improvement on chloramphenicol, 11 had infections with *Ps. aeruginosa*, 3 had obstructive uropathy, and 2 additional patients had *P. vulgaris* infections resistant in vitro to more than 50 gamma of chloramphenicol per ml.

Daily dosage of chloramphenicol varied between 2 and 6 Gm. for an average duration of seven days. The highest incidence of good clinical results was obtained in those patients treated longer than seven days, and concomitantly greater numbers from this group manifested disappearance of bacilluria.

Frequently the antibacterial management of chronic prostatitis has been disappointing,[690] and here, general hygienic measures, correction of urethral obstructions, and local prostatic therapy are indicated in addition to specific treatment. Although the number of reported cases is small, chloramphenicol has been reported to be of value in the antibacterial management of prostatitis.[240] In a small series, chloramphenicol was found to be of definite benefit in the management of recurring epididymitis.[691]

SUMMARY

Ideally, every patient with a urinary tract infection should have urine cultures performed and a stained smear of the sediment of a fresh specimen obtained before antibiotic therapy is instituted. Since this is frequently impractical, many practitioners treat acute urinary tract infections, particularly those of the lower tract, without attempting to identify the causative organism. One of the sulfonamide drugs is most often prescribed as initial therapy. Under these conditions, a Gram stain of the urinary sediment may help identify the offending bacteria.

Chloramphenicol is a valuable antibiotic for the treatment of some urinary tract infections but it should not be used indiscriminately. None of the antibiotics, including chloramphenicol, should be given to patients with urinary tract infections without identification of the bacteria and knowledge of their sensitivity reaction to this antibiotic.

The management of patients with urinary tract infections includes the correction of structural abnormalities of the urinary tract in so far as practicable and elimination of any focal infection outside the urinary tract. Diabetes, if present, should be controlled.

Chloramphenicol should be given for 10 to 14 days in a dosage of 50 mg./Kg. of body weight per day. As discussed in chapter IV, this dosage provides adequate serum levels for treatment of most of the organisms listed in table XIII. Almost all chloramphenicol administered orally is excreted in the urine, in active form sufficient to provide rather satisfactory urine levels. The urine should be kept alkaline with the use of some agent, such as sodium bicarbonate. Follow-up urine cultures and urinalyses should be carried out for a period of months before the infection is considered controlled. Persistence or reappearance of bacilluria warrants re-evaluation of the infectious process with appropriate cultures and sensitivity studies.

Chapter XIV

Therapy of Syphilis, Other Spirochetal Disorders, and Venereal Diseases

SYPHILIS

Syphilis, which is endemic throughout the world, is an infectious constitutional disease caused by *Treponema pallidum*. After an incubation period varying from one to six weeks, the early stage is marked by the appearance of a chancre (initial lesion) and various cutaneous lesions classified as secondary syphilides. The lesions of early syphilis are self-limiting, and in untreated patients, the disorder temporarily assumes a latent phase. Approximately 25 per cent of patients with latent syphilis eventually display one of the various late manifestations, such as involvement of the central nervous system, the cardiovascular apparatus, the skin, mucous membranes, or the skeletal system.

Prior to the advent of antibiotics, syphilis was treated with the trivalent arsenicals and heavy metals administered for a prolonged period. Penicillin therapy has revolutionized the management of this disease, arresting the clinical manifestations in a relatively short period. The broad-spectrum antibiotics, including chloramphenicol, are also of value in the treatment of syphilis.

Clinical Results. Although in vitro studies[25] demonstrated that chloramphenicol had no immobilizing effect on virulent *Spirochaeta pallida*, the course of experimental rabbit syphilis was modified by this antibiotic. When rabbits infected with the *Treponema* of syphilis were given chloramphenicol in a dosage from 50 to 75 mg./Kg./day for eight days, the surface lesions healed, only to relapse at a later date.[20] Rabbits, however, develop a significantly lower serum level of chloramphenicol than man for an equivalent dose of this antibiotic. Hence, higher relative dosage is required. When the dosage was raised to 200 mg./Kg./day, relapse did not occur and the infection in these rabbits was "cured." [162] Similar results have been noted in human syphilis. After a single oral dose of 3 to 4 Gm. of chloramphenicol in patients with primary syphilis, the lesions healed, but relapses usually occurred four to six weeks after treatment.[692]

When given in dosages of 30 mg./Kg./day for eight days, chloramphenicol was only partially effective in "curing" syphilitic patients.[693] When dosages were raised to 60 mg./Kg. for eight days and appraised after a 12 to 15 month follow-up, the clinical results compared favorably with those noted in a series of patients given penicillin for 7 to 10 days.[693] Four pregnant women treated for syphilis at this higher dosage schedule were delivered of healthy infants without the development of clinical or serological evidence of syphilis during a three month follow-up.[693]

A longer follow-up was carried out on a group of 14 patients with early syphilis who were treated with 48 Gm. of chloramphenicol administered during a 15 day period.[694] These patients were observed for two to four years. At the end of the study, 1 patient was lost from observation, 2 had developed serological relapses, and 1 patient developed a mucocutaneous relapse. Five patients remained seronegative, 2 had doubtful serological tests, and the 3 other patients had positive serological tests in low titer. Spinal fluid examinations were negative in all patients.

Intramuscular chloramphenicol is effective in the treatment of early syphilis. Sixty-three patients were given intramuscular chloramphenicol in dosages of 2 to 4 Gm./day for six days and followed for 3 to 13 months.[695] One of the 23 patients, followed three to six months, developed reinfection. All other patients were seronegative or had declining serological titers at the time of last examination.

Summary. Chloramphenicol is an effective antispirochetal drug. This antibiotic could be considered for treatment of patients with syphilis when penicillin is contraindicated for various reasons. The suggested oral dose is 3.0 Gm. followed by 0.5 Gm. every four hours for 15 days (total dosage, 48 Gm.). This antibiotic may be given parenterally in dosage of 1 to 2 Gm. twice daily for six days.

YAWS

Yaws is a constitutional disease caused by *Treponema pertenue* and is endemic in tropical countries. The disease usually begins in childhood and is characterized by the development of ulcerative skin lesions. Although it resembles syphilis in nature, yaws is not a venereal disease, is not transmitted from mother to child, and does not involve the cardiovascular or central nervous systems. Before the advent of penicillin, the trivalent arsenicals were therapeutically useful in yaws but the treatment period was much shorter than that for syphilis. Antibiotic therapy is very effective in the management of yaws.

Clinical Results. In Haiti in 1951, Payne et al [696] employed chloramphenicol for the treatment of patients with yaws. Using various treatment schedules, these investigators treated 63 patients with active clinical lesions. The dosage schedules ranged from 3.0 Gm. of chloramphenicol given during a one and a half hour period to 16.0 Gm. given over five days. Twenty-seven hospitalized patients showed complete clearing of the clinical lesions on a regimen totaling 14.0 to 16.4 Gm. Follow-up studies on 36 ambulatory patients were incomplete, although on last examination the lesions were cured or healing in each case.

Chloramphenicol should be considered for use in patients with yaws, when penicillin therapy is contraindicated.

RELAPSING FEVER

Relapsing fever is an acute infectious disease of moderate severity, endemic in eastern Europe, caused by a spirochete, *Treponema recurrentis* *(Borrelia recurrentis)*. The disease is characterized by paroxysms of fever with interim periods of apparent recovery, and since each relapse is usually less severe than the preceding one, the disease tends to be self-limiting. Before antibiotics were discovered, the trivalent arsenicals were used effectively.

Clinical Results. In vitro studies revealed that chloramphenicol was inhibitory for *Borrelia novyi*,[20] and, subsequently, the antibiotic was found to be effective in treating mice experimentally infected with *Bor. novyi*.[160] Penicillin G and chloramphenicol exhibited similar dose-response relationships in suppressing the marked parasitemia, although larger doses of chloramphenicol were required to produce comparable results. In these tests, the potency ratio of chloramphenicol to penicillin G with treatment by diet was 0.2 and by intraperitoneal injection it was 0.37.

In Korea, Hirschboeck[697] conducted a clinical study in patients with relapsing fever and obtained dramatic results with chloramphenicol. In this series of 27 patients, adults received a total dosage of 2.0 Gm. divided into 4 equal doses in 24 hours, and children received a total dosage of 1.0 Gm. with the same intervals. At the end of 48 hours all bacteriological studies were negative for *Bor. recurrentis*.

OTHER VENEREAL DISEASES

Gonorrhea. Gonorrhea is a venereal disease caused by *Neisseria gonorrhoeae,* a gram-negative intracellular *Diplococcus.* The incubation period is from three to five days. The initial manifestation in the male is a purulent urethral discharge, and when untreated, the inflammation extends to the posterior urethra, the prostate, and the seminal vesicles. In the female, the condition begins as a vaginitis gradually extending to the Fallopian tubes and ovaries. In untreated cases, gonorrhea may involve the skin, joints, and cardiovascular apparatus. Before antibiotics were available, sulfanilamide, sulfathiazole, and sulfapyridine were used effectively in approximately 70 per cent of cases of gonorrhea. Penicillin is unmistakably the most effective antibiotic against gonorrhea. The tetracycline antibiotics and chloramphenicol are also of definite value.

CLINICAL RESULTS. In vitro studies have revealed that chloramphenicol is effective against gonococci, the bacteriostatic concentration of chloramphenicol being of the order of 0.5 gamma/ml.[698] One of the initial clinical studies[699] described complete clearing of gonococcal infections in 13 patients when 3.0 Gm. of chloramphenicol was given in a single dose or in divided doses over 24 hours. Subsequent to this report, larger series have compared the effectiveness of chloramphenicol with penicillin in the treatment of gonorrhea. Barrett and Burton[700] reported negative urethral cultures in 88.7 per cent of 251 patients with gonorrhea treated with 1 Gm. of chloramphenicol in a single dose. This was lower than the 97.4 per cent of negative cultures in 236 patients treated concurrently with 300,000 units of intramuscular penicillin. When chloramphenicol was increased to 2.0 Gm. in a single oral dose, 93.3 per cent of 226 patients with gonorrhea had negative urethral cultures one week after treatment, as compared with 96.6 per cent of 206 patients in a penicillin control series. This difference was not statistically significant.[700] If the patients with probable reinfection are excluded, the figures improve to 97.3 per cent of patients for chloramphenicol and 99.1 per cent for penicillin.

In a separate study, 3.0 Gm. of chloramphenicol given in a single oral dose was compared with 900,000 units of penicillin as a single intramuscular dose in patients with gonorrheal urethritis.[701] When the post-treatment infections believed to be due to reinfection were excluded, all cultures were negative on the ninth post-treatment day in 113 patients receiving chloramphenicol and in 179 patients receiving penicillin.

Although it cannot be said from these data that 3.0 Gm. as a single oral dose is superior to 2.0 Gm. in the treatment of gonorrheal urethritis, most investigators prefer the larger dose.[699] Chloramphenicol is also effective intramuscularly. A cure rate of 96 per cent was reported in 51 patients with gonorrheal urethritis given 1 Gm. of chloramphenicol intramuscularly.[702]

SUMMARY. Chloramphenicol is of significant value in the treatment of gonorrhea. This antibiotic should be restricted for use in those patients who are intolerant of penicillin. The recommended regimen is a single oral dose of 3.0 Gm. of chloramphenicol. Serological tests for syphilis should be performed at periodic intervals for four months after institution of treatment, since it has been demonstrated that a dose of 3.0 Gm. of chloramphenicol will inhibit the appearance of the lesions of early syphilis.[699]

Granuloma Inguinale. Granuloma inguinale is a systemic venereal disease caused by *Donovania granulomatis.* It is endemic in the United States among Southern Negroes of the lower economic strata. The disease is marked by the development of granulomatous lesions, which become progressive and may cause destruction of the external genitals.

CLINICAL RESULTS. When patients with granuloma inguinale were treated with chloramphenicol, Donovan bodies were reported to disappear from the lesions more rapidly than with chlortetracycline or streptomycin.[703] The results in 115 patients treated with either oral or intramuscular chloramphenicol have been encouraging.[695, 703-705] In one series of 23 patients given oral therapy, 2 patients required a second course for complete healing and 2 other patients relapsed.[703] In an additional 20 patients given oral therapy, excellent results were noted in 18, with a single course of therapy; the other 2 patients were greatly improved but were lost to follow-up study.[705] Of 23 patients treated with intramuscular chloramphenicol (12.0 Gm. given during a 6 to 12 day period), excellent results were noted in 22 patients (4 of these patients had previously been treatment failures with streptomycin).[695] For the most part, oral dosage was 2.0 Gm./day for two weeks for these patients. Therapy was continued for an additional two weeks in patients in whom involution of the lesions was delayed.[695]

SUMMARY. Chloramphenicol is an effective antibiotic for treatment of patients with granuloma inguinale. The suggested dosage is 2.0 Gm. orally followed by 0.5 Gm. every six hours for two weeks.

Lymphogranuloma Venereum. When tested under in vitro conditions, chloramphenicol has inhibited the growth of the lymphogranuloma venereum virus, and experimentally produced infections have responded favorably to this antibiotic.[154]

Very few reported cases of lymphogranuloma venereum treated with chloramphenicol are available for evaluation. One patient with lymphogranuloma venereum and syphilis responded to 12.0 Gm. of chloramphenicol,[695] but the results in 3 other patients with a similar dosage schedule were less dramatic.[706] The few reported cases are inadequate for proper evaluation, but it appears that chloramphenicol has little place in the therapy of lymphogranuloma venereum.

Chancroid. In vitro studies have demonstrated an inhibiting action of chloramphenicol on *Hemophilus ducreyi.*[706] There are few reported cases of chancroid treated with chloramphenicol. Based on the available data, it appears that this antibiotic is very effective for treatment of this disease. The involved areas heal promptly in a uniform manner.[695, 706]

Chloramphenicol ointment has been compared with other antibiotic ointments for the treatment of experimental chancroid lesions in man.[707] The efficacy of this agent was compared with that of neomycin, penicillin, chlortetracycline, and erythromycin in 5 volunteers. Chloramphenicol ointment was reported to be "dramatically effective" for both the prevention and the treatment of experimental chancroid lesions. This ointment promptly "cured" all lesions that had failed to respond initially to other antibiotics.[707]

| Chapter XV | Treatment of Dermatological Conditions |

Many dermatological disorders are caused by bacteria, or an underlying dermatosis may be complicated by bacterial infection. The most common organisms producing these infections are *M. pyogenes* and beta-hemolytic *Streptococcus*, although other bacteria (such as *E. coli, P. vulgaris,* and *Ps. aeruginosa*) may be etiological agents. In many patients, antibiotic therapy usually leads to dramatic amelioration of the pyogenic infection. In the treatment of such infections, topical application is preferred, although systemic therapy is preferable when the infection is widespread or deep-seated.

Any drug applied to the skin, particularly inflamed skin, may produce acquired contact sensitivity. Allergic reactions to topical applications of antibiotics predispose to systemic reactions from subsequent parenteral administration. Consequently, antibiotics preferred for topical therapy of bacterial skin infections are those that are not ordinarily administered systemically. Antibiotics such as chloramphenicol are therapeutically effective when administered orally, intramuscularly, and intravenously, and have been found to be effective when given topically for bacterial infections of the skin.

SUPERFICIAL SKIN INFECTIONS

Clinical Results. The superficial skin infections include the primary pyodermas, such as impetigo contagiosa and ecthyma, and also dermatoses when secondary pyogenic infection is superimposed, i.e., allergic dermatoses, eczema, mycoses, seborrheic dermatitis, and stasis ulcer. Chloramphenicol ointment, applied topically, was very effective for treatment of these primary pyodermas and for the secondary pyogenic infections of other superficial dermatoses.[705, 708] One group of investigators considered chloramphenicol ointment as "the most satisfactory" of available medications for superficial pyogenic infections because of excellent clinical response and low incidence of skin sensitization (1 patient sensitive of 226 patients treated).[708]

116

Chloramphenicol ointment* may be applied to the involved area twice daily after the patient has been instructed to remove crusts or surface exudates with warm water compresses.

Summary. Chloramphenicol is a valuable chemotherapeutic drug and is very effective for the topical treatment of superficial pyogenic infections. It should not be used indiscriminately on the skin since host sensitization may occur readily and preclude its use when systemic manifestations require its full therapeutic impact.

DEEP PYOGENIC INFECTIONS

The group of deep-seated pyodermas commonly caused by staphylococci or streptococci includes furuncles, abscesses, carbuncles, folliculitis, cellulitis, and erysipelas. Definite amelioration followed the administration of systemic chloramphenicol in patients with these infections regardless of the concurrent use of surgical drainage. In all these patients, chloramphenicol was given orally.[705] Adults of average size should be given an initial dose of 2.0 Gm. of chloramphenicol followed by 0.5 Gm. every six hours for 7 to 10 days. Children should be given an average dosage of 50 mg./Kg. of body weight divided into four doses over a 24 hour period and continued for 7 to 10 days.

ACNE VULGARIS

Acne vulgaris is a skin disorder of unknown etiology that usually begins at puberty. It is associated with metabolic dysfunction, although pyogenic infection is a significant contributing factor. It is characterized by the appearance of papules and pustules over the face, chest, and back. In some patients the pustular lesions become cystic, and disfiguring scar formation may occur if proper treatment is not instituted.

The most common organisms cultured from the pustular lesions in acne are the staphylococci. Although penicillin exhibits significant in vitro antimicrobial effect for these bacteria,[709] this antibiotic was found to be of little value for treatment of patients with acne.[710] The broad-spectrum antibiotics, given systemically, are of value in the management of these infections.[710] Topical therapy with any antibiotic in patients with acne is generally unsatisfactory.

When chloramphenicol was given exclusively for acne, a few patients showed prolonged improvement,[710] although the over-all results were not uniform. Most patients showed temporary improvement while the drug was continued and suffered recurrence when therapy was stopped. This temporary im-

---

*As a 1 per cent ointment in a base of cetyl alcohol, liquid petrolatum, Duponal C, propylparahydroxybenzoate, and distilled water.

provement has been observed with other antibiotics and has prompted the use of prolonged drug regimens in low dosage. Some patients with acne have responded favorably.[710]

The antibiotics should be considered only as adjunct therapy for management of acne. These drugs do not replace the well-established methods of treatment such as diet restriction and topical and roentgen therapy. The prolonged use of potent antibiotics, even in low dosage, is attended by the hazards of marked alteration in the normal bacterial flora of man. Patients with acne in whom chloramphenicol therapy is to be instituted should be selected wisely and followed carefully.

MISCELLANEOUS DERMATOLOGICAL CONDITIONS

Erythema multiforme is a pleomorphic skin eruption characterized by periods of remission and exacerbation. Patients with this disorder may show temporary involution of their lesions while receiving chloramphenicol, although relapse can be expected when therapy is discontinued.[705]

Chloramphenicol is of no value in modifying the course of discoid or systemic lupus erythematosus.[711, 712]

Although initial reports on the use of chloramphenicol in the treatment of herpes zoster were enthusiastic,[713, 714] this antibiotic is not considered to provoke beneficial action on the course of herpes zoster or other dermatotrophic virus infections such as Kaposi's varicelliform eruption, condyloma acuminata, herpes simplex, molluscum contagiosum, verruca vulgaris, and verruca plana juvenilis.[705, 715]

| Miscellaneous Infections

BACTERIAL ENDOCARDITIS

The control of bacterial infection of the heart valves by antibiotics represents one of the major contributions of medicine, having transformed this disease from one which was invariably fatal to one in which recovery occurs in more than 70 per cent of cases. A review by a distinguished contributor in this field [716] describes the common microbial causes of bacterial endocarditis and the therapeutic considerations, including choice of antibiotic, dosage, and duration of treatment.

Based on the now extensive clinical experience in treatment of bacterial endocarditis, it may be stated unequivocally that penicillin in adequate dosage should be selected as the mainstay of treatment for most cases. This would include patients from whom a specific microorganism has been isolated, doubtful cases of endocarditis for whom a therapeutic decision is forced, and such cases when one must institute treatment before the results of cultures or sensitivity tests are known: Streptomycin in conventional dosage appears to be of real value in supplementing the action of penicillin.

It is true that the broad-spectrum antibiotics including oxytetracycline, chlortetracycline, and chloramphenicol [717] are occasionally effective in some cases of bacterial endocarditis. These antibiotics have been beneficial in a small proportion of cases, but therapeutic results have been much less impressive than those obtained with large dosages of penicillin alone or in combination with streptomycin. Although chloramphenicol and the broad-spectrum antibiotics may effect a favorable clinical response, including their action in controlling the apparent bacteremia, clinical and bacteriological relapses have occurred on cessation of therapy in a large proportion of patients who received these antibiotics.[718-721] It may be concluded that the broad-spectrum antibiotics are not recommended as the drugs of first choice.

Results of Therapy with Chloramphenicol. Some cures of patients with bacterial endocarditis have been attributed to chloramphenicol. Several patients in whom the causative organism was *Streptococcus viridans* made complete

119

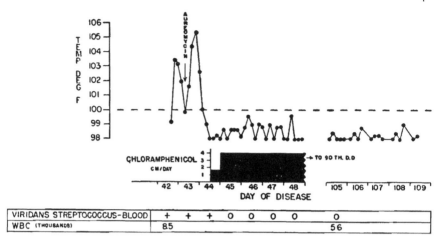

Fig. 19. Graphic record of a 33 year old man with *Str. viridans* endocarditis treated successfully with chloramphenicol.

recoveries with chloramphenicol as the sole effective antibiotic.[721, 722] In other instances of *Str. viridans* endocarditis, penicillin and chloramphenicol combined have led to recovery.[723] Moreover, there are reports of the successful treatment of this type of endocarditis with combinations of oxytetracycline and chloramphenicol.[724]

Shown in figure 19 is the graphic record of a 33 year old man with *Str. viridans* endocarditis treated successfully with chloramphenicol. The patient had known rheumatic heart disease and acquired endocarditis from infected foci in the teeth and gums. Colonies of *Str. viridans* isolated were sensitive to penicillin in the concentration of 0.01 units/ml. The patient was unable to take penicillin because of the development of toxic manifestations, i.e., pyrexia to 104 F. and generalized urticaria. Chlortetracycline evoked a similar unfavorable reaction. The organism was sensitive to chloramphenicol in the concentration of 3 gamma/ml. This antibiotic was first administered on approximately the forty-fourth day of illness, when active clinical manifestations of endocarditis and bacteremia were present. The patient made a complete recovery after a therapeutic course of 46 days with a daily dosage of 4.0 Gm. There was no relapse, and the patient remains cured of endocarditis after a period of six years. This type of clinical result is regarded as the exception rather than the rule.

Chloramphenicol was curative in a patient with endocarditis caused by *M. pyogenes*.[676] A patient with endocarditis caused by *M. pyogenes* failed to respond satisfactorily to penicillin and other antibiotics and recovered fully following the administration of streptomycin and chloramphenicol.[725]

It may be concluded that chloramphenicol and other broad-spectrum antibiotics are second choice, at best, for therapy of patients with bacterial endocarditis. In individual cases when penicillin cannot be given, or is ineffective, and when the knowledge gained from sensitivity tests is appraised carefully, chloramphenicol may be lifesaving. The sensitivity test should be of the tube-dilution type or a modification thereof, with the laboratory attempting to detect synergistic or antagonistic action when combinations of antibiotics are contemplated. The clinician must consider the patient's total clinical response in appraising the effect of treatment.

LEPTOSPIROSIS

The leptospiroses are a group of clinical entities caused by numerous serological types of *Leptospira*. Those types found in the United States include *Leptospira icterohaemorrhagiae, Leptospira canicola, Leptospira pomona, Leptospira autumnalis, Leptospira bataviae,* and *Leptospira grippotyphosa.* With the notable exception of *Lept. icterohemorrhagiae* and *Lept. bataviae,* the illness produced by these microorganisms tends to be relatively benign and of short duration without the occurrence of clinically overt jaundice. Leptospiral infection in man is usually associated with an abrupt onset of fever accompanied by conjunctival injection, gastrointestinal disturbances, and evidence of renal derangement in the form of albuminuria and cylindruria.[726-728] Jaundice may occur in 3 to 40 per cent of patients, depending on the distribution of leptospiral serotypes as well as the diligence with which milder forms of the disease are sought. Mortality is rarely in excess of 10 per cent[726, 729] and may be as low as 0.8 per cent or less.[727, 728]

Evaluation of results after antibiotic therapy of this group of diseases has been attended by a great deal of confusion. Early reports suggested that penicillin favorably altered the course of illness;[730, 731] however, subsequent observations failed to confirm these findings.[732-734] Similarly, opposite conclusions have been drawn from studies wherein tetracycline antibiotics were used to treat these infections.[732, 733] Most recently, Doherty[728] has treated 111 patients infected with several serotypes. He concluded that the febrile period is clearly reduced when 4.0 million units of penicillin are administered daily. It should be emphasized that most leptospiral infections are of relatively short duration; hence an adequate number of untreated control patients must be included in the evaluation of any therapeutic regimen. Further studies may settle the question of penicillin's efficacy in leptospirosis as well as that of the tetracyclines. Until there is some evidence that either of these groups of antibiotics reduces mortality and serious complications, such as renal and hepatic decompensation, encountered in the severe forms of these diseases, the action of antimicrobial agents against *Leptospira* will remain unimpressive.

Whatever one concludes about the efficacy of other antibiotics in the treatment of leptospiroses, there appears to be uniform agreement that chloramphenicol does not alter the course of these diseases, regardless of the serotype involved. In one of the most meticulous evaluations of antibiotic therapy in leptospirosis, Hall and his co-workers[732] concluded that chloramphenicol, penicillin, streptomycin, oxytetracycline, and chlortetracycline did not favorably affect the course of illness in Puerto Rican patients studied by these investigators. In this series, 18 patients received chloramphenicol without benefit, as measured by progress of the clinical manifestations of the disease, renal and hepatic complications, and duration of leptospiremia. Similarly, Fairburn and Semple[735] failed to demonstrate a difference between untreated patients and those who received chloramphenicol or penicillin. Doherty[728] treated 12 patients with chloramphenicol alone and 20 patients with chloramphenicol and penicillin combined. There was no evidence in either group that the illness had been altered appreciably.

Clinical studies to date seem to indicate that chloramphenicol does not affect the course of leptospiral infections when a variety of parameters are employed. Although some investigators feel that penicillin and the tetracyclines may, under certain circumstances, shorten the febrile period, the issue will not be clarified until more patients are studied under rigidly controlled conditions.

SURGICAL INFECTIONS, INCLUDING CELLULITIS AND PERITONITIS

Two factors have influenced appreciably the value of chloramphenicol in single and mixed infections of the surgical type. Some of these infections, such as cellulitis, or peritonitis in particular, arise from a special focus and become an acute, spreading inflammatory process with a very adequate blood supply, which permits ready access for the antimicrobial drug. Chloramphenicol, with its broad range of activity, reaches the inflamed area promptly in high tissue concentration. It should be emphasized, however, that antimicrobial drugs do not eradicate the established focus singlehandedly, and surgical intervention is required in most instances. With the increase in number of organisms resistant to other antibiotics in clinical practice, particularly micrococci (see chapter XII on staphylococcal infections), the therapeutic value of chloramphenicol has increased.

In one large series Altemeier and Culbertson[645] treated patients with various types of surgical infection with chloramphenicol, employing a daily dosage of 25 to 75 μg./Kg. body weight. The average total dosage was 25.0 Gm. given over a period of 16 days. In 37 patients with infections caused by hemolytic and nonhemolytic *M. pyogenes var. aureus,* an excellent result was obtained with improvement beginning in 24 to 36 hours, return of temperature to normal levels within 72 hours or less, and spontaneous resolution in 6 cases of cellulitis, 4 patients with wound infections, 2 with abscess, and 1 with osteomyelitis. In 21 patients the results were classified as good, these infections being usually of long duration necessitating surgical drainage.

In 3 patients, 1 each with cellulitis, wound infection, and osteomyelitis, the results were of questionable significance (see chapter XII on staphylococcal infections).

Forty-five patients with cellulitis or wound infections caused by aerobic streptococci made satisfactory recoveries after chloramphenicol treatment, and in 1 patient the response to antibiotic treatment was difficult to evaluate. Two of 3 patients with chronic infections and draining sinuses caused by anaerobic streptococci responded very satisfactorily.

In 16 of 18 patients with infections such as peritonitis, postoperative wound infections, septicemia, localized typhoid bacillus infections, cholangitis, retroperitoneal cellulitis, and acute urinary tract infections caused by gram-negative bacteria, the response was good or excellent. The bacteria involved were chiefly *E. coli, A. aerogenes, Ps. aeruginosa,* and *S. typhosa.*[645]

In 72 per cent of 91 patients with mixed gram-positive and gram-negative bacterial infections treated with chloramphenicol alone, excellent results were obtained.[645] These infections included peritonitis, peritonitis with intra-abdominal abscess, empyema, perinephritic abscess, sinus tracts, purulent otitis media, chronic osteomyelitis, urinary tract infections, and crepitant cellulitis of the abdominal wall. The initial favorable response was likely to be temporary if adjunct surgical treatment was not employed. In 17 of these patients, the results attributable to chloramphenicol were questionable, and there were 9 therapeutic failures. Of 11 patients with acute spreading peritonitis, a prompt response was observed in 3 and a good result in 6 with use of chloramphenicol in conjunction with surgical procedure.

Management of the typhoid patient with a perforated intestine has changed since the introduction of chloramphenicol and the other broad-spectrum antibiotics.[269, 356] Surgical intervention may be avoided or deferred in some instances with reliance placed on control of the spreading peritoneal infection by antibiotics and well-established supportive measures (see chapter VIII on typhoid fever).

Orr,[736] in describing experiences in treating patients with peritonitis, advises that there be greater discrimination in the selection and use of antibiotics. In the treatment of acute peritonitis, the basic factor in surgical treatment still is good surgery. There is no substitute for good surgical judgment in the prevention and treatment of peritonitis. Altemeier et al [737] emphasized that the timing of surgical intervention with antibiotic therapy is of considerable importance. Care should be taken to perform surgical procedures when indicated in the presence of infections after the start of antibiotic treatment and before the development of bacterial resistance. In the experience of this group,[645, 737] acquired resistance to chloramphenicol during treatment developed in 6.6 per cent of bacterial strains originally susceptible to that agent, to chlortetracycline in 9.8 per cent of the strains, to oxytetracycline in 10.1 per

cent of the strains, to penicillin in 14.6 per cent of the strains, and to streptomycin in 32.3 per cent of the strains.

Antibiotic therapy has had a profound effect on the practice of surgery,
although it is quite clear that these drugs are helpful primarily as supportive
measures to the indicated operative procedure. Antibiotics are not therapeutic
panaceas, and the choice of drugs is based on the clinical experience of the
surgeon, which helps him choose intelligently through his knowledge of the
type of bacterial agent involved, the action of the antibiotic on this microorganism, the type and extent of the infectious process, the time of beginning
treatment, and the limitations of the drug itself.

BIBLIOGRAPHY

1. EHRLICH, J.; BARTZ, Q. R.; SMITH, R. M.; JOSLYN, D. A., AND BURKHOLDER, P. R.: Chloromycetin, a new antibiotic from a soil actinomycete, Science 106:417, 1947.
2. EHRLICH, J.; GOTTLIEB, D.; BURKHOLDER, P. R.; ANDERSON, L. E., AND PRIDHAM, T. G.: Streptomyces venezuelae, n. sp., the source of chloromycetin, J. Bact. 56:467, 1948.
3. SMADEL, J. E., AND JACKSON, E. B.: Chloromycetin, an antibiotic with chemotherapeutic activity in experimental rickettsial and viral infections, Science 106:418-419, 1947.
4. SMITH, R. M.; JOSLYN, D. A.; GRUHZIT, O. M.; MCLEAN, I. W., JR.; PENNER, M. A., AND EHRLICH, J.: Chloromycetin: biological studies, J. Bact. 55:425-448, 1948.
5. CARTER, H. E.; GOTTLIEB, D., AND ANDERSON, H. W.: Comments and communications, Science 107:113, 1947.
6. GOTTLIEB, D.; BHATTACHRYYA, P. K.; ANDERSON, H. W., AND CARTER, H. E.: Some properties of an antibiotic obtained from a species of Streptomyces, J. Bact. 55:409-417, 1948.
7. BARTZ, Q. R.: Isolation and characterization of chloromycetin, J. Biol. Chem. 172:445-450, 1948.
8. REBSTOCK, M. C.; CROOKS, H. M., JR.; CONTROULIS, J., AND BARTZ, Q. R.: Chloramphenicol (Chloromycetin). IV. Chemical studies, J. Am. Chem. Soc. 71:2458-2462, 1949.
9. CONTROULIS, J.; REBSTOCK, M. C., AND CROOKS, H. M., JR.: Chloramphenicol (Chloromycetin). V. Synthesis, J. Am. Chem. Soc. 71:2463-2468, 1949.
10. SMADEL, J. E.; JACKSON, E. B.; LEY, H. L., JR., AND LEWTHWAITE, R.: Comparison of synthetic and fermentation chloramphenicol (Chloromycetin) in rickettsial and viral infections, Proc. Soc. Exper. Biol. Med. 70:191-194, 1949.
11. DUNITZ, J. D.: The crystal structure of chloramphenicol and bromamphenicol, J. Am. Chem. Soc. 74:995-999, 1952.
12. MAXWELL, R. E., AND NICKEL, V. S.: The antibacterial activity of the isomers of chloramphenicol, Antib. & Chemo. 4:289-295, 1954.
13. HAHN, F. E.; WISSEMAN, C. L., JR., AND HOPPS, H. E.: Mode of action of chloramphenicol. II. Inhibition of bacterial D-polypeptide formation by an L-isomer of chloramphenicol, J. Bact. 67:674-679, 1954.
14. HAHN, F. E.; HAYES, J. E.; WISSEMAN, C. L., JR.; HOPPS, H. E., AND SMADEL, J.E.: Mode of action of chloramphenicol. VI. Relation between structure and activity in the chloramphenicol series, Antib. & Chemo. 6:531-543, 1956.
15. SMITH, G. N., AND WORREL, C. S.: Enzymatic reduction of chloramphenicol, Arch. Biochem. 24:216-223, 1949.
16. SMITH, G. N.; WORREL, C. S., AND LILLIGREN, B. L.: The enzymatic hydrolysis of chloramphenicol (chloromycetin), Science 110:297, 1949.
17. SMITH, G. N., AND WORREL, C. S.: The decomposition of chloromycetin (chloramphenicol) by microorganisms, Arch. Biochem. 28:232, 1950.
18. GLAZKO, A. J.; DILL, W. A., AND REBSTOCK, M. C.: Biochemical studies of chloramphenicol (chloromycetin). III. Isolation and identification of metabolic products in the urine, J. Biol. Chem. 183:679-691, 1950.
19. GLAZKO, A. J.; DILL, W. A., AND WOLF, L. M.: Observations of the metabolic disposition of chloramphenicol (Chloromycetin) in the rat, J. Pharmacol. & Exper. Therap. 104:452-458, 1952.
20. MCLEAN, I. W.; SCHWAB, J. L.; HILLEGAS, A. B., AND SCHLINGMAN, A. S.: Susceptibility of microorganisms to chloramphenicol (Chloromycetin), J. Clin. Invest. 28:953-963, 1949.
21. WOODWARD, T. E.; SMADEL, J. E.; LEY, H. L., JR.; GREEN, R., AND MANKIKAR, D. S.: Preliminary report on the beneficial effect of chloromycetin in the treatment of typhoid fever, Ann. Int. Med. 29:131-134, 1948.

22. WELCH, H.; REEDY, R. J., AND WOLFSON, S. W.: A comparison of the effect of nine antibiotics on experimental typhoid infections in mice, J. Lab. & Clin. Med. *35*: 663-666, 1950.
23. BLISS, E. A., AND TODD, H. P.: A comparison of eight antibiotic agents, in vivo and in vitro, J. Bact. *58*:61-72, 1949.
24. PARKER, R. T.; LISTER, L. M.; BAUER, R. E.; HALL, H. E., AND WOODWARD, T. E.: Use of chloramphenicol (Chloromycetin) in experimental and human tularemia, J. A.M.A. *143*:7-12, 1950.
25. ROBINSON, R. C. V.; FOX, L. M., AND DUVALL, R. C.: Effect of chloramphenicol in early syphilis, Am. J. Syph., Gonor. & Ven. Dis. *33*:509-514, 1949.
26. KIRBY, W. M. M.; WADDINGTON, W. S., AND DOORNINK, G. M.: Occurrence of anti-biotic-resistant gram-negative bacilli in urinary tract infections. *In*: Antibiotic Annual 1953-1954, New York, Medical Encyclopedia, Inc., 1954, pp. 285-290.
27. STRAUSS, R. E.; KLIGMAN, A. M., AND PILLSBURY, D. M.: The chemotherapy of actinomycosis and nocardiosis, Am. Rev. Tuberc. *63*:441-448, 1951.
28. GARROD, L. P.: The sensitivity of *Actinomyces israeli* to antibiotics, Brit. M. J. *1*: 1263-1264, 1952.
29. LITTMAN, M.; PHILLIPS, G. E., AND FUSILLO, M. H.: In vitro susceptibility of human pathogenic actinomycetes to chloramphenicol (Chloromycetin), Am. J. Clin. Path. *20*:1076-1078, 1950.
30. FELSENFELD, O.; VOLINI, I. F.; ISHIHARA, S. J.; BACHMAN, M. C., AND YOUNG, V. M.: A study of the effect of neomycin and other antibiotics on bacteria, viruses and protozoa, J. Lab. & Clin. Med. *35*:428-433, 1950.
31. FRANK, P. F.; WILCOX, C., AND FINLAND, M.: In vitro sensitivity of coliform bacilli to seven antibiotics (penicillin, streptomycin, bacitracin, polymyxin, aerosporin, aureomycin and Chloromycetin), J. Lab. & Clin. Med. *35*:188-204, 1950.
32. WAISBREN, B. A., AND SPINK, W. W.: Comparative action of aureomycin, Chloro-mycetin, neomycin, Q-19, and polymyxin B against gram negative bacilli, Proc. Soc. Exper. Biol. & Med. *74*:35-40, 1950.
33. SCHNEIERSON, S.S.: Changes in bacterial sensitivity to aureomycin and chloram-phenicol in the course of the past three years, J. Lab. & Clin. Med. *40*:48-57, 1952.
34. EISENBERG, G. M.; O'LOUGHLIN, J. M., AND FLIPPIN, H. F.: Distribution and in vitro antibiotic susceptibility of Klebsiella (Kauffman), J. Lab. & Clin. Med. *43*: 707-712, 1954.
35. LEMKE, C. E., AND GATES, L. E.: Distribution and antibiotic sensitivity in fifty-five strains of *Klebsiella pneumoniae*, J. Lab. & Clin. Med. *38*:889-892, 1951.
36. RANSMEIER, J. C.; BROWN, H. E., AND DAVIS, N.: Comparison of in vitro sensitivity of freshly isolated pathogenic bacteria to terramycin and other antibiotics (aureo-mycin, chloramphenicol, penicillin and streptomycin), J. Lab. & Clin. Med. *38*: 620-630, 1951.
37. MAY, J. R., AND MORLEY, C. W.: The routine testing of the sensitivity of bacteria to antibiotics, Lancet *1*:636-638, 1952.
38. LUND, E.: Determination of the sensitivity of bacteria to aureomycin, chloromy-cetin and terramycin, Acta. path. et microbiol. Scandinav. *31*:281-288, 1952.
39. REID, J. D.; JONES, M.M., AND BRYCE, E. C.: A study of the comparative activity of five antibiotics alone and in certain combinations against *Escherichia coli, Aerobacter aerogenes, Pseudomonas aeruginosa* and *Proteus sp.*, Antib. & Chemo. *2*:351-356, 1952.
40. BROOKE, M. S.: The occurrence of B5W (*B. anitratum*) strains in Denmark, Acta. path. et microbiol. Scandinav. *28*:338-342, 1951.
41. LUND, E.: Sensitivity of *Bacillus anitratum* to eight antibiotics as determined by means of the tablet method, Acta. path. et microbiol. Scandinav. *34*:329-335, 1954.
42. GOLD, H., AND BOGER, W. P.: Newer antibiotics in the treatment of anthrax, New England J. Med. *244*:391-394, 1951.
43. GARROD, L. P.: Sensitivity of four species of bacteroides to antibiotics, Brit. M. J. *2*:1529-1531, 1955.
44. FISHER, A.M., AND MCKUSICK, V. A.: Bacteroides infections; clinical, bacterio-logical and therapeutic features of fourteen cases, Am. J. M. Sc. *225*:253-273, 1953.
45. WILLICH, G.: Bacteriostatic effectiveness of sulfonamides and penicillin against pathogenic anaerobes, Ztschr. f. Hyg. u. Infektionskr. *134*:573-577, 1952.
46. BATTISTINI, M. G., AND TICSE, A.: In vitro action of Chloromycetin on *Bartonella bacilliformis*, Rev. med. exper., Lima *8*:167-171, 1951.

47. Yow, E. M., AND SPINK, W. W.: Experimental studies on the action of streptomycin, aureomycin and Chloromycetin on brucella, J. Clin. Invest. *28*:871-885, 1949.
48. BECK, O., AND LACY, H.: The effect of certain antibiotics, antimalarial drugs and amebicides on *Candida albicans*, Texas Rep. Biol. & Med. *9*:395-405, 1951.
49. ALTEMEIER, W.A.; MCMURRIN, J. A., AND ALT, L. P.: Chloromycetin and aureomycin in exeprimental gas gangrene, Surgery *28*:621-631, 1950.
50. MAZUREK, C.: Study of the in vitro action of chloromycetin against anaerobic bacteria, Ann. Inst. Pasteur *79*:905-908, 1950.
51. ANWAR, A. A., AND TURNER, T. B.: Prophylactic effect of antibiotics in experimental tetanus. *In*: Antibiotics Annual 1955-1956, New York, Medical Encyclopedia, Inc., 1956, pp. 422-427.
52. KISER, J. S.; DeMELLO, G. C.; REICHARD, D. H., AND WILLIAMS, J. H.: Chemotherapy of experimental Clostridial infections, J. Infect. Dis. *90*:76-80, 1952.
53. COHEN, R., AND MILLER, L.: Inhibiting concentrations of Chloromycetin against *Coccidiodes immitis,* Ann. West. Med. & Surg. *4*:342-343, 1950.
54. HEWITT, L. F.: Use of antibiotics in the treatment of experimental diphtheria infections, Brit. J. Exper. Path. *31*:597-602, 1950.
55. JACKSON, G. G.; CHANG, S.; PLACE, E. H., AND FINLAND, M.: Sensitivity of diphtheria bacilli and related organisms to nine antibiotics, J. Pediat, *37*:718-726, 1950.
56. THIBAULT, J.: The sensitivity of some Corynebacteria from man to certain antibiotics, Compt. rend. Soc. de biol. *146*:143-145, 1952.
57. JACKSON, G. G.; GOCKE, T. M.; WILCOX, C., AND FINLAND, M.: In vitro susceptibility of pneumococci to seven antibiotics, Am. J. Clin. Path. *20*:218-224, 1950.
58. RECINOS, A., JR.; ROSS, S.; OLSHAKER, B., AND TWIBLE, E.: Chloromycetin in the treatment of pneumonia in infants and children. A preliminary report on thirty-three cases, New England J. Med. *241*:733-737, 1949.
59. CHABBERT, Y.: Sensitivity to the antibiotics of 700 strains of aerobic bacteria tested in 1950, Ann. Inst. Pasteur *80*:627-632, 1951.
60. FINLAND, M.; WILCOX, C., AND FRANK, P. F.: In vitro sensitivity of human pathogenic strains of streptococci to seven antibiotics, Am. J. Clin. Path. *20*:208-217, 1950.
61. GUPTA, S. P., AND CHARKRAVARTI, R. N.: Determination of bacterial sensitivity to common antibiotics, Indian J. M. Research *42*:159-164, 1954.
62. FINLAND, M., AND WILCOX, C.: In vitro susceptibility of *Hemophilus influenzae* to seven antibiotics, Am. J. Clin. Path. *20*:335-340, 1950.
63. LOVE, B. D., AND FINLAND, M.: Susceptibility of recently isolated strains of *Hemophilus influenzae* to eleven antibiotics in vitro, J. Pediat. *45*:531-537, 1954.
64. MCCRUMB, F. R., JR.; HALL, H. E.; IMBURG, J.; MEREDITH, A.; HELMHOLD, R.; DeFILLO, J. B., AND WOODWARD, T. E.: Treatment of *Hemophilus influenzae* meningitis with chloramphenicol and other antibiotics, J.A.M.A. *145*:469-474, 1951.
65. TUNEVALL, G.: Studies on *Haemophilus influenzae*. Susceptibility in vitro to antibiotics, Acta path. et microbiol. Scandinav. *29*:203-210, 1951.
66. DAY, E., AND BRADFORD, W. L.: Susceptibility of *Hemophilus parapertussis* to certain antibiotics, Pediatrics *9*:320-326, 1952.
67. JACKSON, G. G.; BARNES, M. W., AND FINLAND, M.: Comparison of seven antibiotics against *Hemophilus pertussis* infection in chick embryos, J. Immunol. *65*:419-424, 1950.
68. WELLS, E. B.; CHANG, S.; JACKSON, G. G., AND FINLAND, M.: Antibiotic spectrum of *Hemophilus pertussis,* J. Pediat. *36*:752-757, 1950.
69. ORSKOV, I.: Sensitivity of *H. pertussis* in vitro to aureomycin, Chloromycetin and terramycin, Acta path. et microbiol. Scandinav. *28*:197-200, 1951.
70. SCHLIPKOTER, H. W., AND BECKERS, M.: The effect of chemotherapeutics and antibiotics on pathogenic leptospira, Ztschr. f. Immunitätsforsch. u. exper. Therap. *108*:301-317, 1951.
71. NORMAN, M.; LONGFELLOW, D., AND LEVIN, J. K.: Effect of aureomycin and chloramphenicol on two recently isolated strains of *Listeria monocytogenes,* Proc. Soc. Exper. Biol. & Med. *76*:435-437, 1951.
72. ODEGAARD, B.; GRELLAND, R., AND HENRIKSEN, S. D.: A case of Listeria infection in man, transmitted from sheep, Acta med. Scandinav. *142*:231-238, 1952.

73. FINLAND, M.; FRANK, P.F., AND WILCOX, C.: In vitro susceptibility of pathogenic staphylococci to seven antibiotics, Am. J. Clin. Path. *20*:325-334, 1950.
74. SPINK, W. W.: Clinical and biologic significance of penicillin-resistant staphylococci, including observations with streptomycin, aureomycin, chloramphenicol and terramycin, J. Lab. & Clin. Med. *37*:278-293, 1951.
75. FINLAND, M., AND HAIGHT, T. H.: Antibiotic resistance of pathogenic staphylococci. Study of five hundred strains isolated at Boston City Hospital from October, 1951, to February, 1952, A.M.A. Arch. Int. Med. *91*:143-158, 1953.
76. LEYTON, G. B.: Some observations on staphylococci and their resistance to antibiotics, Canad. M. A. J. *67*:20-22, 1952.
77. ROUNTREE, P. M., AND THOMSON, E. F.: Incidence of antibiotic-resistant staphylococci in a hospital, Lancet *2*:262-265, 1952.
78. BIRNSTINGL, M. A., AND SHOOTER, R. A.: Sensitivity to five antibiotics of strains of *Staph. pyogenes* isolated from out-patients, Brit. M. J. *2*:253-254, 1952.
79. WALLMARK, G.: Bacteriophage-typing of *Staphylococcus aureus pyogenes*. II. An analysis of strains isolated from purulent lesions in hospitalized patients, including sensitivity tests to antibiotics, Acta path. et microbiol. Scandinav. *34*:497-508, 1954.
80. SPINK, W. W.: Staphylococcal infections and the problem of antibiotic-resistant staphylococci, A.M.A. Arch. Int. Med. *94*:167-196, 1954.
81. YOUMANS, G. P.; YOUMANS, A. S., AND OSBORNE, R. R.: Tuberculostatic action of chloromycetin in vitro and in vivo, Proc. Soc. Exper. Biol. & Med. *67*:426-428, 1948.
82. STEENKEN, W., JR., AND WOLINSKY, E.: Effects of antimicrobial agents on the tubercule bacillus and on experimental tuberculosis, Am. J. Med. *9*:633-653, 1950.
83. CROS, R., AND DERMARCHI, J.: The in vitro action of Chloromycetin against Whitmore's bacillus, Ann. Inst. Pasteur *79*:217-221, 1950.
84. LOVE, B. D., AND FINLAND, M.: In vitro susceptibility of meningococci to eleven antibiotics and sulfadiazine, Am. J. M. Sc. *228*:534-539, 1954.
85. McCRUMB, F. R., JR.; HALL, H. E.; MERIDETH, A. M.; DEANE, G. E.; MINOR, J. V., AND WOODWARD, T. E.: Chloramphenicol in the treatment of meningococcal meningitis, Am. J. Med. *10*:696-703, 1951.
86. GOCKE, T. M.; WILCOX, C., AND FINLAND, M.: Antibiotic spectrum of the gonococcus, Am. J. Syph., Gonor. & Ven. Dis. *34*:265-272, 1950.
87. LOVE, B. D., AND FINLAND, M.: Susceptibility of *Neisseria gonorreae* to eleven antibiotics and sulfadiazine. Comparison of susceptibility of recently isolated strains with results obtained in previous years in the same laboratory, A.M.A. Arch. Int. Med. *95*:66-73, 1955.
88. OLITZKY, I., AND BIERMAN, G. W.: The *in vitro* activity of antibiotics against paracolobactrum bacilli, Antib. & Chemo. *2*:344-346, 1952.
89. MELEN, B.: The susceptibility of pleuropneumonia-like organisms to the in vitro action of some antibiotics, Acta path. et microbiol. Scandinav. *30*:98-103, 1951.
90. LEBERMAN, P. R.; SMITH, P. F., AND MORTON, H. E.: The susceptibility of pleuropneumonia-like organisms to the in vitro action of antibiotics: aureomycin, chloramphenicol, dihydrostreptomycin, streptomycin and sodium penicillin G, J. Urol. *64*:167-173, 1950.
91. FRANK, P. F.; WILCOX, C., AND FINLAND, M.: In vitro sensitivity of *Bacillus proteus* and *Pseudomonas aeruginosa* to seven antibiotics (penicillin, streptomycin, bacitracin, polymyxin, aerosporin, aureomycin and Chloromycetin), J. Lab. & Clin. Med. *35*:205-214, 1950.
92. POTEE, K. G.; WRIGHT, S. S., AND FINLAND, M.: In vitro susceptibility of recently isolated strains of Proteus to ten antibiotics, J. Lab. & Clin. Med. *44*:463-477, 1954.
93. PERCH, B.: Sensitivity of Proteus and Providencia to eight antibiotics and sulfathiazole, Acta path. et microbiol. Scandinav. *35*:278-286, 1954.
94. WRIGHT, S. S.; POTEE, K. G., AND FINLAND, M.: Susceptibility of pseudomonas to ten antibiotics in vitro. Some properties of recently isolated strains, Am. J. Clin. Path. *24*:1121-1132, 1954.
95. ERWIN, C. P.; WAISBREN, B. A., AND KRUSE, R.: Clinical and laboratory studies of infections due to *Pseudomonas aeruginosa* and Pseudomonas species, Am. J. M. Sc. *226*:525-532, 1953.
96. YOW, E. M.: Comparison of the action of varying concentrations of eight antibiotics against *Pseudomonas aeruginosa*, Am. J. Med. *13*:654, 1952.

97. ALIN, K., AND WALLMARK, G.: In vitro susceptibility of typhoid, paratyphoid and dysentery bacilli to aureomycin and chloramphenicol, Nord. med. *43*:663-664, 1950.

98. JACKSON, G. G.; GOCKE, T. M.; COLLINS, H. S., AND FINLAND, M.: In vitro sensitivity of pathogenic enteric bacteria to various antibiotics, J. Infect. Dis. *87*:63-70, 1950.

99. SELIGMANN, E., AND WASSERMANN, M.: Action of Chloromycetin on Salmonella, Proc. Soc. Exper. Biol. & Med. *71*:253-254, 1949.

100. GAULD, R. L.; SCHLINGMAN, A. S.; JACKSON, E. B.; MANNING, M. C.; BATSON, H. C., AND CAMPBELL, C. C.: Chloramphenicol (Chloromycetin) in experimental cholera infections, J. Bact. *57*:349-352, 1949.

101. FELSENFELD, O.; SOMAN, D. W.; ISHIHARA, S. J.; WATERS, T., AND NORSEN, J.: In vitro sensitivity of recently isolated cholera vibrios to ten antibiotics, Proc. Soc. Exper. Biol. & Med. *77*:287-288, 1951.

102. BOGER, W. P.: *Bacillus anthracis*. Observations on in vitro sensitivity to seven antibiotics with a comment on therapeutic implications, A.M.A.. Arch. Dermat. & Syph. *67*:541-545, 1953.

103. FINEGOLD, S. M., AND HEWITT, W. L.: Antibiotic sensitivity pattern of *Bacteroides* species. *In*: Antibiotics Annual 1955-1956, New York, Medical Encyclopedia, Inc., 1956, pp. 794-801.

104. NETER, E., AND GORZYNSKI, G. A.: Relative efficacy upon *Pasteurella multocida* of various antibiotics, aureomycin, terramycin, bacitracin and polymyxin B, Proc. Soc. Exper. Biol. & Med. *74*:328-330, 1950.

105. GAUTHIER, J. L.: Action of Chloromycetin in vitro and in vivo on some Pasteurella organisms from animals, Ann. Inst. Pasteur *79*:470-472, 1950.

106. KYLIN, O., AND LINDBERG, L.: Correlation between resistance characteristics and biochemical reactions in coliform bacteria, Antib. & Chemo. *3*:803-806, 1953.

107. EAGLE, H.: The development of bacterial resistance to penicillin, streptomycin and chloromycetin, Bact. Proc. *1*:101, 1950.

108. DEMEREC, M., AND DEMEREC, R.: Bacterial resistance to neomycin and Chlorochloromycetin, Bact. Proc. *1*:101, 1950.

109. COFFEY, G. L.; SCHWAB, J. L., AND EHRLICH, J.: In vitro studies of bacterial resistance to chloramphenicol, J. Infect. Dis. *87*:142-148, 1950.

110. GOCKE, T. M., AND FINLAND, M.: Development of chloramphenicol-resistant and chloramphenicol-dependent variants of a strain of *Klebsiella pneumoniae*, Proc. Soc. Exper. Biol. & Med. *74*:824-829, 1950.

111. CAVALLI, L. L., AND MACCACARO, G. A.: Chloromycetin resistance in *E. coli*, a case of quantitative inheritance in bacteria, Nature, London *166*:991-992, 1950.

112. MONNIER, J. J., AND SCHOENBACH, E. B.: The resultant sensitivity of microorganisms to various antibiotics after induced resistance to each of these agents, Antib. & Chemo. *1*:472-486, 1951.

113. EAGLE, H.; FLEISCHMAN, R., AND LEVY, M.: Development of increased bacterial resistance to antibiotics. I. Continuous spectrum of resistance to penicillin, chloramphenicol and streptomycin, J. Bact. *63*:623-638, 1952.

114. WRIGHT, S. S.; PURCELL, E. M.; WILCOX, C.; BRODERICK, M. K., AND FINLAND, M.: Antibiotic combinations and resistance to antibiotics. Development of resistance during repeated subcultures of staphylococci and certain streptococci on media containing penicillin, streptomycin, erythromycin, terramycin and chloramphenicol used singly and in pairs, J. Lab. & Clin. Med. *42*:877-895, 1953.

115. PANSY, F. E.; KHAN, P.; PAGANO, J. F., AND DONOVICK, R.: The relationship between aureomycin, chloramphenicol and terramycin, Proc. Soc. Exper. Biol. & Med. *75*:618-620, 1950.

116. FUSILLO, M. H., AND ROMANSKY, M. J.: The simultaneous increase in resistance of bacteria to aureomycin and terramycin upon exposure to either antibiotic, Antib. & Chemo. *1*:107-109, 1951.

117. GOCKE, T. M., AND FINLAND, M.: Cross-resistance to antibiotics. Effect of repeated exposure of bacteria to aureomycin, terramycin, chloramphenicol or neomycin on the resistance of all of these antibiotics and to streptomycin and penicillin, J. Lab. & Clin. Med. *38*:719-735, 1951.

118. GEZON, H. M., AND FASAN, D. M.: Cross resistance of streptococci to five Streptomyces antibiotics, Science *114*:422-423, 1951.

119. PRICE, C. W.; RANDALL, W. A.; WELCH, H., AND CHANDLER, V. L.: Studies of the combined action of antibiotics and sulfonamides, Am. J. Pub. Health 39:340-344, 1949.
120. JAWETZ, E.; GUNNISON, J. B., AND COLEMAN, V. R.: The combined action of penicillin with streptomycin or Chloromycetin on enterococci in vitro, Science 111:254-256, 1950.
121. BIGGER, J. W.: Synergism and antagonism as displayed by certain antibacterial substances, Lancet 2:46-50, 1950.
122. GUNNISON, J. B.; JAWETZ, E., AND COLEMAN, V. R.: The effect of combinations of antibiotics on enterococci in vitro, J. Lab. & Clin. Med. 36:900-911, 1950.
123. JAWETZ, E., AND SPECK, R. S.: Joint action of penicillin with chloramphenicol on an experimental streptococcal infection of mice, Proc. Soc. Exper. Biol. & Med. 74:93-96, 1950.
124. ROMANSKY, M. J.; FUSILLO, M., AND LEVY, B.: Synergistic action of combinations of the antibiotics and their practical application, Am. J. Med. 10:237, 1951.
125. JAWETZ, E.; GUNNISON, J. B.; SPECK, R. S., AND COLEMAN, V. R.: Studies on antibiotic synergism and antagonism: The interference of chloramphenicol with the action of penicillin, A.M.A. Arch. Int. Med. 87:349-359, 1951.
126. ARMSTRONG, C. W. J., AND LARNER, A. E.: The effect of combinations of antibiotics on Pseudomonas aeruginosa and on Proteus vulgaris in vitro and in vivo, J. Lab. & Clin. Med. 37:584-592, 1951.
127. JAWETZ, E.; GUNNISON, J. B., AND SPECK, R. S.: Antibiotic antagonism: The interference of chloramphenicol, aureomycin and terramycin with the action of penicillin in experimental infections and in vitro, Am. J. Med. 10:762, 1951.
128. JAWETZ, E.; GUNNISON, J. B., AND SPECK, R. S.: Studies on antibiotic synergism and antagonism: The interference of aureomycin, chloramphenicol and terramycin with the action of streptomycin, Am. J. M. Sc. 222:404-412, 1951.
129. SPECK, R. S., AND JAWETZ, E.: Antibiotic synergism and antagonism in a subacute experimental streptococcus infection in mice, Am. J. M. Sc. 223:280-285, 1952.
130. AHERN, J. J.; BURNELL, J. M., AND KIRBY, W. M. M.: Lack of interference of chloramphenicol with penicillin in a hemolytic streptococcal infection in mice, Proc. Soc. Exper. Biol. & Med. 79:568-571, 1952.
131. JAWETZ, E., AND GUNNISON, J. B.: Studies on antibiotic synergism and antagonism: a scheme of combined antibiotic action, Antib. & Chemo. 2:243-248, 1952.
132. JAWETZ, E.; GUNNISON, J. B.; BRUFF, J. B., AND COLEMAN, V. R.: Studies on antibiotic synergism and antagonism. Synergism among seven antibiotics against various bacteria in vitro, J. Bact. 64:29-39, 1952.
133. JAWETZ, E.: Antibiotic synergism and antagonism: Review of experimental evidence, A.M.A. Arch. Int. Med. 90:301-309, 1952.
134. THOMPSON, P. E.; DUNN, M. C.; BAYLES, A., AND REINERTSON, J. W.: Action of chloramphenicol (Chloromycetin) and other drugs against Endamoeba histolytica in vitro and in experimental animals, Am. J. Trop. Med. 30:203-215, 1950.
135. BRAUDE, A. I., AND SPINK, W. W.: The action of aureomycin and other chemotherapeutic agents in experimental brucellosis, J. Immunol. 65:185-199, 1950.
136. HEILMAN, F. R.: The effect of combined treatment with aureomycin and dihydrostreptomycin on brucella infections in mice, Proc. Staff Meet., Mayo Clin. 24:133-136, 1949.
137. WERNER, C. A., AND KNIGHT, V.: The suppressive effect of antimicrobial drugs on Brucella melitensis infection in mice, J. Immunol. 65:509-514, 1950.
138. STANTON, M. F.; LASKOWSKI, L., AND PINKERTON, H.: Chemoprophylactic effectiveness of aureomycin and terramycin in murine bartonellosis, Proc. Soc. Exper. Biol. & Med. 74:705-707, 1950.
139. OLEJNIK, E., AND DAVIDOVITCH, S.: Action of terramycin and Chloromycetin on cholera vibrio in mice, Nature 168:654, 1951.
140. JACKSON, E. B.: Comparative efficacy of several antibiotics on experimental rickettsial infections in embryonated eggs, Antib. & Chemo. 1:231-241, 1951.
141. SMADEL, J. E.; JACKSON, E. B., AND CRUISE, A. B.: Chloromycetin in experimental rickettsial infections, J. Immunol. 62:49-65, 1949.
142. ORMSBEE, R. A.; PARKER, H., AND PICKENS, E. G.: The comparative effectiveness of aureomycin, terramycin, Chloromycetin, erythromycin and thiocymetin in suppressing experimental rickettsial infections in chick embryos, J. Infect. Dis. 96:162-167, 1955.

143. KNEELAND, Y., JR., AND PRICE, K. M.: Treatment with chloramphenicol, aureomycin and terramycin of the pneumonia of mice caused by feline pneumonitis virus, J. Immunol. 65:653-660, 1950.
144. TAYLOR, W. I., AND NOVAK, M. V.: Antibiotic prophylaxis of experimental gas gangrene, Bact. Proc. 108 (M 74), 1952.
145. SANDUSKY, W. R.; KEEBLE, C. F.; WHARTON, W. P., AND TAYLOR, R. N.: An evaluation of aureomycin and Chloromycetin in experimental *Clostridium welchii* infection, Surgery 28:632-641, 1950.
146. GELLER, H. O., AND THYGESON, P.: Aureomycin, Chloromycetin and terramycin in experimental herpes-simplex virus infections, Am. J. Ophth. 34:165-174, 1951.
147. UHLENHUTH, P., AND SCHOENHERR, K. E.: Experimental studies on the therapy of leptospiroses, Ztschr. f. Immunitätsforsch. u. exper. Therap. 108:289-301, 1951.
148. LEE, C. T.: Effect of aureomycin, chloramphenicol and para-aminobenzoic acid on myxoma and vaccinia viruses in the egg, Proc. Soc. Exper. Biol. & Med. 75:649-651, 1950.
149. ORMSBEE, R. A., AND PICKENS, E. G.: A comparison by means of the complement-fixation test of the relative potencies of chloramphenicol, aureomycin and terramycin in experimental Q fever infections in embryonated eggs, J. Immunol. 67:437-448, 1951.
150. MEYER, K. F.: Modern therapy of plague, J.A.M.A. 144:982-985, 1950.
151. McCRUMB, F. R., JR.; LARSON, A., AND MEYER, K. F.: The chemotherapy of experimental plague in the primate host, J. Infect. Dis. 92:273-287, 1953.
152. QUAN, S. F.; CHEN, T. S., AND MEYER, K. F.: Protective action of antibiotics against the toxin of *Pasteurella pestis* in mice, Proc. Soc. Exper. Biol. & Med. 75:548-549, 1950.
153. EATON, M. D.: Action of aureomycin and Chloromycetin on the virus of primary atypical pneumonia, Proc. Soc. Exper. Biol. & Med. 73:24, 1950.
154. SMADEL, J. E., AND JACKSON, E. B.: Effect of Chloromycetin on experimental infection with psittacosis and lymphogranuloma venereum viruses, Proc. Soc. Exper. Biol. & Med. 67:478-483, 1948.
155. WELLS, E. B., AND FINLAND, M.: Comparative effect of aureomycin and Chloromycetin on psittacosis infection in chick embryos, Proc. Soc. Exper. Biol. & Med. 72:365-368, 1949.
156. BARSKI, G., AND MAURIN, J.: Action in vitro of penicillin, streptomycin, aureomycin and Chloromycetin on the lymphogranuloma-psittacosis group of viruses, Ann. Inst. Pasteur 78:659-764, 1950.
157. HURST, E. W.; PETERS, J. M., AND MELVIN, P.: The therapy of experimental psittacosis and lymphogranuloma venereum (inguinale). I. The comparative efficacy of penicillin, chloramphenicol, aureomycin and terramycin,, Brit. J. Pharmacol. 5:611-624, 1950.
158. BATES, J. D.: Failure of antibiotics in experimental rabies, Nature, London 166:155-156, 1950.
159. THOMPSON, P. E., AND DUNN, M. C.: Comparison of the actions of chloramphenicol and penicillin G against experimental relapsing fever, Federation Proc. 8:338, 1949.
160. THOMPSON, P. E.; DUNN, M. C., AND WINDER, C. V.: Comparison of the actions of chloramphenicol (Chloromycetin) and penicillin G against relapsing fever in mice, J. Infect. Dis. 86:110-119, 1950.
161. MILNER, K. C., AND SHAFFER, M. F.: Chemotherapy of experimental Salmonella infections in chicks, Bact. Proc. 113 (M 86), 1952.
162. GRUHZIT, O. M., AND FISKEN, R. A.: Chloramphenicol (Chloromycetin) in experimental syphilis of rabbits, Am. J. Syph., Gonor. & Ven. Dis. 34:338-341, 1950.
163. TURNER, T. B., AND SCHAEFFER, K.: The comparative effect of various antibiotics in experimental syphilis, Am. J. Syph. Gonor. & Ven. Dis. 38:81-91, 1954.
164. KOLMER, J. A.: A comparative study of ten antibiotic compounds in the treatment of experimental syphilis of rabbits. *In*: Antibiotics Annual 1955-1956, New York, Medical Encyclopedia, Inc., 1956, pp. 592-595.
165. CROSS, J. B., AND JOSEPH, H.: Chloromycetin and experimental toxoplasmosis, Texas Rep. Biol. & Med. 7:406, 1949.
166. YOUMANS, G. P.: Comparative effectiveness of chemotherapeutic agents upon experimental tuberculosis of mice, Tr. 9th Streptomycin Conf., 1950, Washington, D. C., Veterans Administration, 1950, p. 198.

167. EIGELSBACH, H. T., AND HERRING, R. D.: Prediction of clinical response to antibiotic therapy from data derived from experimental animal studies, Bact. Proc. 122 (M 102), 1952.
168. GRUHZIT, O. M., AND FISKEN, R. A.: Effect of Chloromycetin on experimental *S. typhosa* infection in rabbits, Am. J. Trop. Med. *31*:329-334, 1951.
169. THOMSON, E. F.: The incidence of antibiotic resistance in gram-negative bacilli in a general hospital, J. Clin. Path. *5*:169-174, 1952.
170. GOSLINGS, W. R.; HIEN, T. L., AND BOTS, A. W.: Infections with antibiotic-resistant staphylococci. I. Results of sensitivity tests in staphylococci of various origins, Acta med. Scandinav. *152*:439-449, 1955.
171. BANKS, H. S.: Drug resistance of micro-organisms, Lancet *1*:560, 1952.
172. ANON.: Editorial: Chloramphenicol in penicillin-resistant infection, Lancet *1*:550, 1952.
173. KOCH, M. L., AND BOURGEOIS, R. W.: Report on a further increase in the incidence of drug-resistant pathogenic *staphylococci* encountered in the hospital laboratory, Antib. & Chemo. *2*:229-233, 1952.
174. NEEDHAM, G. M., AND NICHOLS, D. R.: Recent changes in sensitivity of *Micrococcus pyogenes* to various antibiotic agents, J. Lab. & Clin. Med. *41*:150-156, 1953.
175. FINLAND, M.: Some observations on changing patterns of resistance of certain common pathogenic bacteria to antimicrobial agents. *In*: Antibiotics Annual 1954-1955, New York, Medical Encyclopedia, Inc., 1955, pp. 35-50.
176. FINLAND, M.: Changing patterns of resistance of certain common pathogenic bacteria to antimicrobial agents, New England J. Med. *252*:570-580, 1955.
177. FINLAND, M.: Emergence of antibiotic-resistant bacteria, New England J. Med. *253*:909-922, 969-979, 1019-1028, 1955.
178. SANFORD, J. P.; FAVOUR, C. B. AND MAO, F. H.: The emergence of antibiotic-resistant gram-negative bacilli, J. Lab. & Clin. Med. *45*:540-545, 1955.
179. KIRBY, W. M. M., AND AHERN, J. J.: Changing pattern of resistance of staphylococci to antibiotics, Antib. & Chemo. *3*:831-835, 1953.
180. MEADS, M.; HARRIS, C. M.; HASLAM, N. M., AND CLINE, W. A.: Chloramphenicol-fastness: development in vivo and experimental production in vitro, J. Clin. Invest. *29*:1474-1479, 1950.
181. VOUREKA, A.: Bacterial variants in patients treated with chloramphenicol, Lancet *1*:27-28, 1951.
182. VOUREKA, A.: Production of bacterial variants in vitro with chloramphenicol and specific antiserum, Lancet *1*:28-31, 1951.
183. PULVERTAFT, R. J. V.: The effect of antibiotics on growing cultures of *Bacterium coli*, J. Path. & Bact. *64*:75-89, 1952.
184. SMADEL, J. E.: Chloramphenicol (Chloromycetin) and tropical medicine, Tr. Roy. Soc. Trop. Med. & Hyg. *43*:555, 1950.
185. HOBBY, G. L.; LENERT, T. F., AND DOUGHERTY, N.: Newer antibiotics: factors influencing their antimicrobial activity, Ann. New York Acad. Sc. *53*:27-37, 1950.
186. ALEXANDER, H. E.; LEIDY, G., AND REDMAN, W.: Comparison of the action of streptomycin, polymyxin B, aureomycin and Chloromycetin on *H. pertussis, H. parapertussis, H. influenzae* and five enteric strains of gram-negative bacilli, J. Clin. Invest. *28*:867-870, 1949.
187. WATSON, K. C.: In vitro activity of chloramphenicol on *Salmonella typhi*, J. Lab. & Clin. Med. *45*:97-101, 1955.
188. GRAY, J. D.: Antibacterial action of chloramphenicol on a coliform, J. Path. & Bact. *64*:447-452, 1952.
189. PETERSDORF, R. G.; BENNETT, I. L., JR., AND ROSE, M. C.: The sensitivity of pathogenic bacteria to a series of antibiotics, Bull. Johns Hopkins Hosp. *100*:1-13, 1957.
190. BOZEMAN, F. M.; WISSEMAN, C. L., JR.; HOPPS, H. E., AND DANAUSKAS, J. X.: Action of chloramphenicol on T-1 bacteriophage. I. Inhibition of intracellular multiplication, J. Bact. *67*:530-536, 1954.
191. EAGLE, H., AND SAZ, A. K.: Antibiotics, Ann. Rev. Microbiol. *9*:187-191, 1955.
192. GALE, E. F., AND FOLKES, J. P.: The assimilation of amino acids by bacteria. 18. The incorporation of glutamic acid into the protein fraction of *Staphylococcus aureus*, Biochem. J. *55*:721-729, 1953.
193. WISSEMAN, C. L., JR.; SMADEL, J. E.; HAHN, F. E., AND HOPPS, H. E.: Mode of action of chloramphenicol. I. Action of chloramphenicol on assimilation of am-

monia and on synthesis of proteins and nucleic acids in *Escherichia coli*, J. Bact. 67:662-673, 1954.

194. HOPPS, H. E.; WISSEMAN, C. L., JR., AND HAHN, F. E.: Mode of action of chloramphenicol. V. Effect of chloramphenicol on polysaccharide synthesis by *Neisseria perflava*, Antib. & Chemo. 4:857-858, 1954.

195. HAHN, F. E.; WISSEMAN, C. L., JR., AND HOPPS, H. E.: Mode of action of chloramphenicol. III. Action of chloramphenicol on bacterial energy metabolism, J. Bact. 69:215-223, 1955.

196. GLAZKO, A. J.; WOLF, L. M., AND DILL, W. A.: Biochemical studies on chloramphenicol (Chloromycetin). I. Colorimetric methods for the determination of chloramphenicol and related nitro compounds, Arch. Biochem. 23:411-418, 1949.

197. BESSMAN, S. P., AND STEVENS, S.: A colorimetric method for the determination of Chloromycetin in serum or plasma, J. Lab. & Clin. Med. 35:129-135, 1950.

198. HESS, G. B.: Polarographic estimation of chloramphenicol (Chloromycetin), Analyt. Chem. 22:649, 1950.

199. JOSLYN, D. A., AND GALBRAITH, M.: A turbidimetric method for the assay of antibiotics, J. Bact. 54:26, 1947.

200. JOSLYN, D. A., AND GALBRAITH, M.: A turbidimetric method for the assay of antibiotics, J. Bact. 59:711-716, 1950.

201. RANDALL, W. A.; KIRSHBAUM, A.; NIELSEN, J. K., AND WINTERMERE, D.: Diffusion plate assay for chloramphenicol and aureomycin, J. Clin. Invest. 28:940-942, 1949.

202. LEY, H. L., JR.; SMADEL, J. E., AND CROCKER, T. T.: Administration of chloromycetin to normal subjects, Proc. Soc. Exper. Biol. & Med. 68:9-12, 1948.

203. ROSS, S.; BISCHOFF, H.; PREISSER, W., AND ORR, W.: Some observations on the absorption and excretion of aureomycin and chloramphenicol, J. Clin. Invest. 28:1050, 1949.

204. GLAZKO, A. J.; WOLF, L. M.; DILL, W. A., AND BRATTON, A. C., JR.: Biochemical studies on chloramphenicol (chloromycetin). II. Tissue distribution and excretion studies, J. Pharmacol. & Exper. Therap. 96:445-459, 1949.

205. WELCH, H.: Absorption, excretion and distribution of terramycin, Ann. New York Acad. Sc. 53:253-265, 1950.

206. ROY, T. E.; KREIGER, E.; CRAIG, G.; COHEN, D.; McNAUGHTON, G. A., AND SILVERTHORNE, N.: Studies on the absorption of chloramphenicol in normal children in relation to the treatment of meningitis, Antib. & Chemo. 2:505-516, 1952.

207. CALMAN, R. M., AND MURRAY, J.: Chloramphenicol treatment of the newborn, Brit. M. J. 1:759-761, 1953.

208. KELLEY, R. S.; HUNT, A. D., JR., AND TASHMAN, S. G.: Studies on the absorption and distribution of chloramphenicol, Pediatrics 8:362-367, 1951.

209. ALTEMEIER, W. A.; CULBERTSON, W. R., AND COITH, R. L.: The intestinal absorption of oral antibiotics in traumatic shock. An experimental study, Surg., Gynec. & Obst. 92:707-711, 1951.

210. GRAY, J. D.: The concentration of chloramphenicol in human tissue, Canad. M. A. J. 72:778-779, 1955.

211. SMADEL, J. E.; WOODWARD, T. E.; LEY, H. L., JR., AND LEWTHWAITE, R.: Chloramphenicol (chloromycetin) in the treatment of tsutsugamushi disease (scrub typhus), J. Clin. Invest. 28:1196-1215, 1949.

212. WILLIAMS, B., JR., AND DART, R. M.: Chloramphenicol ("chloromycetin") concentrations in cerebrospinal, ascitic and pleural fluids, Boston M. Quart. 1:7-10, 1950.

213. ROSS, S.; BURKE, F. G.; SITES, J.; RICE, E. C., AND WASHINGTON, J. A.: Placental transmission of chloramphenicol (chloromycetin), J.A.M.A. 142:1361, 1950.

214. SCOTT, W. C., AND WARNER, R. F.: Placental transfer of chloramphenicol (chloromycetin), J.A.M.A. 142:1331-1332, 1950.

215. LEOPOLD, I. H.; NICHOLS, A. C., AND VOGEL, A. W.: Penetration of chloramphenicol U.S.P. (chloromycetin) into the eye, A.M.A. Arch. Ophth. 44:22-36, 1950.

216. ABRAHAM, R. K., AND BURNETT, H. H.: Tetracycline and chloramphenicol studies on rabbit and human eyes, A.M.A. Arch. Ophth. 54:641-659, 1955.

217. BENDER, I. B.; PRESSMAN, R. S., AND TASHMAN, S. G.: Studies on the excretion of antibiotics in human saliva. II. Chloramphenicol, J. Dent. Research 32:289-293, 1953.

218. LEBIRO, M., AND VITTORIO, M. P.: Ricerche sulla eliminazione del cloroamfenicolo attraversa il latte di donne, Clin. pediat. 35:830-834, 1953.

219. BORSKI, A. A.; PULASKI, E. J.; KIMBROUGH, J. C., AND FUSILLO, M. H.: Prostatic fluid, semen, and prostatic tissue concentrations of the major antibiotics following intravenous administration, Antib. & Chemo. 4:905-910, 1954.
220. GLAZKO, A. J.; WOLF, L. M., AND DILL, W. A.: Distribution of cholramphenicol (chloromycetin) and its metabolic products between human red cells and plasma, Proc. Soc. Exper. Biol. & Med. 72:602-604, 1949.
221. MAGOFFIN, R. L., AND SPINK, W. W.: The protection of intracellular Brucellae against streptomycin alone and in combination with other antibiotics, J. Lab. & Clin. Med. 37:924-930, 1951.
222. PRAMER, D.: Absorption of antibiotics by plant cells, Science 121:507-508, 1955.
223. BOZEMAN, F. M.; HOPPS, H. E.; DANAUSKAS, J. X.; JACKSON, E. B., AND SMADEL, J. E.: Study on the growth of rickettsiae. I. A tissue culture system for quantitative estimations of Rickettsia tsutsugamushi, J. Immunol. 76:475-488, 1956.
224. BOGER, W. P.; MATTEUCCI, W. V., AND BEATTY, J. O.: "Benemid" p (di-n-propyl sulfamyl)-benzoic acid: lack of effect of aureomycin, chloromycetin, streptomycin and terramycin, Proc. Soc. Exper. Biol. & Med. 76:222-225, 1951.
225. GRAY, J. D.: Some effects of chloramphenicol on the gut, J. Hyg. 51:322-329, 1953.
226. WOODWARD, T. E.; SMADEL, J. E., AND LEY, H. L., JR.: Chloramphenicol and other antibiotics in the treatment of typhoid fever and typhoid carriers, J. Clin. Invest. 29:87-99, 1950.
227. GRONROOS, J. A.: On the excretion of chloramphenicol in the bile, Acta path. et microbiol. Scandinav., suppl. XCIII, pp. 411-414, 1952.
228. DANOPOULOS, E.; ANGELOPOULOS, B.; ZIODROU, C., AND AMIRA, P.: Chloramphenicol excretions in the bile, Brit. J. Pharmacol. 9:260-261, 1954.
229. ROYER, M.; MAZURE, P. A., AND NOIR, B.: Concentración de la cloromycetina en la bilis vesicular humana, Prensa méd. argent. 41:52-54, 1954.
230. SPIERS, A. L.: Stool concentrations and absorption of chloramphenicol and its palmitate in babies, Brit. J. Pharmacol. 9:59-61, 1954.
231. WELCH, H., AND LEWIS, C. N.: Antibiotic Therapy, Washington, D. C., The Arundel Press, Inc., 1951, p. 184.
232. DEANE, G. E.; FURMAN, J. E.; BENTZ, A. R., AND WOODWARD, T. E.: Treatment of meningitis with Chloromycetin Palmitate; results of therapy in twenty-three cases, Pediatrics 11:368-380, 1953.
233. ROSS, S.; PREISSER, W. G.; ORR, W. W.; BURKE, F. G., AND RICE, E. C.: Intramuscular administration of chloramphenicol. A preliminary note, Clin. Proc. Child. Hosp. 7:61, 1951.
234. SCHOENBACH, E. B.; SPENCER, H. C., AND MONNIER, J.: Treatment of H. Influenzae meningitis with aureomycin and chloramphenicol. Experience in thirty consecutive cases, Am. J. Med. 12:263, 1952.
235. ROSS, S.; PUIG, J., AND ZAREMBA, E.: Chloramphenicol acid succinate (sodium salt). Some preliminary clinical and laboratory observations in infants and children. In: Antibiotics Annual 1957-1958, New York, Medical Encyclopedia, Inc., 1958, p. 803.
236. McCRUMB, F. R., JR.; SNYDER, M. J., AND HICKEN, W. J.: The use of chloramphenicol acid succinate in the treatment of acute infections. In: Antibiotics Annual 1957-1958, New York, Medical Encyclopedia, Inc., 1958, p. 837.
237. FLOREY, H.: New antibiotic agents, J.A.M.A. 135:1047, 1947.
238. MARMION, D. E.: The treatment of typhoid fever with chloramphenicol; a clinical study of 330 cases of enteric fever treated in Egypt, Tr. Roy. Soc. Trop. Med. & Hyg. 46:619, 1952.
239. HIRSCH, F. G.: Infectious mononucleosis. Report of a case treated with chloromycetin, U. S. Nav. M. Bull. 49:1081, 1949.
240. HEWITT, W. L., AND WILLIAMS, B.: Chloromycetin (chloramphenicol) in treatment of infections, New England J. Med. 242:119-127, 1950.
241. WILLIAMS, B., JR.: Oral and pharyngeal complications of chloramphenicol (chloromycetin) therapy, Am. Pract. & Digest Treat. 1:897, 1950.
242. FINLAND, M., AND WEINSTEIN, L.: Complications induced by antimicrobial agents, New England J. Med. 248:220, 1953.
243. KLIGMAN, A. M.: Are fungus infections increasing as a result of antibiotic therapy? J.A.M.A. 149:979, 1952.
244. KLIGMAN, A. M.: Editorial: Antibiotic therapy and fungus infections, New England J. Med. 247:491, 1952.

245. NEWMAN, C. R.: Pseudomembranous enterocolitis and antibiotics, Ann. Int. Med. *45*:409, 1956.
246. DEARING, W. H., AND HEILMAN, F. R.: Micrococcic (staphylococcic) enteritis as a complication of antibiotic therapy: its response to erythromycin, Proc. Staff Meet., Mayo Clin. *28*:121, 1953.
247. REINER, L.; SCHLESINGER, M. J., AND MILLER, G. M.: Pseudomembranous enterocolitis following aureomycin and chloramphenicol, A.M.A. Arch. Path. *54*:39, 1952.
248. KRAMER, I. R. H.: Fatal staphylococcal enteritis developing during streptomycin therapy by mouth, Lancet *2*:646, 1948.
249. HERRELL, W. E.; NICHOLS, D. R., AND MARTIN, W. J.: Erythromycin for infections due to micrococcus pyogenes, J.A.M.A. *152*:1601, 1953.
250. HAIGHT, T. H., AND FINLAND, M.: Laboratory and clinical studies with erythromycin, New England J. Med. *247*:227, 1952.
251. NELSON, A. A., AND RADOMSKI, J. L.: Comparative pathological study in dogs of feeding of six broad-spectrum antibiotics, Antib. & Chemo. *4*:1174, 1954.
252. RADOMSKI, J. L., AND NELSON, A. A.: Toxic effects of chloramphenicol in dogs. Synthetic and fermentative products compared with aureomycin, Federation Proc. *12*:358, 1953.
253. REUTNER, T. F.; MAXWELL, R. E.; WESTON, K. E., AND WESTON, J. K.: Chloramphenicol toxicity studies in experimental animals. Part I. The effect of chloramphenicol and various other antibiotics on malnutrition in dogs, with particular reference to the hematopoietic system, Antib. & Chemo. *5*:679, 1955.
254. RADOMSKI, J. L.; NELSON, A. A., AND DEICHMANN, W. B.: The effects on the peripheral blood of the intermittent administration of chloramphenicol. A proposed test for granulocytopenic properties of a drug, Antib. & Chemo. *5*:674, 1955.
255. BLOOMFIELD, A.: Editorial: Effect of antibiotics on bacteria of upper air passages, A.M.A. Arch. Int. Med. *88*:135, 1951.
256. WOODS, J. W.; MANNING, I. H., JR., AND PATTERSON, C. N.: Monilial infection complicating therapeutic use of antibiotics, J.A.M.A. *145*:207, 1951.
257. DUVERNE, J.; MULLER, AND BONNAYME, R.: Les accidents cutanéo-muqueux observés au cours des traitements par chloromycetine dans un service de typhiques, Bull. Soc. franç. de dermat. et syph. *57*:239, 1950.
258. PLANSON, E.: Le traitement de la para B du nourrisson et du jeune enfant par la chloromycetine, Presse méd. *57*:1083, 1949.
259. ROMANSKY, M. J.; OLANSKY, S.; TAGGART, S. R., AND ROBIN, E. D.: The antitreponemal effect of oral Chloromycetin in 32 cases of early syphilis in man. A preliminary report, Science *110*:639, 1949.
260. KNIGHT, V.: Chemotherapy of brucellosis, Ann. New York Acad. Sc. *53*:333, 1950.
261. WOODWARD, T. E.: Unpublished data.
262. STEPHENS, P. R.: Unsuccessful treatment of typhoid fever with chloramphenicol, Lancet *1*:731, 1950.
263. BOCCUZZI, G.: Il colasso nelle febbri tifoidee in cura cloromicetina, Minerva med. *42*:53, 1951.
264. GALPINE, J. F.: Chloramphenicol in typhoid fever, Brit. M.J. *2*:1047, 1949.
265. IZAR, G.: Collasso acuto di circola da cloroamfenicolo, Riforma med. *64*:1237, 1950.
266. FARINAUD, M. E., AND PORTES, L.: La chloromycetine à doses progressives dans le traitement des fièvres typhoides à forme hypertoxique, Presse med. *59*:3, 1951.
267. SMADEL, J. E.; LEY, H. L., JR., AND DIERCKS, F. H.: Treatment of typhoid fever: combined therapy with cortisone and chloramphenicol, Ann. Int. Med. *34*:1, 1951.
268. WOODWARD, T. E.; HALL, N. E.; DIAZ-RIVERA, R.; HIGHTOWER, J. A.; MARTINEZ, E., AND PARKER, R. T.: Treatment of typhoid fever: control of clinical manifestations with cortisone, Ann. Int. Med. *34*:10, 1951.
269. WOODWARD, T. E.; SMADEL, J. E., AND PARKER, R. T.: The therapy of typhoid fever, M. Clin. North America *38*:577, 1954.
270. WALLENSTEIN, L., AND SNYDER, L.: Neurotoxic reaction to chloromycetin, Ann. Int. Med. *36*:1526,1952.
271. GEWIN, H. M., AND FRIOU, G. J.: Manifestations of vitamin deficiency during aureomycin and chloramphenicol therapy of endocarditis due to staphylococcus aureus, Yale J. Biol. & Med. *23*:332, 1951.

272. RICH, M. L.; RITTERHOFF, R. J., AND HOFFMAN, R. J.: A fatal case of aplastic anemia following chloramphenicol (Chloromycetin) therapy, Ann. Int. Med. *33*: 1459-1467, 1950.
273. CLAUDON, D. B., AND HOLBROOK, A.: A. Fatal aplastic anemia associated with chloramphenicol (Chloromycetin) therapy, J.A.M.A. *149*:912-914, 1952.
274. HARGRAVES, M. M.; MILLS, S. D., AND HECK, F. J.: Aplastic anemia associated with administration of chloramphenicol, J.A.M.A. *149*:1293-1300, 1952.
275. HAWKINS, L. A., AND LEDERER, H.: Fatal aplastic anemia after chloramphenicol treatment, Brit. M. J. *4781*:423-426, 1952.
276. LOYD, E. L.: Aplastic anemia due to chloramphenicol, Antib. & Chemo. *2*:1-4, 1952.
277. RHEINGOLD, J. J., AND SPURLING, C. L.: Chloramphenicol and aplastic anemia, J.A.M.A. *149*:1301-1304, 1952.
278. STURGEON, P.: Fatal aplastic anemia in children following chloramphenicol (Chloromycetin) therapy, J.A.M.A. *149*:918-922, 1952.
279. WILSON, L. E.; HARRIS, M. S.; HENSTELL, H. H.; WITHERBEE, O. O., AND KAHN, J.: Aplastic anemia following prolonged use of chloramphenicol, J.A.M.A. *149*: 231-234, 1952.
280. WOLMAN, B.: Fatal aplastic anemia after chloramphenicol, Brit. M. J. *4781*:426-427, 1952.
281. DAMASHEK, W., AND CAMPBELL, E. W.: Hypoplastic anemia following the continued administration of chloramphenicol, Bull. New England M. Center *14*:81-86, 1952.
282. MOSELEY, V., AND BAROODY, W. G.: Parenteral chloromycetin, M. Times *80*:228-232, 1952.
283. GILL, P. F.: Agranulocytopenia following "chloromycetin," M. J. Australia *1*:768-769, 1950.
284. LEWIS, C. N.; PUTNAM, L. E.; HENDRICKS, F. D.; KERLAN, I., AND WELCH, H.: Chloramphenicol (Chloromycetin) in relation to blood dyscrasias wiith observations on other drugs, Antib. & Chemo., *2*:601, 1952.
285. WELCH, H.; LEWIS, C. N., AND KERLAN, I.: Blood dyscrasias: a nationwide survey, Antib. & Chemo. *4*:607, 1954.
286. WOODWARD, T. E.: The chloramphenicol problem, Mod. Med. Jan., 1953.
287. FRIEDMAN, A.: An evaluation of chloramphenicol therapy in typhoid fever in children, Pediatrics *14*:28, 1954.
288. WOOLINGTON, S. S.; ADLER, S. J., AND BOWER, A. G.: Five years' experience with chloramphenicol. *In:* Antibiotics Annual 1956-1957, New York, Medical Encyclopedia, Inc., 1957, p. 365.
289. PAYNE, H. M.; BULLOCK, W.; HACKNEY, R. L.; McKNIGHT, H. V., AND SYPHAX, G. B.: The protracted intramuscular use of chloramphenicol. *In:* Antibiotics Annual 1956-1957, New York, Medical Encyclopedia, Inc., 1957, p. 359.
290. PAYNE, E. H.; SHARP, E. A., AND KMANDT, J. A.: Treatment of epidemic typhus with chloromycetin, Tr. Roy. Soc. Trop. Med. & Hyg. *42*:163, 1948.
291. SMADEL, J. E.; LEON, A. P.; LEY, H. L., JR., AND VARELA, G.: Chloromycetin in the treatment of patients with typhus fever, Proc. Soc. Exper. Biol. & Med. *68*:12, 1948.
292. PINCOFFS, M. C.; GUY, E. G.; LISTER, L. M.; WOODWARD, T. E., AND SMADEL, J. E.: The treatment of Rocky Mountain spotted fever with chloromycetin, Ann. Int. Med. *29*:656, 1948.
293. LEY, H. L., JR.; WOODWARD, T. E., AND SMADEL, J. E.: Chloramphenicol (chloromycetin) in the treatment of murine typhus, J.A.M.A. *143*:217, 1950.
294. GROOT, H. R.: Typhus-syndrome and chloromycetin, Rev. san. mil., Columbia *1*:27, 1950.
295. KNIGHT, V.; McDERMOTT, W., AND RUIZ-SANCHEZ, F.: Aureomycin and chloramphenicol use in typhus, typhoid and brucellosis, J. Clin. Invest. *28*:1052, 1949.
296. RUIZ-SANCHEZ, F.: El tratamiento del tifo exantematico con acido para-amino-benzoico, aureomicina y chloromicetina; estudio comparativo, Medicina, México *30*:165, 1950.
297. MURRAY, E. S.; BAEHR, G.; SCHWARTZMANN, G.; MANDELBAUM, R. A.; ROSENTHAL, N.; DOANE, J. C.; WEISS, L. B.; COHEN, S., AND SNYDER, J. C.: Brill's disease, J.A.M.A. *142*:1059, 1950.
298. KNIGHT, V., AND RUIZ-SANCHEZ, F.: Treatment of endemic and epidemic typhus with antibiotics, Ann. New York Acad. Sc. *55*:992, 1952.

299. BAILEY, C. A.; LEY, H. L., JR.; DIERCKS, F. H.; LEWTHWAITE, R., AND SMADEL, J. E.: Treatment of scrub typhus: evaluation of chloramphenicol, aureomycin, terramycin, and para-aminobenzoic acid, Antib. & Chemo. *1*:16, 1951.
300. BAILEY, C. A., AND LEY, H. L., JR.: The treatment and prophylaxis of scrub typhus with antibiotics, Ann. New York Acad. Sc. *55*:983, 1952.
301. SMADEL, J. E.; BAILEY, C. A., AND DIERCKS, F. H.: Chloramphenicol (chloromycetin) in the chemoprophylaxis of scrub typhus (tsutsugamushi disease). IV. Relapses of scrub typhus in treated volunteers and their prevention, Am. J. Hyg. *51*:229, 1950.
302. SMADEL, J. E.: Influence of antibiotics on immunological responses in scrub typhus, Ricketts, Award Lecture, University of Chicago, May, 1953.
303. SMADEL, J. E.; LEY, H. L., JR.; DIERCKS, F. H., AND CAMERON, J. A. P.: Persistence of *R. tsutsugamushi* in tissues of patients recovered from scrub typhus, Am. J. Hyg. *56*:294, 1952.
304. PARKER, R. T.; MENON, P. G.; MERIDETH, A. M.; SNYDER, M. J., AND WOODWARD, T. E.: Persistence of *R. rickettsii* in a patient recovered from Rocky Mountain spotted fever, J. Immunol. *73*: 383, 1954.
305. PARKER, R. T.; BAUER, R. E.; LISTER, L. M.; WOODWARD, T. E., AND HALL, H. E.: Further experience in the treatment of Rocky Mountain spotted fever with chloramphenicol, Am. J. Med. *9*:308, 1950.
306. CARSON, M. J.; GOWEN, L. F., AND COCHRANE, F. R.: Rocky Mountain spotted fever treated with chloromycetin, J. Pediat. *35*:232, 1949.
307. EDWARDS, E. H.; IRWIN, W. H., AND HOLLEY, H. L.: Chloromycetin therapy in Rocky Mountain spotted fever, J.M.A. Alabama *19*:165, 1949.
308. REILLY, W. A., AND EARLE, A. M.: Rocky Mountain spotted fever treated with chloramphenicol and aureomycin, J. Pediat. *36*:306, 1950.
309. WORKMAN, J. E.; HIGHTOWER, J. A.; BORGES, F. J.; FURMAN, J. E., AND PARKER, R. T.: Cortisone as an adjunct to chloramphenicol in the treatment of Rocky Mountain spotted fever, New England J. Med. *246*:962, 1952.
310. SCHAEFER, L. E., AND RASHKOFF, I. A.: Use of chloromycetin in a case of rickettsialpox, New York State J. Med. *50*:1224, 1950.
311. ROSE, H. M.: The treatment of rickettsialpox with antibiotics, Ann. New York Acad. Sc. *55*:1019, 1952.
312. JANBON, M.; BERTRAND, L., AND COMBIER, C.: Le traitement de la fievre boutonneuse par la chloromycetine, Presse méd. *57*:1026, 1949.
313. FOUQUET, J., AND MORIN, M.: Fièvre boutonneuse contractée dans L'Ile-de-France et traitée par la chloromycetine, Bull. et mém. Soc. méd. d. hôp. de Paris *66*:80, 1950.
314. GEAR, J.: Discussion. *In:* YEO, R. M.: Common tropical diseases encountered at the W.N.L.A. and their treatment with special reference to some of the newer drugs, Proc. Transvaal Mine Med. Officers A. *29*:93, 1950.
315. SMADEL, J. E.: Q fever. *In:* RIVERS, T. M., EDITOR: Viral and Rickettsial Infections in Man, ed. 2, Philadelphia, J. B. Lippincott Co., 1952, pp. 652-664.
316. ZARAFONETIS, C. J. D., AND BATES, R. C.: Q fever. Report of a case treated with chloromycetin, Ann. Int. Med. *32*:982, 1950.
317. CLARK, W. H., AND LENNETTE, E. H.: Treatment of Q fever with antibiotics, Ann. New York Acad. Sc. *55*:1004, 1952.
318. FELLERS, F. X.: An outbreak of Q fever. II. Treatment with aureomycin and chloramphenicol, U. S. Armed Forces M.J. *3*:665, 1952.
319. SCURO, L. A.: La terapie, della febbre Q con cloroamfenicolo, Polie Linico (Sez. Prat.) *56*:269, 1952.
320. WISSEMAN, C. L., JR.; PATERSON, P. Y.; SMADEL, J. E.; DIERCKS, F. H., AND LEY, H. L., JR.: Studies on cortisone and antibiotics for prompt therapeutic control of typhoid fever and scrub typhus, J. Clin. Invest. *33*:264, 1954.
321. WOODWARD, T. E., AND SMADEL, J. E.: Principles of Internal Medicine, New York, The Blakiston Co., 1954, pp. 1052.
322. WOODWARD, T. E.: Chloromycetin and Aureomycin: therapeutic results, Ann. Int. Med. *31*:53, 1949.
323. HORSEFALL, F. L., JR.: Approaches to the chemotherapy of viral diseases, Bull. New York Acad. Med. *31*:783, 1955.
324. RIVERS, T. M., EDITOR: Viral and Rickettsial Infections of Man, ed. 2, Philadelphia, I. B. Lippincott Co., 1952.

325. HARTMAN, F. W.; HORSEFALL, F. L., JR., AND KIDD, J. G., EDITORS: International Symposium. The Dynamics of Virus and Rickettsial Infections, New York, The Blakiston Co., 1953.
326. MCLEAN, I. W., JR.; MILLER, F. A., AND RIGHTSEL, W. A.: Suppression of Growth by Clinical Antibiotics. In: The Dynamics of Virus and Rickettsial Infections, New York, The Blakiston, Co., 1953, p. 431.
327. PARODI, A. S.: La acción de la penicillina en la psittacosis, Rev. d. Inst. bact., Buenos Aires 14:176, 1949.
328. MEYER, K. F.: Early diagnosis of infections by the psittacosis lymphogranuloma venereum group. In: The dynamics of virus and rickettsial infections, New York, The Blakiston Co., 1953, p. 295.
329. LEVADITI, F., AND VAISMAN, A.: Effet curatif, de la penicilline dans la maladie de Nicolas-Favre de la souris, Bull. Acad. de méd., Paris 129:253, 1945.
330. MORGINSON, W. J.: The clinical use of penicillin in dermatology, South. M.J. 38:320, 1945.
331. WRIGHT, L. T.; WHITAKER, J. C.; WILKINSON, R. S., AND BEINFIELD, M. S.: The treatment of lymphogranuloma venereum with terramycin: report of twenty successfully treated cases, Antib. & Chemo. 1:193, 1951.
332. BRAINERD, H.; LENNETTE, E. H.; MEIKLEJOHN, G.; BRUYN, H. B., JR., AND CLARK, W. H.: The clinical evaluation of aureomycin, J. Clin. Invest. 28:992, 1949.
333. GREEN, T. W.: Aureomycin therapy of human psittacosis, J.A.M.A. 144:237, 1950.
334. FAGIN, I. D., AND MANDIBERG, J. N.: Psittacosis treated with penicillin and chloramphenicol, J. Michigan M. Soc. 49:182, 1950.
335. BASSETT, M. A.: Psittacosis; a report of three cases, J. Indiana M.A. 65:119-121, 1952.
336. ALERGOUT, C. D.: Aureomycin in lymphogranuloma inguinale, Lancet 1:950, 1950.
337. WARMROCK, V. S.; GREENBLATT, R. B.; DIENST, R. B.; CHEN, C., AND WEST, R. M.: Aureomycin in treatment of granuloma inguinale and lymphogranuloma venereum, J. Invest. Research 14:427, 1950.
338. MEYER, K. F., AND EDDIE, B.: The knowledge of human virus infections of animal origin, J.A.M.A. 133:822, 1947.
339. MEYER, K. F., AND EDDIE, B.: A review of psittacosis for the years 1948 to 1950, Bull. Hyg. 26:1, 1951.
340. GRACE, A. W.: Lymphogranuloma venereum. In: Clinical Tropical Medicine, New York, Paul B. Hoeber, Inc. 1944, pp. 499-508.
341. LEVADITI, C., AND VAISMAN, A.: Action de la chloromycetine (chloramphenicol) et de l'aureomycin sur le virus lymphogranulomateux (maladie de Nicolas-Faure), Compt. rend. Acad. d.sc. 229:1274, 1949.
342. DARIUS, D. J.: Penicillin treatment of trachoma: preliminary report, Am. J. Ophth. 28:1007, 1945.
343. THYGESON, P.: Diagnosis and treatment of trachoma. Report of 19 cases in military personnel, Mil. Surgeon 97:355, 1945.
344. MITSUI, Y., AND TANAKA, C.: Terramycin, aureomycin and chloramphenicol in the treatment of trachoma, Antib. & Chemo. 1:146, 1951.
345. PIJOAN, M.; PAYNE, E. H., AND DINEEN, J.: Chloromycetin in the treatment of trachoma. Read at American Society of Tropical Medicine, Memphis, Nov., 1949.
346. PAYNE, E. H.: Present status of chloromycetin therapy, New Orleans M. & S.J. 101:597, 1949.
347. GIDDIENS, S. W., AND HOWARD, W. A.: Inclusion blennorrhea in pediatric practice, M. Ann. District of Columbia 9:333, 1940.
348. SORSBY, A.: Local penicillin therapy in ophthalmia neonatorum, Brit. M.J. 1:903, 1945.
349. BRALEY, A. E., AND SANDERS, M.: Aureomycin in ocular infections. A study of its spectrum, Ann. New York Acad. Sc. 51:280, 1948.
350. COLLINS, H. S.; WELLS, E. B.; GOCKE, T., AND FINLAND, M.: Treatment of primary atypical pneumonia with aureomycin, Am. J. Med. 8:4-20, 1950.
351. KNEELAND, Y., AND MELCHER, G. W.: Terramycin in the treatment of primary atypical pneumonia, Ann. New York Acad. Sc. 53:437, 1950.
352. WOOD, E. J.: Atypical pneumonia treated with chloromycetin, Lancet 2:55-56, 1949.
353. WALKER, S. H.: Ineffectiveness of aureomycin in primary atypical pneumonia, Am. J. Med. 15:593-602, 1953.
354. MCCRAE, T.: The symptoms of typhoid fever. In: OSLER, W. AND MCCRAE, T.: Modern Medicine, vol. 2, Philadelphia, Lea Brost Co., 1907, chap. 4, p. 104.

355. SMADEL, J. E.; BAILEY, C. A., AND LEWTHWAITE, R.: Synthetic and fermentative type chloramphenicol (Chloromycetin) in typhoid fever: prevention of relapses by adequate treatment, Ann. Int. Med. *33*:1, 1950.
356. WOODWARD, T. E.; SMADEL, J. E.; PARKER, R. T., AND WISSEMAN, C. L., JR.: Treatment of typhoid fever with antibiotics, Ann. New York Acad. Sc. *55*:1043, 1952.
357. KNIGHT, V.; RUIZ-SANCHEZ, F.; RUIZ-SANCHEZ, A.; SHULTZ, S., AND McDERMOTT, W.: Antimicrobial therapy in typhoid fever, Arch. Int. Med. *85*:44, 1950.
358. EL RAMLI, A. H.: Chloramphenicol in typhoid fever Lancet, *1*:618, 1950.
359. VALDIVIESA, R.; SEPULVEDA, G.; CONTRERAS, V., AND GONZALES, A.: Chloramfenicol en la tratamiento de la fiebre tifoidea, Rev. méd. de Chile *79*:300, 1951.
360. MENEGHELLO, J.; UNDURRAGA, O.; GALLO, A., AND RAIMANN, A.: Tratamiento de 100 casos de fiebre tifoidea en el niño con cloramfenicol (chloromicetina), Rev. méd. de Chile *79*:307, 1951.
361. EL RAMLI, A. H.: Chloramphenicol in typhoid and paratyphoid fevers: new lines of treatment, Lancet *1*:927, 1953.
362. MOLLARET, D.; REILLY, J.; BASTIN, P., AND TOURNIER, P.: Accidents du traitement des fièvres typhoides et paratyphoides par le chloramphenicol (Chloromycetin), Bull. Soc. méd. hôp. de Paris *66*:85, 1950.
363. SEDALLIAN, P.; MARAL, R.; EXBRAYAT, S.; TRAEGER, J., AND GAILLARD, L.: La chloramphenicol dans le traitement de la fièvre typhoide, J. de méd. de Lyon *31*:627, 1950.
364. COOK, A. T., AND MARMION, D. E.: Chloramphenicol in the treatment of typhoid fever, Lancet *2*:975, 1949.
365. EDGE, W.: Typhoid fever treated with chloramphenicol, Lancet *1*:710, 1950.
366. GOOD, R. A., AND MACKENZIE, R. D.: Chloramphenicol in typhoid fever, Lancet *1*:611, 1950.
367. SMADEL, J. E.; WOODWARD, T. E., AND BAILEY, C. A.: Relation of relapses in typhoid to duration of chloramphenicol therapy, J.A.M.A. *141*:129, 1949.
368. LONGCHAMPT, J., AND CARBONEL, J.: Sur une statistique de 140 cas de fièvre typho-paratyphiques traitées par la chloromycetine, Bull. Soc. méd. hôp. de Paris *66*: 1248, 1950.
369. MATTEUCCI, W. V.; SCHIMMEL, N. H., AND BOGER, W. P.: Typhoid fever: chloramphenicol therapy and the problem of relapse, Am. J. M. Sc. *222*:446, 1951.
370. MARMION, D. E.; NAYLOR, R. E., AND STEWART, I. O.: Second attacks of typhoid fever, J. Hyg. *41*:260, 1953.
371. RAPELLINI, M., AND DiNOLA, F.: La terapia vaccino-antibiotica nella febbre tifoidee, Minerva med *42*:107, 1951.
372. STUART, B. M., AND PULLEN, R. L.: Typhoid: clinical analysis of 360 cases, Arch. Int. Med., *78*:629, 1946.
373. BAILEY, C. A., AND SUMEAUX, C. V.: Aureomycin in the treatment of peritonitis, Brit. M. J. *1*:271, 1950.
374. SCOTT, R. B.; BANKS, L. O., AND CRAWFORD, R. D.: Typhoid fever in children, Arch. Pediat. *67*:224, 1950.
375. CLAISSE, R., AND CROSNIER, J.: Perforation in the course of typhoid fever treated with Chloromycetin. Healing by only the medical treatment, Presse méd. *58*:99, 1950.
376. LEWIS, L. A., AND PAGE, I. H.: Studies with protective power of adrenal extract and steroids against bacterial toxins in adrenalectomized rats. *In:* KENDALL, E. C.: The chemistry and partial synthesis of adrenal steroids, appendix I, Ann. New York Acad. Sc. *50*:547, 1949.
377. REILLY, J.: Les accidents du traitement des fièvres typhoides par la chloromycetine: étude experimentale et deductions therapeutiques, Ann. méd. *51*:597, 1950.
378. ROSS, S.; BURKE, F. G.; RICE, E. C.; WASHINGRON, J. A., AND STEVENS, S.: Chloromycetin in treatment of salmonella enteritis, New England J. Med. *242*:145, 1950.
379. REINMAN, H. A., AND LIAN, P. T.: Chloramphenicol in paratyphoid A, A.M.A. Arch. Int. Med. *96*:777, 1955.
380. ROSS, S.; BURKE, F. G.; RICE, E. C.; WASHINGTON, J. A., AND STEVENS, S.: Chloramphenicol (chloromycetin) therapy in shigella enteritis, J.A.M.A. *143*:1459, 1950.
381. CHRISTIE, A. B.: Chloromycetin, Post-Grad. M.J. *24*:410, 1949.
382. GARBER, M. D.: Streptomycin, aureomycin, chloromycetin and their application in pediatric practice, J. Indiana M.A. *43*:105, 1950.

383. MOZER, J. J.; ANDEROUD, R., AND DELETRA, J.: Chloromycetin in the treatment of typhoid fever, Rev. méd de la Suisse Rom 69:653, 1949.
384. WEINTRAUB, A.: Two cases of paratyphoid B treated with chloromycetin, Schweiz. med. Wchnschr. 79:1268, 1949.
385. WOODWARD, T. E.: Unpublished data.
386. FITZGERALD, J., AND SNYDER, M. J.: An unusual case of Salmonella cholerasuis meningitis: cure following surgical excision of an infected subarachnoid cyst, Ann. Int. Med. In press.
387. NEVA, F. A.; NELSON, R. J., AND FINLAND, M.: Hospital outbreak of infections with Salmonella newington, New England J. Med. 244:252, 1951.
388. HEWITT, W. L.: Antibacterial agents in gastro-intestinal disease, M. Clin. North America 36:1083, 1952.
389. BENGTSSON, E.; HEDLUND, P.; NISELL, A., AND NORDENSTAM, H.: Epidemic due to salmonella typhimurium occurring in Sweden in 1953 with special reference to clinical complications, bacteriology, serology, antibiotic treatment and morbid anatomy, Acta med. Scandinav. 153:1, 1955.
390. HARDY, A. V.; MASON, R. P., AND MARTIN, G. A.: The antibiotics in acute bacillary dysentery, Ann. New York Acad. Sc. 55:1070, 1952.
391. CHEEVER, F. S.: The treatment of shigellosis with antibiotics, Ann. New York Acad. Sc. 55:1063, 1952.
392. LIEBERMAN, D., AND JAWETZ, E.: Treatment of shigella infection with polymyxin, J. Pediat. 8:249, 1951.
393. SIME, D. A., AND CAMERON, D.: Persistent bacillary dysentery treated with chloramphenicol, Brit. M.J. 1:997, 1951.
394. MARTIN, G. A.; GARFINKEL, B. T.; BROOKE, M. M.; WEINSTEIN, P. P., AND FRYE, W. W.: Comparative efficacy of amebacides and antibiotics in acute amoebic dysentery, J.A.M.A. 151:1055, 1953.
395. BERCOVITZ, Z. T.: Chloramphenicol in chronic ulcerative colitis: clinical results and blood counts over a 4½ year period in 67 patients, and sensitivity studies of predominating organisms in stools. In: Antibiotics Annual 1953-1954, New York, Medical Encyclopedia, Inc., 1954, p. 261.
396. GILPIN, B. E., AND ROHRS, L. C.: Chloromycetin (chloramphenicol) in the treatment of pneumococcic pneumonia and miscellaneous infections, Am. Pract. & Digest Treat. 2:937-943, 1951.
397. FLIPPIN, H. F.; MATTEUCCI, W. V.; SCHIMMEL, N. H., AND BOGER, W. P.: Aureomycin, chloramphenicol and penicillin in treatment of bacterial pneumonia, J.A.M.A. 147:918-921, 1951.
398. KIRBY, W. M. M.; MICHEL, J. C.; COLEMAN, D. H.; HAVILAND, J. W., AND SPARKMAN, D. R.: Comparison of aureomycin and chloramphenicol in treatment of bacterial pneumonia, J.A.M.A. 147:110-115, 1951.
399. SCADDING, J. C., CHAIRMAN: The treatment of clinical pneumonia with antibiotics. Report by a subcommittee of the Antibiotics Clinical Trials (Non-tuberculous) Committee of the Medical Research Council, Brit. M.J. 2:1361-1365, 1951.
400. EBELING, W. C.; PARKER, R. T.; HAGAN, R. C.; COHEN, J. E., AND BENNETT, V. D.: Chloramphenicol in the treatment of pneumonia: a comparison with penicillin Am. J. Med. 13:643, 1952 (abstr.).
401. AUSTRIAN, R.; CLUFF, L. E.; MIRICK, G. S.; SESSOMS, S. M., AND ZUBROD, C. G.: A comparison of the efficacy of chloramphenicol (chloromycetin) and of penicillin in the treatment of pneumococcal lobar pneumonia, Bull. Johns Hopkins Hosp. 91:323-329, 1952.
402. WEISS, W.; EISENBERG, G. M.; ALEXANDER, J. D., JR.; MANN, L., AND FLIPPIN, H. F.: Antibiotic combination in treatment of pneumococcic pneumonia, J.A.M.A. 154:1167-1170, 1954.
403. DAVIS, W. M.: Successful treatment of pneumococcal pneumonia with combination of chloramphenicol and penicillin, Am. J. M. Sc. 227:391-397, 1954.
404. VAN METRE, T. E., JR.: Pneumococcal pneumonia treated with antibiotics. The prognostic significance of certain clinical findings, New England J. Med. 251:1048-1052, 1954.
405. HEFFRON, R.: Pneumonia with Special Reference to Pneumococcus Lobar Pneumonia, New York, Commonwealth Fund, 1939, 1086 pp.
406. DOWLING, H. F.; LEPPER, M. H., AND HIRSCH, H. L.: Treatment of pneumococcal pneumonia with large doses of repository penicillin compared with lower doses of penicillin: study of 686 patients, Am. J. M. Sc. 220:17-22, 1950.

407. DOWLING, H. F., AND LEPPER, M. H.: The effect of antibiotics (penicillin, aureomycin and terramycin) on the fatality rate and incidence of complications in pneumococcic pneumonia. A comparison with other methods of therapy, Am. J. M. Sc. *222*:396-403, 1951.

408. FINN, J. J., JR.; KANE, L. W., AND FINN, R. E.:Chloromycetin palmitate in the treatment of pneumococcal pneumonia, Bull. New England M. Center *14*:61-63, 1952.

409. BARBER, J. M., AND GRANT, A. P.: Friedländer's pneumonia: a report of six cases, Brit. M.J. *2*:752-755, 1952.

410. OBINSKY, W.; DERMONT, R. E.; FOWLER, R. E. L., AND RUHSTALLER, F.: Friedländer-Aerogenes infections in infancy, A.M.A. Am. J. Dis. Child. *80*:621-657, 1950.

411. HOLMES, R. B.: Friedländer's pneumonia, Am. J. Roentgenol. *75*:728-745, 1956.

412. POMERANTZ, H. Z.; WASSERMAN, E., AND KATZ, K. H.: Friedländer's pneumonia, Boston M. Quart. *2*:23-28, 1951.

413. GILL, R. J.: Treatment of Friedländer's pneumonia, Am. J. M. Sc. *221*:5-9, 1951.

414. KAUFFMANN, F.: On serology of Klebsiella group, Acta path. et Microbiol. Scandinav. *26*:381, 1949.

415. EDWARDS, P. R., AND FIFE, M. A.: Studies on the Klebsiella-Aerobacter group of bacteria, J. Bact. *70*:382, 1951.

416. WEISS, W.; EISENBERG, G. M.; SPIVAK, A.; NADEL, J.; KAYSER, H. L.; SATHAVARA, S., AND FLIPPIN, H. F.: Klebsiella in respiratory disease, Ann. Int. Med. *45*:1010-1026, 1956.

417. LIMSON, B. M.; ROMANSKY, M. J., AND SHEA, J. G.: An evaluation of twenty-two patients with acute and chronic pulmonary infection with Friedländer's bacillus, Ann. Int. Med. *44*:1070-1081, 1956.

418. JERVEY, L. P., JR., AND HAMBURGER, M.: The treatment of acute Friedländer's bacillus pneumonia, A.M.A. Arch. Int. Med. *99*:1-7, 1957.

419. SCOTT, N. M., JR.: The treatment of Friedländer's pneumonia, M. Bull. European Command *8*:367-370, 1951.

420. STEINBERG, H., AND TOWBIN, M. N.: Chronic Friedländer's pneumonia infection treated with chloromycetin: case report, Dis. of Chest *21*:455-459, 1952.

421. WASSERMAN, E., AND POMERANTZ, H. Z.: Friedländer's pneumonia: report of two cases treated with chloromycetin, M. Ann. District of Columbia *20*:435-436, 1951.

422. KIRBY, W. M. M., AND COLEMAN, D. H.: Antibiotic therapy of Friedländer's pneumonia, Am. J. Med. *11*:179-187, 1951.

423. POMERANTZ, H. Z., AND WASSERMAN, E.: Chronic Friedländer's pneumonia, Canad. M.A.J. *66*:137-139, 1952.

424. KOULUMIES, R., AND LAITINEN, H.: Friedländer pneumonia. Ann. med. int. Fenniae *43*:27-38, 1954; Bull. Hyg. *29*:917, 1954 (abstr.).

425. MAY, H. E.: Use of ACTH in a case of Friedländer's pneumonia, Ohio State M.J. *49*:501-502, 1953.

426. SARBER, R. W., AND HEMANS, M.J.: *In vitro* and chemotherapeutic studies with chloramphenicol (chloromycetin) against *Hemophilus pertussis*, J. Infect. Dis. *88*:50-53, 1951.

427. PAYNE, E. H.; LEVY, M.; ZAMORA, G. M.; VILLARROEL, M. S., AND CANELAS, E. Z.: Pertussis treated with chloramphenicol, J.A.M.A. *141*:1298-1299, 1949.

428. PAYNE, E. H.; LEVY, M.; CANELAS, E. Z.; ZAMORA, G. M., AND VILLARROEL, M. S.: Chloromycetin as a treatment for pertussis: continued observations, J. Michigan M. Soc. *49*:450-452, 1950.

429. DEGENHARDT, D. P.: Whooping cough treated with chloromycetin, Lancet *2*:579-580, 1949.

430. GRAY, J. D.: Aureomycin and chloramphenicol in whooping cough, Lancet *2*:800-802, 1950.

431. KHALIL, A., AND ABDIN, Z. H.: Chloramphenicol in whooping cough, Lancet *2*:307, 1950.

432. MACRAE, J.: Chloramphenicol in whooping cough, Lancet *1*:400, 1950.

433. BOOHER, C. E.; FARRELL, J. B., AND WEST, E. J.: Pertussis: clinical comparison of the new antibiotics, J. Pediat. *39*:411-422, 1951.

434. BOGDAN, A.: Control of pertussis in day-nursery contacts with chloramphenicol, Lancet *2*:1204-1205, 1951.

435. HAZEN, L. N.; JACKSON, G. G.; CHANG, S.; PLACE, E. H., AND FINLAND, M.: Antibiotic treatment of pertussis, J. Pediat. *39*:1-15, 1951.

436. LASSEN, H. C. A., AND GRANDJEAN, L. C.: Chloramphenicol in the treatment of pertussis. Review of a hundred cases, Lancet *1*:763-764, 1951.
437. WEINSTEIN, L.; SELTSER, R., AND MARROW, C. T., III: The treatment of pertussis with aureomycin, chloramphenicol and terramycin, J. Pediat. *39*:549-559, 1951.
438. ANON.: Whooping-Cough Subcommittee of the Antibiotics Clinical Trials (Nontuberculous Conditions) Committee of the Medical Research Council: Treatment of whooping-cough with antibiotics, Lancet *1*:1109-1112, 1953.
439. CHRISTENSEN, A.: Behandling af kighoste. Oversight samt erfaringer fra 2½ aars med antibiotica, Ugesk. f. laeger *117*:147-167, 1955; Bull. Hyg. *30*:397, 1955 (abstr.).
440. CLAESSON, U., AND LINDQUIST, B.: Pertussis och antibiotica, Nord. Med. *53*:799-801, 1955; Bull. Hyg. *31*:5-6, 1956 (abstr.).
441. DE RUDDER, B., AND VETTERMANN, H.: Antibiotische Pertussisbehandlung, Deutsche med. Wchnschr. *79*:1317-1318, 1954; Bull. Hyg. *30*:10, 1955 (abstr.).
442. VOLCKER, W., AND STEIN, H.: Ergebnisse der neuzeitlichen Keuchhustentherapie, Ztschr. f. ärtzl. Fortbildung *49*:632-634, 1955; Bull. Hyg. *31*:241, 1956 (abstr.).
443. WILLIAMS, S.: The value of broad-spectrum antibiotics in the treatment of pertussis, In: Antibiotics Annual 1956-1957, New York, Medical Encyclopedia, Inc., 1957, pp. 316-318.
444. WEHRLE, P. F., AND LEPPER, M. H.: Aureomycin treatment of pertussis, J. Pediat. *39*:435-441, 1951.
445. MORRIS, D., AND COCKBURN, W. C.: Treatment of early whooping-cough with chloramphenicol palmitate, Lancet *2*:724-736, 1954.
446. WEINSTEIN, L.: The chemoprophylaxis of infection, Ann. Int. Med. *43*:287-298, 1955.
447. GRUTTOLA, G.: L'ACTH per via intradermica nella terapia della pertosse. Gior. di malattie infettive e parassit. *7*:226-227, 1955; Bull. Hyg. *31*:6, 1956 (abstr.).
448. SYVERTON, J. T.: Non-bacterial pneumonias, Dis. of Chest *18*s456-477, 1952.
449. DINGLE, J. H.: Respiratory disease caused by viruses, Mil. Med. *117*:252-258, 1955.
450. DINGLE, J. H., AND FELLER, A. E.: Non-influenzal viral infections of the respiratory tract, New England J. Med. *254*:465-471, 1956.
451. REIMANN, H. A.: Viral pneumonias, J.A.M.A. *161*:1078-1079, 1956.
452. MEIKLEJOHN, G.: Viral pneumonia, M. Clin. North America *31*:1442-1456, 1947.
453. HILLEMAN, M. R.; WERNER, J. H.; ADAIR, C. V., AND DREISBACH, A. R.: Outbreak of acute respiratory illness caused by RI-67 and Influenza A viruses, Fort Leonard Wood, 1952-1953, Am. J. Hyg. *61*:163-173, 1955.
454. HILLEMAN, M. R.; WERNER, J. H.; DASCOMB, H. E., AND BUTLER, R. L.: Epidemiologic investigations with respiratory disease virus RI-67, Am. J. Pub. Health *45*: 203-210, 1955.
455. LIU, C.; EATON, M. D., AND HEYL, J. T.: Studies on primary atypical pneumonia, Bull. New York Acad. Med. *32*:170-171, 1956.
456. COHEN, P., AND SCHWARTZ, R.: Use of chloromycetin in infections. I. In nonbacterial (atypical undifferentiated) respiratory infections, J. Pediat. *37*:23-36, 1950.
457. GRAVES, F. B., AND BELL, W. O.: Evaluation of the treatment of primary atypical pneumonia with aureomycin, chloromycetin and terramycin, J. Pediat. *39*:155-167, 1951.
458. PECK, G. A., AND BERRY, J. W.: Antibiotic therapy in primary atypical pneumonia: the use of aureomycin, chloromycetin, streptomycin, and penicillin in controlled studies, Antib. & Chemo. *1*:291-298, 1951.
459. FINLAND, M.: Antimicrobial treatment of viral and related infections. I. Antibiotic treatment of primary atypical pneumonia, New England J. Med. *247*:317-325, 1952.
460. GALLAGHER, C. D., AND GALLAGHER, J. R.: Effect of aureomycin on the development of cold agglutinins in primary atypical pneumonia, New England J. Med. *247*:314-316, 1952.
461. MEIKLEJOHN, G.; THALMAN, W. G.; WALIGORA, J. D.; KEMPE, C. H., AND LENNETTE, E. H.: Chemotherapy of primary atypical pneumonia, J.A.M.A. *154*:553-557, 1954.
462. STEVENS, A. R.: Chloro-tetracycline in primary atypical pneumonia, Northwest Med. *55*:772-776, 1956.
463. WOLF, R. L., AND BROWN, L. T.: Primary atypical non-bacterial pneumonia. An evaluation of the efficacy of antibiotic therapy in one hundred eighteen cases, A.M.A. Arch. Int. Med. *97*:593-598, 1956.

464. SEIBERT, R. H.; JORDAN, W. S., JR., AND DINGLE, J. H.: Clinical variations in the diagnosis of psittacosis, New England J. Med. *254*:925-930, 1956.
465. CHAPMAN, E. M.: Psittacosis: a case in Cape Cod, J.A.M.A. *147*:1343-1344, 1951.
466. BACON, A. P. C.: Psittacosis: two further human cases, Lancet *2*:376-378, 1953.
467. HÄNDEL, F., AND KÜHNLEIN, E.: Epidemiologische und klinische Beobachtungen anlässlich einer Psittakose-epidemie, Med Klin. *48*:1469-1473, 1953.
468. LOGAN, G. B.: The diagnosis and treatment of acute laryngotracheobronchitis, Dis. of Chest *15*:85-91, 1949.
469. NEFFSON, A. H.: Acute Laryngotracheobronchitis, New York, Grune and Stratton. 1949, pp. 1-197.
470. SIMPSON, J. R.: Management of acute laryngotracheobronchitis, Arch. Otolaryng. *50*:724-731, 1950.
471. THOMPSON, J.: Acute laryngo-tracheo-bronchitis, J. Laryng. & Otol. *64*:667-670, 1950.
472. EVERETT, A. R.: Acute laryngotracheobronchitis. An analysis of 1,175 cases with 98 tracheotomies, Laryngoscope *61*:113-123, 1951.
473. EMERY, J. L.: Acute laryngotracheobronchitis in children. A study of incidence and pathology, Brit. M.J. *2*:1067-1070, 1952.
474. HIGH, H. C., JR.: The treatment of acute laryngotracheobronchitis, Wisconsin M. J. *51*:367-370, 1952.
475. EVERETT, A. R.: The problem of acute laryngotracheobronchitis, Eye, Ear, Nose & Throat Monthly *32*:142-146, 1953.
476. RABE, E. F.: Infectious croup. I. Etiology, Pediatrics *2*:255-265, 1948.
477. RABE, E. F.: Infectious croup. II. "Virus" croup, Pediatrics *2*:415-427, 1948.
478. RABE, E. F.: Infectious croup. III. *Hemophilus influenzae* type B croup, Pediatrics *2*:559-566, 1948.
479. MILLER, A. N.: *Hemophilus influenzae* type B epiglottitis or acute supraglottic laryngitis in children, Laryngoscope *58*:514-526, 1948.
480. CHANOCK, R. M.: Association of a new type of cytopathogenic myxovirus with infantile croup, J. Exper. Med. *104*:555-576, 1956.
481. DAVIDSON, F. W.: Acute laryngotracheobronchitis. Further studies on treatment, Arch. Otolaryng. *47*:455-464, 1948.
482. MONCRIEFF, A., AND WELLER, D. V.: Acute laryngotracheobronchitis treated with chloromycetin, Lancet *2*:748, 1949.
483. EMERY, F. C.: Acute laryngotracheobronchitis, Arch Pediat. *67*:116-123, 1950.
484. FORFAR, J.O.; KEAY, K. R., AND THOMSON, J.: Acute obstructive laryngotracheitis and laryngotracheobronchitis, Lancet *1*:181-185, 1951.
485. BATY, J. M., AND KREIDBERG, M. B.: Acute laryngotracheobronchitis, M. Clin. North America, *36*: pp. 1279-1288. Sept., 1952.
486. BRIGGS, J. N., AND HESSELTINE, J. R.: Tracheotomy in acute obliterative laryngotracheobronchitis, Brit. M.J. *2*:1064-1067, 1952.
487. THOMAS, J. W.; KELLY, F. R., JR.; EDMONDS, A. M., AND KENDIG, E. L., JR.: Chloromycetin palmitate-clinical evaluation in allergic and non-allergic children and adults, Virginia M. Monthly *79*:272-274, 1952.
488. BARACH, A. L.; BICKERMAN, H. A., AND BECK, G. J.: Antibiotic therapy in infections of the respiratory tract, A.M.A. Arch. Int. Med. *90*:808-849, 1952.
489. WYNN-WILLIAMS, N., AND MOYES, E. N.: Bronchiectasis treated with chloramphenicol, Edinburgh M.J. *58*:503, 1951.
490. HARRIS, M. S.; GORNELL, L.; SHORE, C., AND LOVITZ, H.: Chloramphenicol in the control of bronchopulmonary suppuration, Dis. of Chest. *21*:450-454, 1952.
491. HEWITT, W. L.: Antibiotic therapy of abscess of the lung and bronchiectasis, California Med. *76*:319-324, 1952.
492. FRANKLIN, A. W., AND GARROD, L. P.: Chloramphenicol treatment of bronchiectasis in children, Brit. M.J. *2*:1067-1069, 1953.
493. BURKE, F. G.; ROSS, S.; PARROTT, R. H., AND RICE, E. C.: Non-tuberculous bacterial meningitis in infants and children, GP *12*:98, 1955.
494. ROSS, S.; RICE, C.; BURKE, F. G.; McGOVERN, J. J.; PARROTT, R. H., AND McGOVERN, J. P.: Treatment of meningitis due to *Haemophilus influenzae;* use of chloromycetin and sulfadiazine, New England J. Med. *247*:541, 1952.
495. PARKER, R. T.; SNYDER, M. J.; LIU, R. S. J.; LOOPER, J. W., JR., AND WOODWARD, T. E.: Therapeutic range of chloramphenicol in purulent meningitis, Antib. Med. *1*:192, 1955.
496. SMITH, M. H. D.: Acute bacterial meningitis, Pediatrics *17*:258, 1956.

497. PRATHER, G. W., AND SMITH, M. H. D.: Chloramphenicol in treatment of Hemophilus influenzae meningitis, J.A.M.A. 143:1405, 1950.
498. SCOTT, J. R.; WALCHER, D. N.: Intravenous chloramphenicol in the treatment of meningitis due to Hemophilus influenzae (type B), J. Pediat. 41:442, 1952.
499. GREEN, R.; MANKIKAR, D. S., AND MILLETTI, J. S.: Influenzal meningitis treated with chloramphenicol, Brit. M.J. 2:1154, 1950.
500. ALEXANDER, H. E.: Guides to optimal therapy in bacterial meningitis, J.A.M.A. 152:662, 1953.
501. MENON, P. G.; RASKIN, H. F., AND WOODWARD, T. E.: Further experience with chloramphenicol in the treatment of meningococcal meningitis, Antib. & Chemo. 4:1113, 1954.
502. KNIGHT, V., AND COLLINS, H. S.: Problem cases of infection, M. Clin. North America 38:905, 1954.
503. DIRIART, H.; POUJOL, J., AND RAULINE, J.: Intramuscular chloromycetin in a case of acute meningococcic meningitis, Presse méd. 60:1363, 1952.
504. DOWLING, H. F.; SWEET, L. F.; ROBINSON, J. A.; ZELLER, W. W., AND HIRSH, H. L.: The treatment of pneumococcic meningitis with massive doses of systemic penicillin, Am. J. M. Sc. 217: 149, 1949.
505. LEPPER, M. H., AND DOWLING, H. F.: Treatment of pneumococcic meningitis with penicillin compared with penicillin plus aureomycin, A.M.A. Arch. Int. Med. 88: 489, 1951.
506. SPECK, R. S.; JAWETZ, E., AND GUNNISON, J. R.: Studies on antibiotic synergism and antagonism, A.M.A. Arch. Int. Med. 88:167, 1951.
507. HAGAN, R. C.; COHEN, J. E., AND EBELING, W. C.: Alpha streptococcus meningitis; report of case successfully treated with chloramphenicol, Antib. & Chemo. 2:147, 1952.
508. ANDERSON, K. F., AND ELLIS, F. G.: Intrathecal chloramphenicol in staphylococcal meningitis resistant to penicillin and streptomycin, Brit. M. J. 2:1067, 1951.
509. BOETTNER, C. M. R., AND CARRIZOSA, A.: Typhoid meningitis cured with chloramphenicol: case. South M. J. 44:197, 1951.
510. SMITH, C. E. G., AND MARSDEN, A. T. H.: Fatal meningitis in typhoid treated with chloramphenicol, Lancet 2:430, 1951.
511. RIPY, H. W.: Typhoid fever in infant complicated by typhoid meningitis; therapeutic failure with chloromycetin (chloramphenicol); but response to aureomycin, J. Pediat. 36:376, 1950.
512. HANSEN, S.: Chloramphenicol in therapy of purulent meningitis caused by Salmonella typhimurium, Monatschr. f. Kinderh. 99:154, 1951.
513. EIGNER, J.: Heilung einer meningitis purulenta verursacht durch Salmonella Newport, Kinderarzti Prax. 22:162-163, April, 1954.
514. RALSTON, E. L.: Osteomyelitis of spine due to Salmonella choleraesuis, J. Bone & Joint Surg. 37:580, 1955.
515. TRINDADE, O., AND NASTARI, F.: Treatment of meningitis by intracisternal injection of chloramphenicol, J.A.M.A. 147:1757, 1951.
516. WOODWARD, T. E.: Unpublished data.
517. DARNLEY, J. D.: Chloromycetin and streptomycin in the treatment of meningitis due to B. Proteus, Neurology 2:69, 1951.
518. LEPPER, M. H.; BLATT, N. H.; WEHRLE, P. F., AND SPIES, H. W.: Treatment of bacterial meningitis of unusual etiology and purulent meningitis of unknown origin, A.M.A. Am. J. Dis. Child. 85:295, 1953.
519. EBSWORTH, J. S., AND LEYS, D. G.: Recovery of a newborn child from bacteria coli meningitis, Lancet 2:914, 1951.
520. FISCH, G. H.: A case of E. coli meningitis in the newborn treated with intrathecal chloramphenicol, Guy's Hosp. Rep. 101:229, 1953.
521. ETTELDORF, J. N.: Management of purulent meningitis, J.A.M.A. 159:746, 1955.
522. SMITH, R. T.: Septicemia and meningitis in a newborn infant, J. Pediat. 47:740, 1955.
523. MARTIN, R.; SUREAU, B.; LEMER, G., AND MOUSSET, H.: Postoperative meningitis due to Friedländer's bacteria; chloramphenicol therapy following failure of streptomycin, Arch. franç. pédiat. 7:721, 1950.
524. CORCOS, V.: Meningitis due to Friedländer's pneumobacillus (Klebsiella pneumoniae) in an eight year old infant: sensitivity of the bacteria to chloromycetin; recovery, Arch. franç. pédiat. 10:647,1953.

525. BALMES, J.; BERTRAND, L., AND MALLET, H.: Meningitis due to Friedländer's pneumobacillus; cure after chloramphenicol therapy following various therapeutic attempts, Arch. franç. pédiat. 9:1108, 1952.
526. FINEGOLD, S. M.; BRADLEY, J. G.; CAMPBELL, M. K., AND GREENBERG, A. J.: *Listeria monocytogenes* meningitis. Summation of literature and report of two new cases, A.M.A. Arch. Int. Med 93:515, 1954.
527. BENNETT, I. L., JR.; RUSSELL, P. E., AND DERIVAUX, J. H.: Treatment of Listeria meningitis, Antib. & Chemo. 2:142, 1952.
528. BERRY, J. F.: *Listerella monocytogenes* meningitis. Report of a case, U. S. Armed Forces M. J. 1:894, 1950.
529. LINE, F. G., AND APPLETON, F. G.: Listeria meningitis in a premature infant, J. Pediat. 41:97, 1952.
530. WOODWARD, T. E.; SMADEL, J. E.; HOLBROOK, W. A., AND RABY, W. T.: The beneficial effect of chloromycetin in brucellosis, J. Clin. Invest. 28:968, 1949.
531. McDERMOTT, W.: Antimicrobial therapy, Proc. Inst. Med. Chicago 18:2, 1950.
532. KNIGHT, V.; RUIZ-SANCHEZ, F., AND McDERMOTT, W.: Chloramphenicol in the treatment of the acute manifestations of brucellosis, Am. J. M. Sc. 219:627, 1950.
533. HARRIS, H. J.: Aureomycin and chloramphenicol in brucellosis with special reference to side effects, J.A.M.A. 142:161, 1950.
534. VIOLINI, I. F.; GREENSPAW, I.; EHRLICH, L.; GONNER, J. A.; FELSENFLEND, O., AND SCHWARTZ, S. O.: Hemopoietic changes during administration of chloramphenicol (chloromycetin), J.A.M.A. 142:1333, 1950.
535. WALLEY, J. F. L., AND COOPER, T. V.: A case of undulant fever treated by chloramphenicol, Brit. M. J. 2:265, 1949.
536. FULLERTON, C. W., AND FAY, K. J.: Acute brucellosis treated with chloromycetin, Canad. M.A.J. 62:596, 1950.
537. KILLOUGH, J. H.; MAGILL, G. B., AND SMITH, R. C.: Terramycin, chloramphenicol and aureomycin in acute brucellosis: preliminary report, J.A.M.A. 145:553, 1951.
538. HALL, W. H.: Brucellosis in man. A study of thirty-five cases due to *Brucella abortus*, Minnesota Med. 36:460, 1953.
539. SPINK, W. S.; HALL, W. H., AND MAGOFFIN, R.: Follow-up study of therapy in forty-eight culturally proven cases of brucellosis, A.M.A. Arch. Int. Med. 88:419, 1951.
540. HERRELL, W. E., AND BARBER, T. E.: A new method for treatment of brucellosis, J.A.M.A. 144:519, 1950.
541. MAGILL, G. B., AND KILLOUGH, J. H.: Oxytetracycline-streptomycin therapy in brucellosis due to *Brucella melitensis*, A.M.A. Arch. Int. Med. 9:204, 1953.
542. McDOUGAL, J. L.: The immediate clinical results following the use of chloromycetin in the treatment of chronic brucellosis, J. Am. Osteo. A. 49:194, 1949.
543. RALSTON, R. J., AND PAYNE, E. H.: Treatment of chronic brucellosis with chloramphenicol and aureomycin, J.A.M.A. 142:159, 1950.
544. GRIGGS, J. F.: Effects of chloramphenicol in chronic brucellosis, Antib. & Chemo. 2:300, 1952.
545. SPINK, W. W.: Some biologic and clinical problems related to intracellular parasitism in brucellosis, New England J. Med. 247:603, 1952.
546. WOODWARD, T. E.: Unpublished data.
547. SPINK, W. W.: What is chronic brucellosis? Ann. Int. Med. 35:358, 1951.
548. MAGILL, G. B.; KILLOUGH, J. H., AND SAID, S. I.: Cortisone and combined antibiotic therapy of acute *Brucellosis melitensis*, Am. J. Med. 16:810, 1954.
549. EIGELSBACH, H. T., AND HERRING, R. D.: Effectivness of chloromycetin and aureomycin for treatment of experimental tularemia, Abstracts Soc. Am. Bacteriologists, 49th meeting, May, 1949, pp. 67-68.
550. KARCHER, F.: Two cases of tularemia treated with chloramphenicol, Presse méd. 58:96, 1950.
551. McCRUMB, F. R., JR.; SNYDER, M. J., AND WOODWARD, T. E.: Studies on human infection with *Pasteurella tularensis*. Comparison of streptomycin and chloramphenicol in the prophylaxis of clinical disease, Tr. A. Am. Physicians 70:74, 1957.
552. MEYER, K. F.; QUAN, S. F.; McCRUMB, F. R., AND LARSON, A.: Effective treatment of plague, Ann. New York Acad. Sc. 55:1228, 1952.
553. SMADEL, J. E.; WOODWARD, T. E.; AMIES, C. R., AND GOODNER, K.: Antibiotics in the treatment of bubonic and pneumonic plague in man, Ann. New York Acad. Sc. 55:1275, 1952.

554. McCRUMB, F. R., JR.; MERCIER, S.; ROBIC, G.; BOULLIAT, M.; SMADEL, J. E.; WOOD-WARD, T. E., AND GOODNER, K.: Chloramphenicol and terramycin in the treatment of pneumonic plague, Am. J. Med. *14*:284, 1953.

555. SPINK, W. W.: Nature of Brucellosis, Minneapolis, University of Minnesota Press, 1956.

556. RYLE, J. A.: Staphylococcal infections. I. The natural history, prognosis and treatment of staphylococcal fever, Guy's Hosp. Rep. *80*:137-152, 1930.

557. ROGERS, D. E.: The current problem of staphylococcal infections, Ann. Int. Med. *45*:748-781, 1956.

558. ELEK, S. D.: Experimental staphylococcal infections in the skin of man, Ann. New York Acad. Sc. *65*:85-89, 1956.

559. LACK, C. H.: Biological characteristics of staphylococci recovered from pathologic materials, Ann. New York Acad. Sc. *65*:103-108, 1956.

560. RAMMELKAMP, C. H., JR., AND LEBOVITZ, J. L.: The role of coagulase in staphylococcal infections, Ann. New York Acad. Sc. *65*:144-151, 1956.

561. JACKSON, G. G.; DOWLING, H. F., AND LEPPER, M. H.: Pathogenicity of staphylococci. A comparison of alpha-hemolysin production with the coagulase test and clinical observations of virulence, New England J. Med. *252*:1020-1025, 1955.

562. EVANS, J. B.; BUETTNER, L. G., AND NIVEN, C. F., JR.: Evaluation of the coagulase test in the study of staphylococci associated with food poisoning, J. Bact. *60*:481-484, 1950.

563. TAGER, M.: Problems in the coagulation of plasma by staphylocoagulase, Ann. New York Acad. Sc. *65*:109-118, 1956.

564. SMITH, W., AND HALE, J. H.: The nature and mode of action of staphylococcal coagulase, Brit. J. Exper. Path. *25*:101-110, 1944.

565. SMITH, W.; HALE, J. H., AND SMITH, M.: The role of coagulase in staphylococcal infections, Brit. J. Exper. Path. *28*:57-67, 1947.

566. BOAKE, W. C.: Antistaphylocoagulase in experimental staphylococcal infections, J. Immunol. *76*:89-96, 1956.

567. SURGALLA, M. J., AND DACK, G. M.: Enterotoxin produced by micrococci from cases of enteritis after antibiotic therapy, J.A.M.A. *158*:649-650, 1955.

568. KELLAWAY, C. H.; MACCALLUM, P., AND TEBBUTT, A. H.: Report of the Royal Commission of Inquiry into the fatalities at Bundaberg. *In:* Parliamentary Papers of the Commonwealth of Australia, Canberra, H. J. Green, 1928. (M.J. Australia *2*:2, 38, 1928; J.A.M.A. *91*:262, 1928).

569. THAL, A., AND EGNER, W.: Local effect of staphylococcal toxin. Studies on blood vessels with particular reference to phenomena of dermonecrosis, A.M.A. Arch. Path. *57*:392-404, 1954.

570. THAL, A. P., AND EGNER, W.: The mechanism of shock produced by means of staphylococcal toxin, A.M.A. Arch. Path. *61*:488-495, 1956.

571. THAL, A.: Selective renal vasospasm and ischemic renal necrosis produced experimentally with staphylococcal toxin. Observations on the pathogenesis of bilateral cortical necrosis, Am. J. Path. *31*:233-259, 1955.

572. DINGLE, J. H.; HOFF, E. H.; NAHUM, L. H., AND CAREY, B. W., JR.: The effect of *Staphylococcus aureus* exotoxin on the rabbit heart, J. Pharmacol. & Exper. Therap. *61*:121-129, 1937.

573. SKINNER, D., AND KEEFER, C. S.: Significance of bacteremia caused by *Staphylococcus aureus*, Arch. Int. Med. *68*:851-875, 1941.

574. KLEIGER, B., AND BLAIR, J. E.: Correlation between clinical and experimental findings in cases showing invasion of the blood stream by staphylococci, Surg., Gynec. & Obst. *71*:770-777, 1940.

575. KLEIGER, B., AND BLAIR, J. E.: Role of toxin and use of antitoxin in systemic staphylococcic infections, Arch. Surg. *46*:548-554, 1943.

576. KLEIGER, B.; BLAIR, J. E., AND HALLMAN, F. A.: Behavior of rabbits after infection with toxigenic and nontoxigenic staphylococci. An experimental study, Arch. Surg. *45*:571-577, 1942.

577. WISE, R. I., AND SPINK, W. W.: The influence of antibiotics on the origin of small colonies (G variants) of *Micrococcus pyogenes* var. *aureus*, J. Clin. Invest. *33*:1611-1622, 1954.

578. WISE, R. I.: Small colonies (G variants) of staphylococci: isolation from cultures and infections, Ann. New York Acad. Sc. *65*:169-174, 1956.

579. GOUDIE, J. G., AND GOUDIE, R. B.: Recurrent infections by a stable dwarf colony variant of *Staphylococcus aureus*, J. Clin. Path. *8*:284-287, 1955.

580. Spink, W. W.: The clinical problem of antimicrobial resistant staphylococci, Ann. New York Acad. Sc. 65:175-190, 1956.
581. Dowling, H. F.; Lepper, M. H., and Jackson, G. G.: Clinical significance of antibiotic resistant bacteria, J.A.M.A. 157:327-331, 1954.
582. Prissick, F. H.: Antibiotic-resistant staphylococci and related infections, Am. J. M. Sc. 225:299-319, 1953.
583. Welch, H.: Editorial: The antibiotic-resistant staphylococci, Antib. & Chemo. 3:561-570, 1953.
584. Knight, V., and Holzer, A. R.: Studies on staphylococci from hospital patients. I. Predominance of strains of group III phage patterns which are resistant to multiple antibiotics, J. Clin. Invest. 33:1190-1198, 1954.
585. Knight, V., and Collins, H. S.: A current view on the problem of drug resistant staphylococci and staphylococcal infection, Bull. New York Acad. Med. 31:549-568, 1955.
586. Hopps, H. E.; Wisseman, C. L., Jr., and Whelan, J.: Relation of antibiotic resistance of staphylococci to prevalence of antibiotic therapy in diverse geographic areas, Antib. & Chemo. 4:270-276, 1954.
587. Lepper, M. H.: Microbial resistance to antibiotics, Ann. Int. Med. 43:299-315, 1955.
588. Pulaski, E. J., and Isokane, R. K.: Novobiocin therapy of pyogenic surgical infections, Surg., Gynec. & Obst. 104:310-318, 1957.
589. Bryson, V.: Genetics of antimicrobial resistance, Ann. New York Acad. Sc. 65: 161-168, 1956.
590. McDermott, W.: The problem of staphylococcal infections, Ann. New York Acad. Sc. 65:58-65, 1956.
591. Smith, J. M., and Dubos, R. J.: The behavior of virulent and avirulent staphylococci in the tissues of normal mice, J. Exper. Med. 103:87-108, 1956.
592. Smith, J. M., and Dubos, R. J.: The effect of nutritional disturbances on the susceptibility of mice to staphylococcal infections, J. Exper. Med. 103:109-118, 1956.
593. Smith, J. M., and Dubos, R. J.: The effect of dinitrophenol and thyroxin on the susceptibility of mice to staphylococcal infections, J. Exper. Med. 103:119-126, 1956.
594. Schaedler, R. W., and Dubos, R. J.: Reversible changes in the susceptibility of mice to bacterial infections. II. Changes brought about by nutritional disturbances, J. Exper. Med. 104:67-84, 1956.
595. Collins, H. S.; Helper, A. N.; Blevins, A., and Olenberg, G.: Staphylococcal bacteremia, Ann. New York Acad. Sc. 65:222-234, 1956.
596. Dubos, R. J.: The unknowns of staphylococcal infection, Ann. New York Acad. Sc. 65:243-246, 1956.
597. Young, G.: Experimental staphylococcus infection in the hamster cheek pouch: the process of localization, J. Exper. Med. 99:299-306, 1954.
598. Myrvik, Q. N.: Serum bactericidins active against gram-positive bacteria, Ann. New York Acad. Sc. 66:391-400, 1956.
599. Pillemer, L.: The nature of the properdin system and its interaction with polysaccharide complexes, Ann. New York Acad. Sc. 66:233-243, 1956.
600. Hirsch, J. G.: Phagocytin. a bactericidal substance from polymorphonuclear leucocytes, J. Exper. Med. 103:589-611, 1956.
601. Skarnes, R. C., and Watson, D. W.: Characterization of leukin: an antibacterial factor from leucocytes active against gram-positive pathogens, J. Exper. Med. 104:829-845, 1956.
602. Landy, M., and Shear, M. J.: Similarity of host responses elicited by polysaccharides of animal and plant origin and by bacterial endotoxins, J. Exper. Med. 106:77-97, 1957.
603. Miles, A. A.: Reactions to bacterial invasion, Lectures on the Scientific Basis of Medicine 3:235-258, 1953-1954.
604. Lyons, C.: Bacteremic staphylococcal infection, Surg., Gynec. & Obst. 74:41-46, 1942.
605. Rogers, D. E.: The blood stream clearance of staphylococci in rabbits, Ann. New York Acad. Sc. 65:73-84, 1956.
606. Rogers, D. E., and Tompsett, R.: The survival of staphylococci within human leukocytes, J. Exper. Med. 95:209-230, 1952.

607. TOMPSETT, R.: The survival of staphylococci within phagocytic cells, Bull. New York Acad. Med. *30*:480, 1954.
608. TOMPSETT, R.: Protection of pathogenic staphylococci by phagocytes, Tr. A. Am. Physicians *69*:84-92, 1956.
609. SMITH, J. M.: Studies on the fate of virulent and avirulent staphylococci in mice, Ann. New York Acad. Sc. *65*:67-72, 1956.
610. McCURE, R. M., JR.; DINEEN, P. A. P., AND BATTEN, J. C.: The effect of antimicrobial drugs on an experimental staphylococcal infection in mice, Ann. New York Acad. Sc. *65*:91-102, 1956.
611. MILES, A. A.; WILLIAMS, R. E. O., AND CLAYTON-COOPER, B.: The carriage of *Staphylococcus* (pyogenes) *aureus* in man and its relation to wound infection, J. Path. & Bact. *56*:513-524, 1944.
612. GOULD, J. C., AND McKILLOP, E. J.: The carriage of *Staphylococcus pyogenes* var. *aureus* in the human nose, J. Hyg. *52*:304-310, 1954.
613. ROUNTREE, P. M.; FREEMAN, B. A., AND BARBOUR, R. G. H.: Nasal carriage of Staphylococcus aureus in the general population and its relationship to hospitalization and to penicillin therapy, M. J. Australia *2*:457-460, 1954.
614. GOULD, J. C., AND ALLAN, W. S. A.: Staphylococcus pyogenes cross-infection, Lancet *2*:988-989, 1954.
615. LOWBURY, E. J. L.: Cross-infection of wounds with antibiotic-resistant organisms, Brit. M. J. *1*:985-990, 1955.
616. BLAIR, J. E.: Epidemiological implications of staphylococcal phage typing, Ann. New York Acad. Sc. *65*:152-159, 1956.
617. LEPPER, M. H.; DOWLING, H. F.; JACKSON, G. G., AND HIRSCH, M. M.: Epidemiology of penicillin- and aureomycin-resistant staphylococci in a hospital population, A.M.A. Arch. Int. Med. *92*:40-50, 1953.
618. RAVENHOLT, R. T., AND LAVECK, G. D.: Staphylococcal disease—an obstetric pediatric, and community problem, Am. J. Pub. Health *46*:1287-1296, 1956.
619. EDMUNDS, P. N.; ELIAS-JONES, T. F.; FORFAR, J. O., AND BALF, C. L.: Pathogenic staphylococci in the environment of the new born infant, Brit. M. J. *1*:990-994, 1955.
620. HUTCHISON, J. G. P.; GREEN, C. A., AND GRINISON, T. A.: Nasal carriage of *Staphylococcus aureus* in nurses, J. Clin. Path. *10*:92-95, 1957.
621. RIPPON, J. E., AND VOGELSANG, T. M.: Carriage of pathogenic staphylococci in the upper respiratory tract of children, Acta path. et microbiol. Scandinav. *39*:284-296, 1956.
622. HIRSHFELD, J. W., AND LAUBE, P. J.: Surgical masks. An experimental study, Surgery *9*:720-730, 1941.
623. TORREY, J. C., AND REESE, M. K.: Initial flora of newborn (premature) infants. Nature, source and relation to ultraviolet irradiation and face marks, Am. J. Dis. Child. *67*:89-99, 1944.
624. HARE, R., AND THOMAS, C. G. A.: The transmission of *Staphylococcus aureus,* Brit. M. J. *2*:840-844, 1956.
625. WEBB, J. F.: Newborn infections and breast abscesses of staphylococcal origin, Canad. M. A. J. *70*:382-388, 1954.
626. SHAFFER, T. E.; BALDWIN, J. N.; RHEINS, M. S., AND SYLVESTER, R. F., JR.: Staphylococcal infections in newborn infants. I. Study of an epidemic among infants and nursing mothers, Pediatrics *18*:750-761, 1956.
627. GOULD, J. C.: The effect of local antibiotic on nasal carriage of Staphylococcus pyogenes, J. Hyg. *53*:379-385, 1955.
628. ROUNTREE, P. M.; HESSELTINE, M.; RHEUBEN, J., AND SPEARMAN, R. P.: Control of staphylococcal infection of the newborn by the treatment of nasal carriers in the staff, M. J. Australia *1*:528-532, 1956.
629. CLARKE, A. J. R.; McGEOCH, A. H., AND SIPPE, G. R.: Neonatal infection of the skin by Staphylococcus pyogenes, M. J. Australia *1*:655-658, 1950.
630. GILLESPIE, W. A., AND ALDER, V. G.: Control of an outbreak of staphylococcal infection in a hospital, Lancet *1*:632-634, 1957.
631. FELDMAN, F., AND ANNUNZIATA, D.: *Staphylococcus aureus* infections in the newborn infant, J. Pediat. *41*:399-402, 1952.
632. FORFAR, J. O.; BALF, C. L.; ELIAS-JONES, T. F., AND EDMUNDS, P. N.: Staphylococcal infection of the newborn, Brit. M. J. *2*:170-174, 1953.
633. HARDYMENT, A. F.: The control of infections in the newborn, Canad. M. A. J. *70*: 379-382, 1954.

634. GILLESPIE, W. A.; POPE, R. C., AND SIMPSON, K.: Pemphigus neonatorum caused by *Staphylococcus aureus* type 71, Brit. M. J. *1*:1044-1046, 1957.
635. SPITTLEHOUSE, K. E.: Phage types of *Staphylococcus pyogenes* isolated from impetigo and sycosis barbae, Lancet *2*:378, 1955.
636. BARROW, G. I.: Clinical and bacteriological aspects of impetigo, J. Hyg. *53*:495-508, 1955.
637. PARKER, M. T.; TOMLINSON, A. J. H., AND WILLIAMS, R. E. O.: Impetigo contagiosa. The association of certain types of *Staphylococcus aureus* and of *Streptococcus pyogenes* with superficial skin infections, J. Hyg. *53*:458-473, 1955.
638. LIVINGOOD, C. S., AND MULLINS, J. F.: Management of bacterial infections of the skin, Postgrad. Med. *12*:15-26, 1952.
639. SNEDDON, I. B.: Drug resistance of micro-organisms, Lancet *1*:668, 1952.
640. HOWE, C. W.: The treatment of staphylococcal infections, M. Clin. North America *37*:1461-1479, 1953.
641. VALENTINE, F. C. O., AND HALL-SMITH, S. P.: Superficial staphylococcal infection, Lancet *2*:351-354, 1952.
642. HOWE, C. W.: Postoperative wound infections due to *Staphylococcus aureus*, New England J. Med. *251*:411-417, 1954.
643. BLOWERS, R.; MASON, G. A.; WALLACE, K. R., AND WALTON, M.: Control of wound infection in a thoracic surgery unit, Lancet *2*:786-794, 1955.
644. HOWE, C. W.: Discussion of SPINK, W. W.: [580] Ann. New York Acad. Sc. *65*:189-190, 1956.
645. ALTEMEIER, W. A., AND CULBERTSON, W. R.: Chloramphenicol (Chloromycetin) and aureomycin in surgical infections, J.A.M.A. *145*:449-456, 1951.
646. FLINT, M. H.; GILLIES, H., AND REID, D. A. C.: Local use of chloramphenicol in wound infections, Lancet *1*:541-544, 1952.
647. DEARING, W. H.: Micrococcic enteritis and pseudomembranous enterocolitis as complications of antibiotic therapy, Ann. New York Acad. Sc. *65*:235-241, 1956.
648. CHICKERING, H. T., AND PARK, J. H., JR.: Staphylococcus pneumonia, J.A.M.A. *72*:617-626, 1919.
649. KANOF, A.; KRAMER, B., AND CARNES, M.: Staphylococcus pneumonia, J. Pediat. *14*:712-724, 1939.
650. CLEMENS, H. H., AND WEENS, H. S.: Staphylococcic pneumonia in infants: occurrence of pyopneumothorax, J. Pediat. *20*:281-296, 1942.
651. BLUMENTHAL, S., AND NEUHOF, H.: Staphylococcic (suppurative) pneumonia in infancy and childhood and its surgical aspects, Am. J. Dis. Child. *72*:691-719, 1946.
652. GUTHRIE, K. J., AND MONTGOMERY, G. L.: Staphylococcal pneumonia in childhood: pathologic considerations, Lancet *2*:752-755, 1947.
653. MCLETCHIE, N. G. B.: Staphylococcal pneumonia in childhood, Canad. M. A. J. *60*:352-356, 1949.
654. FINLAND, M.; PETERSON, O. L., AND STRAUSS, E.: Staphylococcic pneumonia occurring during an epidemic of influenza, Arch. Int. Med. *70*:183-205, 1942.
655. KANOF, A.; EPSTEIN, B.; KRAMER, B., AND MAUSS, I.: Staphylococcal pneumonia and empyema, Pediatrics *11*:385-392, 1953.
656. TAFT, L. I.: Recent experiences with staphylococcal infection in childhood, M. J. Australia *2*:970-976, 1955.
657. WALLMAN, I. S.; GODFREY, R. C., AND WATSON, J. R. H.: Staphylococcal pneumonia in infancy, Brit. M. J. *2*:1423-1426, 1955.
658. LEFROY, R. B.: Pneumonia, Australasian Ann. Med. *4*:70-76, 1955.
659. DISNEY, M. E.; WOLFF, J., AND WOOD, B. S. B.: Staphylococcal pneumonia in infants, Lancet *1*:767-771, 1956.
660. HAUSMANN, W., AND KARLISH, A. J.: Staphylococcal pneumonia in adults, Brit. M. J. *2*:845-847, 1956.
661. GRESHAM, G. A., AND GLEESON-WHITE, M. M.: Staphylococcal bronchopneumonia in debilitated hospital patients. A report of fourteen fatal cases, Lancet *1*:651-653, 1957.
662. SCADDING, J. G.: Lung changes in influenza, Quart. J. Med. n. s. *6*:425-465, 1937.
663. HUNMELWEIT, F.: Influenza B virus isolated from a fatal case of pneumonia, Lancet *2*:793-794, 1943.
664. BURNET, F. M.; STONE, J. D., AND ANDERSON, S. G.: An epidemic of influenza B in Australia, Lancet *1*:807-811, 1946.
665. LEFROY, R. B.: Staphylococcal pneumonia occurring during an influenza epidemic, Australasian Ann. Med. *3*:299-304, 1954.

666. EVANS, A. D., AND EVANS, M.: Staphylococcal infection of the lower respiratory tract in adults with influenza, Lancet *1*:771-773, 1956.
667. SULLIVAN, J.: Staphylococcal pneumonia, M. J. Australia *1*:700-702, 1956.
668. WARREN, W. R., AND KEHOE, E. L.: Psittacosis complicated by staphylococcal pneumonia, Ann. Int. Med. *44*:796-806, 1956.
669. BLOOMER, W. E.; GIAMONA, S.; LINDSKOG, G. E., AND COOKE, R. E.: Staphylococcal pneumonia and empyema in infancy, J. Thoracic Surg. *30*:265-271, 1955.
670. BEAVEN, D. W., AND BURRY, A. F.: Staphylococcal pneumonia in the newborn, Lancet *2*:211-215, 1956.
671. BRIGGS, J. N.: Staphylococcic pneumonia in infants and young children, Canad. M. A. J. *76*:269-272, 1957.
672. DOWLING, H. F.; LEPPER, M.; CALDWELL, E. R., AND SPIES, H. W.: Staphylococcic endocarditis: an analysis of 25 cases treated with antibiotics together with a review of the recent literature, Medicine *31*:155-176, 1952.
673. SCHIRGER, A.; MARTIN, W. J., AND NICHOLS, D. R.: Micrococcal bacteremia without endocarditis: clinical data and therapeutic considerations in 109 cases, Ann. Int. Med. *47*:39-48, 1957.
674. FINLAND, M., AND JONES, W. F., JR.: Staphylococcal infections currently encountered in a large municipal hospital: some problems in evaluating antimicrobial therapy in such infections, Ann. New York Acad. Sc. *65*:191-205, 1956.
675. WILSON, R., AND HAMBURGER, M.: Fifteen years' experience with staphylococcus septicemia in a large city hospital, Am. J. Med. *22*:437-457, 1957.
676. SPRING, M., AND WARDELL, H.: Tetralogy of Fallot with subacute bacterial endocarditis. Successful treatment with chloromycetin, Am. Heart J. *43*:918-921, 1952.
677. MILLER, G.; HANSEM, J. E., AND POLLOCK, B. E.: Staphylococcal endocarditis. A report of three cured cases, Am. Heart. J. *47*:453-461, 1954.
678. WISE, R. I.: Staphylococcal sepsis: control with antibiotics, Minnesota Med. *37*: 857-861, 1954.
679. CARMICHAEL, D. B., JR.: Fatal bacterial endocarditis due to *Staphylococcus aureus,* U. S. Armed Forces M. J. *4*:287-294, 1953.
680. FISHER, A. M.; WAGNER, H. N., JR., AND ROSS, R. S.: Staphylococcal endocarditis: some clinical and therapeutic observations on thirty-eight cases, A.M.A. Arch. Int. Med. *95*:427-437, 1955.
681. O'BRIEN, R. M.: Acute and chronic osteomyelitis, Postgrad. Med. *12*:133-136, 1952.
682. HEIMBERG, F.: The roles of antibiotics and surgical intervention in the therapy of acute osteomyelitis in children, Bull. Hosp. Joint Dis. *13*:328-341, 1952.
683. VENABLE, C. S., AND PULASKI, E. J.: Planned timing in treatment of chronic osteomyelitis under antibiotic control, Am. J. Surg. *80*:649-651, 1950.
684. ALTEMEIER, W. A., AND LARGEN, T.: Antibiotics and chemotherapeutic agents in infections of the skeletal system, J.A.M.A. *150*:1462-1468, 1950.
685. BOYES, J.; BREMNER, A. E., AND NELIGAN, G. A.: Haematogenous osteitis in the newborn, Lancet *1*:544-548, 1957.
686. DENNISON, W. M.: Haematogenous osteitis in the newborn, Lancet *2*:474-476, 1955.
687. RHOADS, P. S.; BILLINGS, C. E., AND O'CONNOR, V. J.: Antibacterial management of urinary tract infections, J.A.M.A. *148*:165-170, 1952.
688. BEESON, P. B.: Factors in the pathogenesis of pyelonephritis, Yale J. Biol. & Med. *28*:81-104, 1955.
689. CHITTENDEN, G. E.; SHARP, E. A.; VONDER HEIDE, E. C.; BRATTON, A. C.; GLAZKO, A. J., AND STIMPERT, F. D.: The treatment of bacillary urinary infections with chloromycetin, J. Urol. *62*:771-790, 1949.
690. ALYEA, E. P.: Infections and inflammations of the male genital tract, *In:* Campbell, M.: Urology, Philadelphia, W. B. Saunders Co., 1954, pp. 643-652.
691. REDEWILL, F. H.: Chloromycetin in the successful treatment of recurrent epididymitis, J. Urol. *62*:581-589, 1949.
692. SMADEL, J. E.; BAILEY, C. A., AND MANKIKAR, D. S.: Preliminary report on the use of chloramphenicol (chloromycetin) in the treatment of acute gonorrheal urethritis. Presented before the Second National Symposium on Recent Advances in Antibiotics Research, Washington, D. C., April 11-12, 1949.
693. TAGGART, S. R.; ROMANSKY, M. J., AND LANDMAN, G. S.: Treatment of syphilis with aureomycin and chloromycetin, Am. J. Syph., Gonor. & Ven. Dis. *36*:174-178, 1952.

694. ROBINSON, H. M., AND ROBINSON, H. M., JR.: Broad-spectrum antibiotic therapy of early syphilis, Am. J. Syph., Gonor. & Ven. Dis. *37*:243-246, 1953.
695. OLANSKY, S.; HARB, F. W.; WOOD, C. E., AND RAMBO, D. S.: Intramuscular chloromycetin (chloramphenicol) in the treatment of venereal disease, Am. J. Syph., Gonor. & Ven. Dis. *37*:253-258, 1953.
696. PAYNE, E. H.; BELLERIVE, A., AND JEAN, L.: Chloromycetin as a treatment for yaws and tropical ulcer, Antib. & Chemo. *1*:88-91, 1951.
697. HIRSCHBOECK, M. M.: The use of chloramphenicol in relapsing fever, Am. J. Trop. Med. & Hyg. *3*:712-713, 1954.
698. CHEN, C. H.; DIENST, R. B., AND GREENBLAT, R. B.: The treatment of gonorrhea with chloramphenicol, South. M. J. *42*:986-988, 1949.
699. ROBINSON, H. M., AND ROBINSON, H. M., JR.: Studies on chloramphenicol in early syphilis and gonorrhea, South. M.J. *42*:988-991, 1949.
700. BARRETT, C. D., JR., AND BURTON, M. E.: Chloromycetin treatment of gonorrhea, Am. J. Syph., Gonor. & Ven. Dis. *37*:165-176, 1953.
701. BUTLER, P. G.; BREWER, A. F.; CONDIT, P. K., AND JOHNSTON, J.: Chloromycetin (chloramphenicol) and penicillin in gonorrheal urethritis. Two effective single-dose plans, Am. J. Syph., Gonor. & Ven. Dis. *36*:269-271, 1952.
702. ROBINSON, R. C. V., AND WELLS, T. L.: Intramuscular chloramphenicol in the treatment of gonorrhea and granuloma inguinale, Am. J. Syph., Gonor. & Ven. Dis. *36*: 264-268, 1952.
703. GREENBLATT, R. B.; BARFIELD, W. E.; DIENST, R. B.; WEST, R. M., AND ZISES, M.: A five-year study of antibiotics in the treatment of granuloma inguinale, Am. J. Syph., Gonor. & Ven. Dis. *36*:186-191, 1952.
704. ZISES, M., AND SMITH, G. C.: Nine cases of granuloma inguinale treated with chloromycetin, Am. J. Syph., Gonor. & Ven. Dis. *35*:294-296, 1951.
705. ROBINSON, H. M., JR.; ZELIGMAN, I.; SHAPIRO, A., AND COHEN, M. M.: Chloromycetin in the treatment of dermatoses, Bull. School Med. Univ. Maryland *38*:109, 1953.
706. ROBINSON, R. C. V.: Newer antibiotics in the treatment of venereal diseases, Am. J. Syph., Gonor. & Ven. Dis. *34*:273-288, 1950.
707. DEACON, W. E.; OLANSKY, S.; ALBRITTON, D. C., AND KAPLAN, W.: VDRL chancroid studies. IV. Experimental chancroid, prophylaxis and treatment, Antib. Med. *2*:143-147, 1956.
708. NEWMAN, B. A., AND FELDMAN, F. F.: Treatment of pyogenic dermatoses with topical chloramphenicol (chloromycetin), A.M.A. Arch. Dermat. & Syph. *64*:212-214, 1951.
709. BECKER, F. T.: The acne problem, A.M.A. Arch. Dermat. & Syph. *67*:173-181, 1953.
710. ROBINSON, H. M., JR.: Role of antibiotic therapy of acne, A.M.A. Arch. Dermat. & Syph. *69*:414-417, 1954.
711. JOHNSON, S. A. M.; MEYER, O. O.; BROWN, J. W., AND RASMUSSEN, A. F., JR.: Failure of chloramphenicol (chloromycetin) in the treatment of three cases of lupus erythematosus disseminatus, J. Invest. Dermat. *14*:305-307, 1950.
712. ROBINSON, H. M.: Chloramphenicol (chloromycetin) in the treatment of chronic discoid lupus erythematosus: preliminary report, J. Invest. Dermat. *14*:309-314, 1950.
713. DAWSON, L. M., AND SIMON, H. E.: Herpes zoster treatment with chloramphenicol, South. M. J. *42*:696, 1949.
714. WINTERTON, W.: Report of two cases of herpes zoster treated with chloromycetin, M. J. Australia *1*:706, 1951.
715. BEINHAUER, L. G.: Therapeutic value of chloramphenicol in a group of dermatoses of established or questionable virus etiology, Arch. Dermat. & Syph. *62*:290-292, 1950.
716. FRIEDBERG, C. K.: Diseases of the heart. *In:* Bacterial Endocarditis. Philadelphia, W. B. Saunders Co., 1956, chap. 34.
717. FINLAND, M.: Treatment of bacterial endocarditis, New England J. Med. *250*:419, 1954.
718. BRUNSDON, D. F. V., AND GOULDING, R.: Benemid in treatment of streptococcal endocarditis, Lancet *2*:197, 1952.
719. CATES, J. E.; CHRISTIE, R. J., AND GARROD, L. P.: Penicillin-resistant subacute bacterial endocarditis treated by combination of penicillin and streptomycin, Brit. M. J. *1*:653, 1951.

720. FRIEDBERG, C. K.: Treatment of subacute bacterial endocarditis with aureomycin, J.A.M.A. *148*:98, 1952.
721. KANE, L. W., AND FINN, J. J.: The treatment of subacute bacterial endocarditis with aureomycin and chloromycetin, New England J. Med. *244*:623, 1951.
722. CURTIN, M.: Chloramphenicol in subacute bacterial endocarditis, Lancet *2*:804, 1950.
723. AHERN, J. J., AND KIRBY, W. M. M.: Cure of subacute bacterial endocarditis with penicillin and chloramphenicol, J.A.M.A. *150*:33, 1952.
724. GARRIDO LECCA, G., AND TOLA, A.: Subacute bacterial endocarditis treated with chloramphenicol and oxytetracycline, J.A.M.A. *152*:913, 1953.
725. BAETJER, W. A.: Personal communication.
726. WALCH-SORGDRAGER, B.: Leptospiroses, Bull. Health Organ., League of Nations *8*:143-386, 1939.
727. MCCRUMB, F. R., JR.; STOCKARD, J. L.; ROBINSON, C. R.; TURNER, L. H.; LEVIS, D. L.; KELLEHER, M. F.; GLEISER, C. A., AND SMADEL, J. E.: Leptospirosis in Malaya. I. Sporadic cases among military and civilian personnel, Am. J. Trop. Med. *6*:238-256, 1957.
728. DOHERTY, R. L.: A clinical study of leptospirosis in North Queensland, Australasian Ann. Med. *4*:53-63, 1955.
729. GARDNER, A. D., AND WYLIE, J. A. H.: Laboratory diagnosis of Weil's diseases; six years' observations, Lancet *1*:955-958, 1946.
730. BULMER, E.: Weil's disease in Normandy; its treatment with penicillin, Brit. M. J. *1*:113-114, 1945.
731. SUCHETT-KAYE, A. I.: Penicillin in Weil's disease, Lancet *1*:90-92, 1957.
732. HALL, H. E.; HIGHTOWER, J. A.; DIAZ-RIVERA, R.; BYRNE, R. J.; SMADEL, J. E., AND WOODWARD, T. E.: Evaluation of antibiotic therapy in human leptospirosis, Ann. Int. Med. *35*:981-998, 1951.
733. GSELL, O.: Discussion, U. S. Army Medical Service Graduate School, Symposium on the Leptospiroses. Medical Science Publication No. 1, Washington, D. C., U. S. Government Printing Office, 1953, pp. 212-219.
734. BROOM, J. C.: Leptospirosis in England and Wales, Brit. M. J. *2*:689-697, 1951.
735. FAIRBURN, A. C., AND SEMPLE, S. J. G.: Chloramphenicol and penicillin in the treatment of leptospirosis among British troops in Malaya, Lancet *1*:13-16, 1956.
736. ORR, T. G.: Twenty-five years of progress in the treatment of acute peritonitis, Am. Surgeon *21*:873, 1955.
737. ALTEMEIER, W. A.; CULBERTSON, W. R.; SHERMAN, R.; COLE, W., AND ELSTUN, W.: Critical reevaluation of antibiotic therapy in surgery, J.A.M.A. *157*:305, 1955.
738. KIRBY, W. M. M.: Treatment of bacterial pneumonia, A.M.A. Arch. Int. Med. *96*: 809-817, 1955.

INDEX

INDEX

Absorption of chloramphenicol, 13-15
Achromobacter species, 7
Acne vulgaris, 117-118
Actinomyces bovis, 7
Acute brucellosis, 85-88, 93
Acute hematogenous osteomyelitis, 103-104
Administration method, 19-23
  serum concentration and, 20-23
  see also specific methods
Aerobacter aerogenes, 7
  surgical infections caused by, 123
  urinary tract infections caused by, 107 *(tab.)*
Alcaligenes faecalis, 7
Allergic reactions to chloramphenicol, 25 *(tab.)*, 26-28
Amebiasis, 59-60, 62
Amebic dysentery, 59-60, 62
Anemia, 26, 29, 31
Angioneurotic edema, 26
Antagonisms of chloramphenicol, 9, 11
Antibiotics, resistance to, 123-124
Aplastic anemia, 30-31
Ascitic fluids, chloramphenicol in, 14
Assay methods for chloramphenicol, 12

Bacillary dysentery, 58-59, 62
Bacillus species, 7
Bacitracin in staphylococcal septicemia, 103
Bacterial endocarditis, 119-121
Bacteroides species, 7
Bartonella bacilliformis, 7
Bartonellosis, 10
Bile, chloramphenicol in, 15, 16-17
Biological activity of chloramphenicol, structure and, 3-4
Blood, chloramphenicol in, 13-14, 15, 16
Blood dyscrasias, chloramphenicol and, 25 (tab.), 28-32
Body fluids, chloramphenicol absorption and distribution in, 13-15
Borrelia novyi, 112
Borrelia recurrentis, 112
Bowel flora, chloramphenicol and, 25
Brain, chloramphenicol in, 14
Bratton-Marshall diazo procedure in chloramphenicol assay, 12
Brill's disease, 34-35, 37
Bronchiectasis, 72-73
Brucella species, 7
Brucellosis, 10, 85-89, 93
Bubonic plague, 91-92, 93

Candida albicans, 7
Cells, chloramphenicol penetration into, 15
Cellulitis, 122-123
Chancroid, 114-115
Chemistry of chloramphenicol, 3
Chloramphenicol, absorption of, 13-15
  in acne vulgaris, 117-118
  amebic dysentery and, 59-60, 62
  antagonisms of, 9, 11
  assay methods for, 12
  in bacterial endocarditis, 119-121
  biological activity of, configuration and, 3-4
  bronchiectasis and, 72-73
  brucellosis and, 85-89, 93
  in cellulitis, 122-123
  chemistry of, 3
  in chronic ulcerative colitis, 61, 62
  cortisone plus, for typhoid fever, 54-55
  for dermatological conditions, 116, 118
  distribution of, 13-15
  dosage forms of, 19-23
  enzymes and, 3-4
  excretion of, 15-17
  genitourinary tract infections and, 105-109
  history of development of, 2-4
  in infectious croup (nondiphtheritic), 71-72
  in vitro results with, 6-9
  in vivo results with, 9-11
  Klebsiella pneumoniae and, 65-67
  laboratory studies of, 5-12
  in leptospirosis, 121-122
  lymphogranuloma venereum and, 44
  in meningitis, 74-84
  metabolism of, 15-17
  methods of administration for, 19-23
  mode of action of, 11-12
  penetration of, into cells, 15
  pharmacological properties of, 13-18
  in plague, 91-93
  pneumococcic lobar pneumonia and, 63-65
  primary atypical pneumonia and, 45
  psittacosis and, 43, 70-71
  in pyogenic skin infections, 116-117
  in relapsing fever, 112
  resistance to, 8-9, 11
  rickettsial diseases and, 33-41
  Salmonella species and, 49, 56-58, 62
  Shigella species and, 58-59
  side effects of, 24-32
  in staphylococcal infections, 94-104

155